Praise for Ellie Krieger's books

"Besides being vibrant, flavorful, and healthy, these recipes make it easy to put a good, homemade meal on the table even when you have no time to cook. Way to go, Ellie!"

—**CARLA HALL**
Chef and television personality

"I have long been a fan of Ellie's balanced approach to food and I love the recipes and stunning photos in this book! The fact that they are all make-ahead is a huge help for busy people who want to eat healthy."

—**GINA HOMOLKA**
Author of the *Skinnytaste* cookbook series

"Cooking at home can be easy but it's challenging to make the right food choices. There is so much to choose from and so many decisions to make. . . . With Ellie Krieger's new book, she leads you on a clear path to good eating that strikes a great balance between healthy and delicious. She teaches self-sufficiency through simplicity and makes anything from a yogurt parfait to a homemade braise doable. Give it a try!"

—**ALEX GUARNASCHELLI**
Chef

"We all need a break, but we also deserve good, nutritious food. This is what you get with the fast, diverse recipes in *Weeknight Wonders*."

—**JACQUES PÉPIN**
Cookbook author and PBS-TV cooking series host

"Krieger maintains that 'there is no need to deprive yourself or go to extremes to be healthy . . . balance is the key.' She suggests time-saving shortcuts, like using prewashed greens or canned or frozen foods, but avoids highly processed ingredients and artificial additives, and focuses on common and easy-to-find ingredients...Krieger delivers on her promise—the recipes are fast and fresh."

—*PUBLISHERS WEEKLY*

whole
in
one

whole
in
one

complete, healthy meals
in a single pot,
sheet pan, or skillet

ellie
krieger

Photographs by Randi Baird

LIFE
LONG

Lifelong Books
Hachette Book Group
1290 Avenue of the Americas
New York, NY 10104
HachetteBooks.com
Twitter.com/HachetteBooks
Instagram.com/HachetteBooks

Printed in the United States of
America

First Edition: October 2019

Published by Lifelong Books, an
imprint of Perseus Books, LLC, a
subsidiary of Hachette Book Group,
Inc. The Lifelong Books name and
logo is a trademark of the Hachette
Book Group.

The Hachette Speakers Bureau
provides a wide range of authors for
speaking events. To find out more,
go to www.hachettespeakersbureau
.com or call (866) 376-6591.

The publisher is not responsible for
websites (or their content) that are
not owned by the publisher.

Print book interior design
by Shubhani Sarkar,
sarkardesignstudio.com

Library of Congress Cataloging-in-
Publication Data has been applied
for.

ISBNs: 978-0-7382-8504-7 (hardcover),
978-0-7382-8505-4 (ebook)

LSC-C

10 9 8 7 6 5 4 3 2 1

For
Thom
and
Isabella

contents

acknowledgments

Many talented people contributed their extraordinary passion, skill, and hard work to bring this book to fruition. I am grateful to have the opportunity to recognize them here. A heartfelt thank-you to:

My work family at Flutie Entertainment, for always seeing the big picture while sorting out every detail.

Jane Dystel, literary agent, for your unflagging support, expertise, and guidance.

Renée Sedliar, editor, and the whole team at Hachette/Da Capo, for fueling my fire with your enthusiasm for this book and for your excellence in every way.

Chef Irbania Tavares, for your dedication and culinary prowess. I can't think of anyone I'd rather cook alongside.

Natalie Rizzo, MS, RD, for your hard work on the nutrition analysis.

Randi Baird, photographer, Suzanne Lenzer, food stylist, and Maeve Sheridan, prop stylist, for creating the stunning images that bring the recipes to life on the page.

Suzanne Katz, makeup artist, for helping me look my very best.

Janell Mallios and the team at Sunshine and Sachs, for spreading the word so well.

whole
in
one

introduction

Life can be so overwhelming and chaotic—if you are anything like me, you feel like you are always balancing and juggling at the same time, constantly grasping for a moment to pause and catch your breath. Getting a good, nourishing meal on the table—one that everyone will like—and then cleaning up afterward might feel downright impossible most days. We want the food we love and we strive to be healthy, but who has the time or energy to figure it all out? That's exactly why I created this book—to have a place where it is figured out. Well, at least the dinner part, anyway. *Whole in One* reins in the chaos, focusing everything neatly in a single pan, making a delicious, wholesome meal suddenly doable. More than a cookbook, it is a survival kit of 125 recipes—nutritionally complete meals, plus better-for-you desserts—which can each be prepared entirely and simply in one pot, sheet pan, or skillet.

Many one-pot cookbooks are out there, but this one is different in several ways. Besides being flavor-forward and enticing, each recipe in this book (except the desserts, of course) is a complete meal on its own—one that's well-balanced, packed with healthy protein and colorful produce, and dietitian approved (by me!). Each recipe also includes a full nutritional profile so you have all the details about it that you could want. And because I take my promises seriously, when I say one pan, I mean it. There are no cheats, such as calling for cooked pasta as an ingredient. (That's something I spotted in several "one-pot" books I perused in my research. Hello, you need an extra pot to make that happen.) Instead, I make use of easy culinary tricks and favorite whole-food convenience items here and there to create true one-pot wonders. And since a major point here is to minimize dishes I have also made sure that none of these recipes leaves you with a sink full of mixing bowls. For most of them, you'll just need one or two, if that.

The dishes here may be streamlined and simple, but they are anything but boring. Flip through these pages and you'll find on-trend favorites that use everyday ingredients in exciting new ways, such as loaded potato nachos, zucchini noodle stir-fry, luscious lettuce wraps, and grain bowls chock-full of tasty goodies. There are opportunities to explore enticing world flavors in easy, accessible ways with recipes, such as Brazilian-style seafood stew, masala-spiced chicken, and Filipino-style beef stew. And there are fresh takes on more familiar dishes, such as spaghetti and meatballs (yes, all made in one pot!), crispy chicken breast with broccoli, tacos, chocolate sheet cake, and more. If you know me from my TV shows, newspaper and magazine columns, and social media, you know my mission is to hit what I call the "sweet spot" where delicious and healthy meet—and the recipes in this book are a perfect bull's eye. I am thrilled to share this collection of one-pot wonders with you—I hope it offers an oasis from the daily whirlwind, and makes your life easier, healthier, and tastier.

My Usually-Sometimes-Rarely Food Philosophy

Each recipe in this book follows my tried-and-true *Usually-Sometimes-Rarely* food philosophy, which I put forth in my very first book *Small Changes, Big Results*, and has been the underpinning of every recipe I have created since. Notice there is no "never" category. That's because ruling out foods entirely—as many diets have us do—tends to fuel an unhealthy, all-or-nothing mind-set that in most cases prevents us from being truly, holistically healthy. When you let go of the notion of a forbidden fruit, you invite a way of eating driven by joy and balance rather than deprivation and fear.

There is no one ideal diet (despite what many marketers like to tell us). The truth is, humans can thrive on a wide spectrum of different eating patterns when they have a selection of wholesome foods to choose from. Instead of forcing you into a single, narrowly defined dietary lane, the *Usually-Sometimes-Rarely* approach gives you the freedom to enjoy the full spectrum of wonderful foods available and tailor your choices to what works best for you at any given time.

The idea is to make the *Usually* foods—delicious choices with the most health benefits—the backbone of what you eat each day, so I use them most plentifully in my recipes: vegetables, whole fruit, beans, nuts and seeds, lean proteins, seafood, whole grains, healthy oils, and dairy products, such as yogurt. I sprinkle in *Sometimes* foods here and there, for flavor and variety. Those are somewhat more processed,

such as a baguette; a little higher in saturated fat, such as chicken thighs; or best used in modest amounts, such as honey and maple syrup. *Rarely* foods—such as refined sugar, cream, bacon, and butter—are those many nutritionists forbid but many cooks use with a heavy hand. I have found the ideal balance by using them strategically in small amounts for maximum impact.

Once you start to eat (and think) this way you realize there is no need to deprive yourself or go to extremes to be healthy. If you are enjoying mostly nutrient-rich, whole foods, there is room for a dab of butter in a pan sauce, a little chorizo tossed into a shrimp dish, or a piece of chocolate cake now and then.

I also believe in focusing on seasonal, local produce and whole-food ingredients as much as possible while steering clear of artificial additives. But I am a realist (being a mom with a full-time job will do that to you), so I am happy to take advantage of smart shortcuts, such as prewashed greens, frozen peas, or canned beans, for example. But I always make sure the packaged products I use are minimally processed and have simple ingredient lists.

If you are a fan of my other books—first, thank you, I know you will love this one, too! Second, I'd like to point out something new in the layout here. Instead of the more traditional chapter sequence starting with meat dishes, followed by poultry, seafood, and then vegetarian recipes, I have reversed that order here to highlight the enticing possibilities and reflect the value (to both our health and that of the environment) of eating lower on the food chain. I'm an enthusiastic (and conscientious) omnivore and there are wonderful meat recipes in this book, but I believe in, and enjoy, eating mostly plants, and so I have positioned the plant-protein chapter first in this book, followed by seafood, poultry, meat, and then dessert.

About the Nutrition Facts

I don't cook with a calculator at hand to get a certain nutrient profile from a recipe. Rather, I set out to make a delicious dish and use the principles laid out in my *Usually-Sometimes-Rarely* food philosophy. Remarkably, when I do that, the numbers tend to land in the healthy zone on their own. I also think it's easy to get bogged down by data when you are better off simply focusing on cooking and enjoying wholesome foods. But because numbers can also be a helpful guide I have included the nutrition facts for each recipe, with the amount of calories, fat, protein, carbohydrate, fiber, cholesterol, sodium, and sugars in each serving.

Since some fats are beneficial and others are not, I further break down total fat into saturated (unhealthy fat), monounsaturated and polyunsaturated (healthy fats). Added sugars (the amount put into food to make it sweeter) is also separated out from total sugars. As far as I am concerned, you can ignore total sugars, which includes the sugars inherent in nourishing foods, such as whole fruit and milk. It would be misguided to limit those solely based on their sugar content since those are "packaged" with fiber, antioxidants, and other important nutrients—not to mention they are delicious and satisfying. (If you are concerned about high blood sugar, it's more helpful to pay attention to total carbohydrate than total sugar.) It's a good idea to keep an eye on added sugars, though. The American Heart Association recommends that women keep added sugars to 6 teaspoons (25 g) a day; and men, to 9 teaspoons (36 g) a day. I use sweeteners sparingly, even in my desserts, and I mostly use unrefined ones, such as honey and maple syrup, so it is not much of a concern here, but it's good to have the info if you are keeping track.

I have also listed good and excellent sources of essential nutrients in each recipe. To qualify as a good source a serving must contain at least 10 percent of the Daily Value (the standard daily recommended intake), and to be called an excellent source it needs to provide at least 20 percent of the Daily Value. I encourage you not to get hung up on these values, but you can factor them in when planning your meals and let them serve as a reminder that vitamins and minerals are not just found in powders and pills, as so many marketers would have us believe. They are bountifully present in delicious, wholesome foods.

Keep in mind that the nutrition information excludes optional ingredients or anything added to taste, and if there is a choice of ingredients, such as "low-fat or whole-milk yogurt," I always use the first option listed for the analysis. Also, the type of salt I use throughout is finely ground. If you use course ground or flaked salt, you may need to add a bit more depending on your taste.

Regarding portion size and calories, since people have different appetites and calorie needs, there will always be a range of how many servings a given recipe makes. Also, our appetites can vary meal to meal and day to day. But to do the nutrition analysis, I had to pick one standard, so I chose to base the serving sizes on amounts that would satisfy most moderately active women. With that, the majority of meals in this book fall between 400 and 500 calories per portion, but a range of lighter meals come in at about 300 to 400 calories, and heartier ones have more than 500 calories. Sometimes I suggest serving with whole-grain bread or other easy accompaniments to round out the meal or accommodate heartier appetites. If you are serving a group of high school football players, you are training for a marathon, or you are not as active as you'd like to be, adjust the portions accordingly.

The Essential Six

Besides the fact that each recipe here is cooked in a single skillet, pot, or sheet pan, I also pared down the pots and pans you need for making any of the recipes in this book to just six items. If you are an avid cook, you likely already have this basic equipment. If you are starting fresh, stocking a new kitchen, or your pots and pans could use replacing, these are the essential six to get.

Sheet pan with a rack: A sheet pan, also called a rimmed baking sheet, has a 1-inch raised lip around its edge so food won't slip off and juices won't drip in the oven. Sheet pans come in several different sizes, but the most common, and the one used to test all the sheet pan recipes in this book, is known as a half sheet, measuring 13 by 18 inches. It's best to have one that is sturdy with a good weight to it, as flimsier pans can warp in the oven. Plain stainless steel or aluminum is fine—you don't need to get one with a nonstick surface. You will also want a wire rack that fits inside your sheet pan—the two are often sold together. Although called cooling racks, they are very useful in the oven, too, particularly when you want to elevate food so it can brown under the broiler.

Large, wide-mouthed pot: For many of the soups and stews here, you'll need a heavy, 6- to 8-quart soup pot or Dutch oven that has a lid and, ideally, is wide (with about a 10-inch bottom) rather than tall, so there is plenty of surface to brown meats and poultry before simmering them. It's helpful if the pot and its lid are also oven-safe.

Medium-size pot: A 3- to 4-quart pot or saucepan is ideal for cooking grain-based dishes and making some of the desserts here, such as poached apricots and puddings. A heavy-duty one will conduct heat more evenly than a lightweight one, so go for that if you can. Also make sure it has a lid.

Large, high-sided skillet: Also called a sauté pan, a 12-inch skillet gives you plenty of surface area for browning food and its high sides allow for plenty of room to add liquid for braising, make a bountiful sauce, or stir in a pile of leafy greens. They typically come with a lid, which you will definitely want. Look for one that is oven-safe.

Large, nonstick skillet: A nonstick skillet is a must-have for cooking delicate foods, such as eggs, or for shallow-frying without using a lot of oil. I recommend having a sturdy, 12-inch nonstick pan that is oven-safe.

Medium cast-iron (or ovenproof) skillet: A 10-inch cast-iron skillet is a kitchen workhorse that transitions beautifully from stovetop to oven to table. Serving food—whether it is savory, such as a frittata, or sweet, such as a fruit crisp—right in a cast-iron skillet (with a towel wrapped around its handle for safety) is the very definition of rustic elegance, and is the ultimate in one-pan convenience. If you don't have cast iron, any 10-inch heavy, ovenproof skillet will work.

Ingredient Notes

CHICKEN CONSIDERATIONS

Here are a few helpful buying and prepping tips for the dozens of wonderful chicken recipes in this book. For recipes that involve skinless, boneless chicken breast, if it is not cut into small pieces, I typically call for pounding the chicken to a ½-inch thickness. That ensures even cooking (and a juicy, tender final product), remedying the issue of one side of the breast being considerably thicker than the other. To pound the chicken, just put it between two layers of plastic wrap on a cutting board and smash it with a mallet or rolling pin. It just takes a couple of minutes. Alternatively, you can skip the pounding step by purchasing chicken labeled "thin cut" or cutlets. However, I have found that the thickness of the pieces, even those in the same package, vary widely, from ¼ to ¾ inch. It is fine to use and extra-convenient; just remember to adjust the cooking times depending on the thickness of each piece.

No matter what type of chicken you are buying, the size of the pieces can vary widely, even in the same package. I typically call for boneless breast pieces that are 6 ounces each and bone-in breast pieces that are about 12 ounces each, which are on the small side of what is found in a typical grocery store. If the pieces you get are much larger than that, particularly for chicken on the bone where you are not pounding it to a uniform thickness, you will likely need to increase the cooking time somewhat to ensure an internal temperature of 165°F.

Also note that for the bone-in chicken breast recipes here, I cook it with the skin on so the chicken stays moist inside and gets crispy and golden brown outside. It's up to you whether you want to eat all or part of the skin once the dish is plated (I personally usually eat at least part of the skin), but note that the nutrition analysis is done with the skin removed. For the record, including the skin adds about 60 calories and 2.5 g of saturated fat per portion to the total.

WHOLE GRAIN CONVENIENCE

It used to be that dishes best served over rice were a challenge, if not impossible, to turn into a one-pot dinner. Not anymore. Now thanks to the wide availability of packaged, precooked grain options, it's easy to have brown rice (and other whole grains) ready in minutes in a microwave—no extra pot needed. I have found that frozen grains yield the best results—coming out as fresh tasting and fluffy as just-cooked. And when you buy the plain variety, it has just one ingredient on the label: the cooked grain. I call for frozen brown rice in several recipes in this book, noting in the method the best time in the cooking process to heat it up. If you are halving or doubling the recipe, keep in mind that the microwave time for the grain depends on how much you are heating, from 1½ to 2 minutes per cup. Also it's worth noting that 1 cup of frozen, cooked rice yields ¾ cup of heated rice (which makes sense if you think about how ice takes up more space than when it melts into water). If you prefer, shelf-stable pouches of cooked grain will also work as an alternative to frozen.

STOCK OPTIONS

In many of the recipes in the plant-protein chapter, I give you the option of using either chicken or vegetable broth (both low-sodium), since the chapter is not vegetarian per se and I generally prefer the clean, more neutral taste of chicken broth (or stock) over that of most vegetable broths. To make those recipes vegetarian (or in some cases vegan), use whichever vegetable broth you prefer. (The difference between stock and broth is that stock is made with bones and tastes somewhat richer than broth. Otherwise, for the recipes in this book, you can use either broth or stock interchangeably.)

Regarding the seafood stock I call for in some of the fish and shellfish recipes, several boxed brands are available and you can often find seafood or fish stock in the freezer section and in a jar as a bouillon base. Also, many fishmongers sell house-made stock. The salt content of these products vary widely and I have not been able to find a brand labeled "low-sodium." I typically use the stock my fishmonger makes, which is relatively low in salt, or I buy the boxed version with the lowest sodium level available.

GLUTEN-FREE SWAPS

Many of the recipes here are inherently gluten-free, but for those that are not, I provide gluten-free ingredient alternatives where I am confident they will work. If you are cooking for someone who is strictly gluten-free, be sure to check that any condiments you use, such as prepared spice mixtures and mustards, are made without gluten-containing ingredients, and only use grain products specifically labeled "gluten-free" because even grains that do not naturally contain gluten may be contaminated if processed in the same facility as wheat, barley, or rye.

plant protein, eggs, & dairy

potato swiss chard frittata

Potatoes add just the right heft to a frittata to make it a substantial main course. Here, creamy Yukon golds are diced and sautéed in olive oil with onions, then tossed with Swiss chard (you could substitute spinach or kale) and seasoned with fragrant smoked paprika and garlic. Eggs are added to the skillet and the mixture cooks mostly on the stovetop, then finishes in the oven. The recipe takes its flavor cues from the omelet-like Spanish dish called a *tortilla*, but omits the copious amounts of oil and the potentially stressful technique of flipping it onto a plate used to make that dish. Here, you get all the luscious satisfaction in a lighter, fuss-free way. Serve it with sliced ripe tomatoes, drizzled with extra-virgin olive oil, and sprinkled with sea salt, alongside.

½ bunch Swiss chard (8 ounces)

¼ cup olive oil, divided

1 pound Yukon gold potatoes, unpeeled, diced into ½-inch pieces

1 medium-size onion, chopped

1 garlic clove, minced

½ teaspoon smoked paprika

½ teaspoon salt

¼ teaspoon freshly ground black pepper

6 large eggs, beaten

1. Remove the leaves from the stems of the Swiss chard. Trim any tough edges off the bottom of the stems and chop the remaining tender parts. Chop the chard leaves, keeping them separate from the chopped stems.

2. Heat 1 tablespoon of the oil over medium heat in a 10-inch cast-iron or nonstick, ovenproof skillet. Add the Swiss chard stems and cook, stirring occasionally, until they are firm-tender, 3 to 4 minutes, then add the leaves and cook until they are just wilted, 1 minute more. Transfer the chard to a bowl. Lower the heat to medium-low and add the remaining 3 tablespoons of oil to the skillet. Add the potatoes and onion and cook, stirring occasionally, until the potatoes are tender but not browned, about 15 minutes. Stir in the garlic and cook for 1 minute more. Return the Swiss chard to the skillet, add the smoked paprika, salt, and pepper, and stir to combine.

3. Pour the eggs evenly over the potato mixture and cook until the egg mixture has set around the edges and somewhat, but not entirely, set in the middle, 6 to 8 minutes.

4. While the eggs cook, preheat the broiler. Place the skillet under the broiler and cook until the surface is set and golden brown, 1 to 2 minutes. Allow to rest for 5 minutes before cutting into four wedges.

The frittata will keep in an airtight container in the refrigerator for up to 4 days. Serve warm or at room temperature.

Makes 4 servings

SERVING SIZE: 1 wedge

PER SERVING: Calories 330; Total Fat 21 g (Sat Fat 4 g, Mono Fat 13 g, Poly Fat 3 g); Protein 13 g; Carb 26 g; Fiber 4 g; Cholesterol 280 mg; Sodium 560 mg; Total Sugar 3 g (Added Sugar 0 g)

EXCELLENT SOURCE OF: iodine, iron, molybdenum, protein, riboflavin, selenium, vitamin A, vitamin C, vitamin K

GOOD SOURCE OF: calcium, fiber, folate, magnesium, manganese, pantothenic acid, phosphorous, potassium, vitamin B$_6$, vitamin B$_{12}$, vitamin D

warm chipotle red bean dip

There's your average bean dip, and then there's this one: warm, creamy red beans laced with the smoky zing of chipotle chile, covered in bubbly melted cheese and served right in the skillet. It's the kind of dish that makes people want to gather round and dig in, and they won't stop until it has disappeared. You can certainly serve this as a nibble at a party, but this recipe treats it as the centerpiece of a complete dinner, where various vegetables and warm corn tortillas are put out along with it for a communal dipping (or DIY bean taco)–style dinner. It's a fun and filling meal that will make dinner feel like an extended happy hour.

DIP:

1 tablespoon olive oil

1 small onion, diced

2 garlic cloves, minced

½ teaspoon ground cumin

¼ teaspoon ground coriander

2 (15-ounce) cans low-sodium pinto or other red beans, drained and rinsed, divided

2 tablespoons freshly squeezed lime juice

1 canned chipotle chile in adobo, seeded, plus 2 teaspoons of the adobo sauce

½ teaspoon salt

3 tablespoons coarsely chopped fresh cilantro leaves, plus more for serving

½ cup shredded Monterey Jack cheese

TO SERVE:

8 (6-inch) corn tortillas

1 medium-size jicama, cut into wide sticks

16 small hearts of romaine lettuce leaves

4 radishes, cut into wedges

1. Prepare the dip: Preheat the oven to 425°F. Heat the oil in a 10-inch ovenproof skillet over medium heat. Add the onion and cook until it softens, about 3 minutes. Stir in the garlic, cumin, and coriander and cook for 30 seconds more. Remove from the heat and set aside to cool slightly.

2. Put half of the beans, 2 tablespoons of water, the lime juice, chipotle and adobo sauce, salt, and the onion mixture in the small bowl of a food processor and process until smooth.

3. Return the bean puree to the skillet. Stir in the remaining beans and the cilantro. Sprinkle with the cheese and place in the oven. Bake until the cheese is melted, about 15 minutes. Remove from the oven and let rest for 5 minutes.

4. Just before serving, while the dip is resting, wrap the tortillas in foil and place in the oven to warm for 3 to 5 minutes.

5. Serve the dip in the skillet (with a towel around the handle!), garnished with cilantro, with the tortillas, jicama, lettuce, and radishes for scooping. Alternatively, you can serve taco style with the jicama and radishes cut into matchsticks and the lettuce shredded.

Makes 4 servings

SERVING SIZE: ¼ cup dip, 2 tortillas, and 1½ cups vegetables

PER SERVING: Calories 460; Total Fat 10 g (Sat Fat 3.5 g, Mono Fat 4 g, Poly Fat 1 g); Protein 19 g; Carb 73 g; Fiber 17 g; Cholesterol 15 mg; Sodium 470 mg; Total Sugar 6 g (Added Sugar 0 g)

EXCELLENT SOURCE OF: calcium, fiber, folate, iron, magnesium, phosphorous, potassium, vitamin A, vitamin C, vitamin K, zinc

GOOD SOURCE OF: iodine, manganese, molybdenum, riboflavin, thiamine, vitamin B_6

spinach and artichoke shakshuka

Shakshuka has earned a fashionable following these days, appearing on all the trendy restaurant menus and Instagram feeds. It is a traditional Middle Eastern dish of eggs simmered in a skillet of spiced tomato sauce that can be served for pretty much any meal of the day. But while the red-sauce version is most typical, there are many creative variations possible. This version goes all green with a base of spinach and artichokes seasoned with cumin, coriander, garlic, and a hint of peppery heat, then topped with salty, creamy feta and fronds of fresh dill. It is out of the ordinary in the best possible way. Enjoy it scooped up with warm pita bread.

2 tablespoons olive oil

1 large onion, diced (2 cups)

3 garlic cloves, minced

1 small green hot chile pepper, such as serrano or jalapeño, seeded and finely chopped

½ teaspoon ground cumin

½ teaspoon ground coriander

¼ teaspoon salt, plus more to taste

¼ teaspoon freshly ground black pepper, plus more to taste

10 ounces baby spinach (10 cups lightly packed), coarsely chopped

1 tablespoon freshly squeezed lemon juice

1½ cups frozen artichoke hearts, thawed and chopped

4 large eggs

½ cup crumbled feta cheese

2 tablespoons fresh dill fronds

4 whole wheat pita breads, lightly toasted

1. Heat the oil in a large, high-sided skillet over medium heat. Add the onion and cook, stirring occasionally, until softened, 4 to 5 minutes. Add the garlic, chile pepper, cumin, coriander, salt, and black pepper and cook for 30 seconds more.

2. Add half of the spinach and then the lemon juice and cook, stirring, adding the rest of the spinach in a couple of batches as it wilts and there is room in the pan for more. Once the spinach is all wilted but still bright green, stir in the artichoke hearts and cook for 1 minute more.

3. Spread out the mixture evenly in the pan. Break one of the eggs into a small ramekin or bowl. Form a well in the mixture and transfer the egg into it. Repeat with the remaining three eggs, creating separate wells for them. Scatter the cheese around the surface. Cover and cook until the egg whites become opaque and the yolks are still slightly runny, about 4 minutes. Serve garnished with dill, seasoned with additional salt and pepper to taste, with the pita alongside.

Makes 4 servings

SERVING SIZE: 1 egg, ¾ cup vegetable mixture, and 1 pita

PER SERVING: Calories 400; Total Fat 17 g (Sat Fat 5 g, Mono Fat 7 g, Poly Fat 2 g); Protein 19 g; Carb 47 g; Fiber 2 g; Cholesterol 205 mg; Sodium 785 mg; Total Sugar 6 g (Added Sugar 0 g)

EXCELLENT SOURCE OF: calcium, folate, magnesium, manganese, phosphorous, protein, riboflavin, selenium, thiamine, vitamin A, vitamin B$_6$, vitamin C, vitamin K

GOOD SOURCE OF: fiber, iodine, iron, molybdenum, niacin, pantothenic acid, potassium, vitamin B$_{12}$, vitamin D, zinc

zucchini pancakes
with yogurt-feta sauce

initially made these savory pancakes as a way to put a dent in an overload of summer zucchini, but I have since found myself making them over and over, year-round. They make a homey and fast dinner, lunch, or weekend breakfast, and are also an elegant brunch entrée and (in mini-size) a cocktail party food. The shredded zucchini is squeezed of its liquid (an essential step for keeping these light and crisp) and is held together with egg and a little whole wheat flour. Simply seasoned with onion and salt, the pancakes are panfried in olive oil until they are soft and tender inside with a supple crispness outside. Served hot with a cool dollop of creamy yogurt-feta sauce perfumed with fresh dill, I'm willing to bet that you too will start plotting to make them again as soon as you have your first taste. A cup-for-cup gluten-free flour may be substituted for the whole wheat pastry flour.

3 medium-size zucchini, trimmed (about 8 ounces each)

¾ teaspoon salt, divided

¾ cup plain low-fat or whole-milk Greek yogurt

½ cup crumbled feta cheese

3 tablespoons chopped fresh dill

2 teaspoons freshly squeezed lemon juice

1 small garlic clove, grated or finely minced

¼ cup plus 1 teaspoon olive oil, divided

3 large eggs

6 tablespoons whole wheat pastry flour, plus more as needed

2 tablespoons grated or finely minced onion

1 teaspoon baking powder

¼ teaspoon freshly ground black pepper

1. Shred the zucchini on the large holes of a box grater or in a food processor using the shredding attachment. Transfer it to a strainer or colander, toss with ½ teaspoon of the salt, and let drain for 10 minutes. Then, squeeze it with your hands to press out as much liquid as possible.

2. While the zucchini is draining, make the sauce: Stir together the yogurt, feta, dill, lemon juice, garlic, and 1 teaspoon of the olive oil in a medium-size bowl.

3. Beat the eggs in a large bowl. Add the drained zucchini, flour, onion, baking powder, the remaining ¼ teaspoon of salt, and the pepper and stir to combine. Add more flour by the tablespoon if the batter seems too loose.

4. Heat 2 tablespoons of the oil in a large, nonstick skillet over medium heat until the oil is shimmering. Use a ¼-cup measure to scoop the batter into the pan, using a bit less than the full measure for each dollop, and spreading out the batter with the bottom of the measuring cup after each mound is placed in the pan, so that the pancakes are each about 3½ inches in diameter. You should wind up with about six pancakes in the pan. Cook until they are well browned and crisp on the outside and warmed through, about 3 minutes per side, then transfer to a plate and repeat with the remaining oil and batter. Serve immediately with the sauce alongside.

These are best just-cooked, but you can also make them up to a day ahead, refrigerate them, and then reheat in a 350°F oven.

Makes 4 servings

SERVING SIZE: 3 pancakes and ¼ cup sauce

PER SERVING: Calories 330; Total Fat 24 g (Sat Fat 7 g, Mono Fat 13 g, Poly Fat 3 g); Protein 15 g; Carb 15 g; Fiber 2 g; Cholesterol 160 mg; Sodium 550 mg; Total Sugar 7 g (Added Sugar 0 g)

EXCELLENT SOURCE OF: calcium, magnesium, molybdenum, phosphorous, protein, riboflavin, selenium, vitamin B$_6$, vitamin C, vitamin K

GOOD SOURCE OF: folate, iodine, iron, manganese, pantothenic acid, potassium, vitamin A, vitamin B$_{12}$, zinc

herbed lentil skillet with spinach, tomatoes, and ricotta

You can have this meal on the table in less time than it takes me to run a mile. Okay, I admit I am the slowest runner I know (I am more of a jogger, really)—but still, that is a fast dinner. The key is taking advantage of canned lentils for a tender and hearty instant protein, as well as vegetables that require very little prep—prewashed baby spinach and grape tomatoes. They are seasoned in the skillet with chopped shallot, fresh thyme, and balsamic vinegar, then dolloped with creamy, rich ricotta cheese that is warmed slightly in the skillet, too. A sprinkle of fresh basil leaves takes you, deliciously, to the finish line for the win. I like to serve mine with some whole-grain, sourdough toast or baguette.

2 tablespoons olive oil

⅓ cup chopped shallot

1 garlic clove, minced

2 teaspoons chopped fresh thyme leaves, or ¾ teaspoon dried

2 (15.5-ounce) cans lentils, drained and rinsed (about 3 cups)

1 tablespoon aged balsamic vinegar

½ teaspoon salt

¼ teaspoon freshly ground black pepper

1 cup grape tomatoes, quartered

2 cups lightly packed baby spinach leaves, coarsely chopped

1 cup part-skim ricotta cheese

6 large fresh basil leaves, cut into ribbons

1. Heat the oil in a 10-inch skillet over medium heat. Add the shallots and cook until they have softened, about 1 minute. Stir in the garlic and cook for 30 seconds more. Stir in the thyme, then add the lentils, balsamic vinegar, salt, and pepper, and stir just enough to combine. Add the tomatoes and spinach, lower the heat to medium-low, cover, and cook, stirring occasionally, until warmed through and the vegetables have wilted, 5 minutes.

2. Make a well in the lentil mixture and dollop ¼ cup of the ricotta cheese into it. Repeat with the remaining ricotta, creating separate wells. Cover and cook until the cheese is slightly warmed but not melted, 2 minutes. Sprinkle with the basil and serve.

Leftovers will keep in an airtight container in the refrigerator for up to 4 days.

Makes 4 servings

SERVING SIZE: 1 cup lentil mixture and ¼ cup ricotta cheese

PER SERVING: Calories 340; Total Fat 12 g (Sat Fat 4 g, Mono Fat 7 g, Poly Fat 1 g); Protein 22 g; Carb 38 g; Fiber 17 g; Cholesterol 20 mg; Sodium 630 mg; Total Sugar 6 g (Added Sugar 0 g)

EXCELLENT SOURCE OF: calcium, fiber, iron, manganese, protein, vitamin A, vitamin C, vitamin K

GOOD SOURCE OF: folate, phosphorous, selenium

broccoli cheddar skillet strata

A strata (a savory bread pudding) is, to me, a perfect example of how magical cooking can be. You take a handful of humble ingredients—eggs, milk, bread, broccoli, cheese—and in minutes, with one skillet, turn them into a marvelous, elegant meal. Here, once baked, the egg-soaked bread becomes soufflélike inside—light and puffed—but with a golden brown, crisped top. It is jeweled with flecks of broccoli, and made sumptuous with Cheddar cheese melted throughout. Using whole-grain bread and extra-sharp cheese means a modest amount brings lots of flavor—and means it's a healthfully balanced meal, too.

2 tablespoons olive oil, divided

3 cups cubed whole wheat baguette or other crusty bread (½-inch cubes)

1 small onion, diced

3 cups chopped broccoli (about ½ head, chopped into ½-inch pieces)

6 large eggs

¾ cup low-fat or whole milk

1½ teaspoons Dijon mustard

½ teaspoon salt

½ teaspoon freshly ground black pepper

½ cup packed shredded extra-sharp Cheddar cheese

1. Preheat the oven to 450°F. Heat 1 tablespoon of the oil in a 10-inch ovenproof skillet over medium heat. Add the bread to the skillet and cook, tossing frequently, until it is golden brown, about 6 minutes. Transfer the bread to a plate and carefully wipe any crumbs out of the pan.

2. Add the remaining tablespoon of oil to the skillet, then add the onion and cook until it has softened slightly, 2 minutes. Add the broccoli and cook, stirring frequently, until it begins to soften, 3 minutes.

3. Whisk together the eggs, milk, mustard, salt, and pepper in a medium-size bowl. Add the cheese and the bread and toss to combine, then pour the bread mixture over the vegetables in the skillet.

4. Cover with foil and bake for 10 minutes, then uncover and continue to bake until the strata is set in the center, 5 to 8 minutes more. Remove from the oven and allow to sit for 5 minutes. To serve, scoop out portions with a large spoon or cut into wedges, whichever you prefer.

The strata will keep in an airtight container in the refrigerator for up to 4 days.

Makes 4 servings

SERVING SIZE: ¼ strata

PER SERVING: Calories 350; Total Fat 21 g (Sat Fat 7 g, Mono Fat 8 g, Poly Fat 3 g); Protein 20 g; Carb 21 g; Fiber 2 g; Cholesterol 295 mg; Sodium 710 mg; Total Sugar 6 g (Added Sugar 0 g)

EXCELLENT SOURCE OF: calcium, folate, iodine, manganese, phosphorous, protein, riboflavin, selenium, vitamin C, vitamin K

GOOD SOURCE OF: fiber, iron, magnesium, molybdenum, pantothenic acid, potassium, thiamine, vitamin A, vitamin B$_6$, vitamin B$_{12}$, vitamin D, zinc

halloumi and fig salad with balsamic

I n this delightfully different main course salad, sweet balsamic-basted figs and slabs of salty halloumi cheese yield to the skillet heat to become beautifully browned. They are served warm atop a mound of cool, peppery arugula and crisp fennel tossed with olive oil and salt. A sprinkle of toasted walnuts adds a savory crunch, and a drizzle of aged balsamic vinegar ties all the elements together and adorns the plate. The sweet-tart, deep flavor of aged balsamic is a defining element of this salad, so make sure you use that rather than a more acidic variety. Aged balsamic tends to be on the more expensive side, with a syrupy texture and gentle tanginess. If you don't have that, you can simmer a thinner, more acidic balsamic vinegar with a little honey until the mixture approximates the consistency of maple syrup, then let it come to room temperature, to achieve something similar to the real deal.

1 cup walnut pieces

8 fresh figs, stemmed and halved lengthwise

6 teaspoons aged balsamic vinegar, divided

2 tablespoons olive oil, divided

4 (¼-inch-thick) slabs halloumi cheese (4 ounces)

4 cups baby arugula

1 fennel bulb, thinly sliced (2 cups)

¼ teaspoon salt

Freshly ground black pepper

1. Toast the walnuts in a dry, large, nonstick skillet over medium-high heat until fragrant and golden, 3 minutes. Transfer the nuts to a plate.

2. Brush the figs on both sides with 2 teaspoons of the balsamic vinegar. Heat 1 tablespoon of the oil in the same skillet over medium-high heat. Place the cheese in the skillet and cook until it is warmed through and a nice brown crust has formed on both sides, about 2 minutes per side. Transfer the cheese to a cutting board. Place the figs, cut side down, in the same skillet and cook until caramelized and beginning to soften, 2 minutes, then flip and cook for 1 minute more. Cut the halloumi slabs each into two triangular pieces, so you have eight pieces total.

3. Toss the arugula and fennel in a medium-size bowl with the remaining tablespoon of oil and the salt.

4. To serve, divide the greens among four salad plates. Top each with four pieces of fig, two cheese triangles, and ¼ cup of the walnuts. Drizzle each plate with 1 teaspoon of the remaining balsamic vinegar each and pepper to taste.

Makes 4 servings

SERVING SIZE: 1 salad

PER SERVING: Calories 460; Total Fat 34 g (Sat Fat 8 g, Mono Fat 7 g, Poly Fat 15 g); Protein 13 g; Carb 30 g; Fiber 7 g; Cholesterol 20 mg; Sodium 490 mg; Total Sugar 22 g (Added Sugar 0 g)

EXCELLENT SOURCE OF: calcium, copper, fiber, manganese, protein, vitamin A, vitamin C, vitamin K

GOOD SOURCE OF: folate, iron, magnesium, molybdenum, phosphorous, potassium, thiamine, vitamin B$_6$

falafel burger plate

I have long sought a homemade falafel that was healthier; that is, not deep-fried. The answer, it turns out, is not baking them in the oven, but cooking them on the stovetop. By shaping the falafel mixture into flat patties and cooking them in a skillet with a little olive oil, you get the magical combination of craveable crispness outside and moist inside, in a better-for-you way. Here, the falafel "burgers," which are gorgeously green from an extra handful of fresh herbs and fragrant with cumin, coriander, and garlic, are served over a mound of colorful slaw drizzled with a lemony tahini sauce. I still go out occasionally to get my fix of a real-deal, deep-fried falafel, but this beautiful, flavorful plate grants me my falafel wishes in a way that I can enjoy healthfully anytime. I especially like that everything on this plate can be prepped ahead and pulled together at the last minute. To make this gluten-free, substitute chickpea flour or cup-for-cup gluten-free flour.

FALAFEL BURGERS:

½ cup lightly packed fresh cilantro leaves

½ cup lightly packed fresh parsley leaves

¼ small onion, coarsely chopped

2 garlic cloves, coarsely chopped

¾ teaspoon ground cumin

½ teaspoon salt

½ teaspoon ground coriander

⅛ teaspoon crushed red pepper flakes

1 (15-ounce) can no-salt-added chickpeas, drained, rinsed, and patted dry

3 tablespoons whole wheat pastry flour

½ teaspoon baking powder

2½ tablespoons olive oil

TAHINI SAUCE:

3 tablespoons tahini

1 tablespoon freshly squeezed lemon juice

1. Prepare the falafel burgers: Place the cilantro, parsley, onion, garlic, cumin, salt, coriander, and red pepper flakes in the small bowl of a food processor. Process until all the ingredients are finely minced. Add the chickpeas to the processor and pulse until everything is well incorporated but the mixture is still coarse and grainy, stopping to scrape down the bowl as needed. Sprinkle in the flour and baking powder and stir to combine. Shape the mixture into four flat patties about 3 inches in diameter each. Put the patties on a plate, cover, and refrigerate for at least 1 hour or up to 2 days ahead.

2. Prepare the sauce: Stir together the tahini and lemon juice, then stir in about 2 tablespoons of water, adding them one at a time, until the sauce is the consistency of pancake batter. (The mixture will seize up at first, but don't worry—it will become smooth again as you add the water.)

3. Prepare the salad: Combine all the salad ingredients in a medium-size bowl and toss.

4. To cook the falafel burgers, heat 1½ tablespoons of the oil in a large, nonstick skillet over medium-high heat. Place the patties into the pan, lower the heat to medium, and cook until browned and crisped on the bottom, 2 to 3 minutes. Flip the patties, add the remaining tablespoon of oil to the skillet, and cook the other side for 2 to 3 minutes.

5. Serve the burgers with a mound of the salad, drizzled with the tahini sauce and with the pita alongside, if using.

The tahini sauce and the salad will keep for up to 3 days in the refrigerator, stored in separate airtight containers.

SALAD:

2 cups thinly sliced red cabbage

1 cup grated carrot

¼ cup thinly sliced scallion

1 tablespoon extra-virgin olive oil

1 tablespoon freshly squeezed lemon juice

¼ teaspoon salt

⅛ teaspoon freshly ground black pepper

Whole-grain pita bread, cut into wedges (optional)

Makes 4 servings

SERVING SIZE: 1 burger, ¾ cup salad, and about 1 tablespoon sauce

PER SERVING: Calories 330; Total Fat 19 g (Sat Fat 2.5 g, Mono Fat 11 g, Poly Fat 4 g); Protein 10 g; Carb 32 g; Fiber 8 g; Cholesterol 0 mg; Sodium 560 mg; Total Sugar 5 g (Added Sugar 0 g)

EXCELLENT SOURCE OF: copper, fiber, folate, phosphorous, vitamin A, vitamin C, vitamin K

GOOD SOURCE OF: calcium, iron, magnesium, manganese, potassium, protein, thiamine, zinc

mushroom white bean toasts with frisée

These impressive toasts are piled high with layers of savory flavor and contrasting textures. First, a garlicky, olive oil–enriched white bean mash is spread generously onto crunchy whole-grain toast. That is layered with thyme-scented, sautéed mushrooms, and then a stunning frisée salad is mounded on top. The frisée, with its curly texture and tangy mustard vinaigrette dressing, offers a delicious counterpoint to the soft savoriness of the beans and the meatiness of the mushrooms. (Arugula or watercress would work well as a substitute.) The dish makes a definite statement both on the plate and on your palate, and can be enjoyed as a meal in itself or served on smaller pieces of bread as a starter or small plate at a party.

4 large or 8 medium-size (½-inch thick) slices crusty whole-grain bread (8 ounces total)

5 tablespoons olive oil, divided

4 teaspoons sherry vinegar, divided

1 teaspoon Dijon mustard

¾ teaspoon salt, divided

¼ teaspoon freshly ground black pepper, divided

3 cups lightly packed, torn frisée (1 large head)

1 small garlic clove, minced

1 (15-ounce) can low-sodium white beans, such as cannellini, drained and rinsed

12 ounces mixed sliced mushrooms (such as shiitake, cremini, oyster, or button)

¼ cup chopped shallots

2 teaspoons chopped fresh thyme

1. Toast the bread in a toaster or toaster oven. Whisk 2 tablespoons of the olive oil in a medium-size bowl with 2 teaspoons of the sherry vinegar, the mustard, ¼ teaspoon of the salt, and ⅛ teaspoon of the pepper. Add the frisée and toss to coat.

2. Place the minced garlic on a cutting board and sprinkle with ¼ teaspoon of the salt; using the broad side of a knife blade, mash together the garlic and salt to form a paste. Transfer the paste to a medium-size bowl, add the beans and 2 tablespoons of the olive oil, and mash with a fork until most of the mixture is smooth but there are still some intact beans.

3. Heat the remaining tablespoon of oil in a large skillet over medium-high heat. Add the mushrooms and shallots and cook, stirring occasionally, until the mushrooms have released their liquid and begin to brown, 4 to 5 minutes. Add the thyme and remaining ¼ teaspoon of salt and ⅛ teaspoon of pepper and cook for 1 minute more. Then, stir in the remaining 2 teaspoons of vinegar.

4. To serve, spread each toast generously with the mashed beans; top each with the mushrooms and then a mound of the frisée salad.

The bean mixture and the sautéed mushrooms may be made ahead and kept separately in air-tight containers in the refrigerator for up to 4 days.

Makes 4 servings

SERVING SIZE: 1 large or 2 medium toasts

PER SERVING: Calories 420; Total Fat 20 g (Sat Fat 3 g, Mono Fat 12 g, Poly Fat 3 g); Protein 16 g; Carb 47 g; Fiber 13 g; Cholesterol 0 mg; Sodium 730 mg; Total Sugar 7 g (Added Sugar 0 g)

EXCELLENT SOURCE OF: copper, fiber, folate, iron, magnesium, manganese, niacin, pantothenic acid, phosphorous, potassium, protein, riboflavin, selenium, thiamine, vitamin A, vitamin K, zinc

GOOD SOURCE OF: calcium, vitamin B_6, vitamin C

coconut curry carrot lentil soup

Pureed vegetable soups are central to my everyday cooking repertoire. The core idea is simple: sauté aromatics, add a vegetable and broth plus seasonings, simmer until the vegetable is tender, then whir until smooth. This recipe turns that basic concept into a complete one-pot meal with the addition of red lentils. Once pureed, the lentils blend in seamlessly to the curried carrots, so you'd never guess they are there, but they do a big job of thickening the soup and adding essential protein, minerals, and fiber. A finishing touch of honey balances the spices and brings out the sweetness of the vegetable, and coconut milk adds a fragrant richness. Try it with some toasted naan, or other flatbread, to dunk into the soup.

1 tablespoon olive oil

1 medium-size onion, diced

2 garlic cloves, minced

1 tablespoon curry powder

1 teaspoon salt, plus more to taste

¼ teaspoon freshly ground black pepper

Pinch of cayenne pepper

6 cups low-sodium chicken or vegetable broth

1 cup dried red lentils, rinsed

1 pound carrots (3 to 4 medium-size), cut into ¼-inch-thick coins

1½ tablespoons honey

1 cup light coconut milk

1. Heat the oil in a large pot over medium heat. Add the onion and cook, stirring occasionally, until softened, about 3 minutes. Add the garlic, curry powder, salt, black pepper, and cayenne and cook, stirring, for 30 seconds. Add the broth, cover, and bring to a boil over high heat.

2. Add the lentils; lower the heat to medium-low and simmer, partially covered, stirring once or twice, for 10 minutes. Add the carrots and cook, partially covered, until the carrots are tender, about 15 minutes more.

3. Stir in the honey and coconut milk, then use an immersion blender to puree until smooth. (Alternatively, allow to cool, then puree in several batches in a regular blender.)

The soup will keep in an airtight container in the refrigerator for up to 4 days, or in the freezer for 3 months.

Makes 4 servings

SERVING SIZE: 2¼ cups

PER SERVING: Calories 320; Total Fat 8 g (Sat Fat 3 g, Mono Fat 3 g, Poly Fat 2 g); Protein 13 g; Carb 52 g; Fiber 7 g; Cholesterol 0 mg; Sodium 860 mg; Total Sugar 14 g (Added Sugar 6 g)

EXCELLENT SOURCE OF: copper, fiber, folate, iron, manganese, vitamin A

GOOD SOURCE OF: phosphorous, potassium, protein, thiamine, vitamin B$_6$, vitamin C, vitamin K, zinc

mushroom stroganoff soup

This soup is pure comfort food that is good for you, too. It takes its cues from a classic beef Stroganoff—a dish of sautéed beef and mushrooms in a sour cream–based sauce that's typically served over egg noodles—but here it is reimagined into a sumptuously creamy, hearty soup that's much more healthfully balanced. Doubling down on the mushrooms provides lots of meaty texture without any beef, and low-fat milk thickened with a little flour as a creamy base makes the soup protein-rich and keeps the saturated fat in balance, allowing for the essential tanginess of real sour cream to be used strategically both in the broth and as a cool final dollop. Tender whole wheat egg noodles add heartiness and make it a memorable meal in a bowl. To make this vegetarian, use vegetable broth and a vegetarian Worcestershire sauce.

2 tablespoons olive oil

2 medium-size shallots, chopped (about ⅔ cup)

1 (10-ounce) package white button mushrooms, trimmed and sliced

1 (10-ounce) package cremini mushrooms, trimmed and sliced

2 garlic cloves, minced

4 cups low-sodium chicken or vegetable broth

1 tablespoon Worcestershire sauce

1 teaspoon Dijon mustard

¾ teaspoon salt, plus more to taste

¼ teaspoon freshly ground black pepper

1 cup whole wheat egg noodles

1 cup 1% low-fat milk

⅔ cup sour cream, divided

2 tablespoons all-purpose flour

2 tablespoons chopped fresh parsley

1. Heat the oil in a soup pot over medium heat. Add the shallots and cook, stirring occasionally, until they are softened, 2 minutes. Add the mushrooms, increase the heat to medium-high, and cook, stirring occasionally, until the mushrooms have released their liquid and they begin to brown, about 8 minutes. Stir in the garlic and cook for 30 seconds more. Add the broth, Worcestershire, mustard, salt, and pepper and bring to a boil. Add the egg noodles and boil gently, uncovered, until the noodles are nearly tender, 5 minutes.

2. Whisk together the milk, ⅓ cup of the sour cream, and the flour in a pitcher or medium-size bowl, until the flour is dissolved. Ladle ½ cup of the broth from the pot into the milk mixture and whisk well, then pour the milk mixture into the pot and, stirring, bring to a gentle boil, then lower the heat and simmer until it is thickened, 2 minutes. Season with additional salt to taste.

3. Serve garnished with a dollop of the remaining sour cream and the parsley.

The soup will keep in an airtight container in the refrigerator for up to 4 days.

Makes 4 servings

SERVING SIZE: 1⅔ cups

PER SERVING: Calories 310; Total Fat 15 g (Sat Fat 6g, Mono Fat 5 g, Poly Fat 1 g); Protein 11 g; Carb 34 g; Fiber 2 g; Cholesterol 45 mg; Sodium 740 mg; Total Sugar 10 g (Added Sugar 0 g)

EXCELLENT SOURCE OF: copper, fiber, manganese, phosphorous, potassium, protein, riboflavin, selenium, vitamin B₆, vitamin K

GOOD SOURCE OF: calcium, folate, iron, niacin, pantothenic acid, thiamine, vitamin C, zinc

ancho black bean chili with orange essence

In this hearty chili, the essence of orange—both juice and zest—brightens the deep, savory taste of the black beans and tomatoes, which are simmered with an earthy, smoky blend of spices including cumin, ancho chile powder, and a kick of cayenne. Ancho chile powder is made from smoked poblano peppers—it has a mild heat level and subtle sweetness, and adds a uniquely aromatic and robust flavor dimension. You can substitute regular chili powder for this recipe if need be—just add the cayenne judiciously, depending on how hot your chili powder is.

3 tablespoons olive oil

1 medium-size onion, diced (about 1½ cups)

1 large red bell pepper, seeded and diced (about 1 cup)

4 garlic cloves, minced

1 tablespoon ancho chile powder

2 teaspoons ground cumin

1¼ teaspoons salt, plus more to taste

1 teaspoon dried oregano

½ teaspoon cayenne pepper, plus more to taste

2 tablespoons tomato paste

2 cups canned crushed tomatoes

3 (15-ounce) cans low-sodium black beans, drained and rinsed

2 teaspoons finely grated orange zest, divided

1 tablespoon honey

2 tablespoons freshly squeezed orange juice

½ cup plain Greek yogurt

⅓ cup lightly packed fresh cilantro leaves

1. Heat the oil in a large pot over medium heat. Add the onion and bell pepper and cook, stirring occasionally, until softened, 5 minutes. Add the garlic, ancho chile powder, cumin, salt, oregano, cayenne, and tomato paste and cook, stirring, for 1 minute more.

2. Add the crushed tomatoes, beans, 1 teaspoon of the orange zest, the honey, and ½ cup of water and bring to a boil. Lower the heat to low, cover, and cook, stirring occasionally, until the ingredients have melded, 20 minutes. Stir in the orange juice. Add additional water by the tablespoon if the chili is thicker than you'd like, and more salt and cayenne to taste.

3. Serve each bowl garnished with a dollop of yogurt, cilantro leaves, and a pinch of the remaining orange zest.

The chili will keep in an airtight container in the refrigerator for up to 4 days, or in the freezer for 3 months.

Makes 4 servings

SERVING SIZE: 1⅔ cups

PER SERVING: Calories 320; Total Fat 9 g (Sat Fat 1 g, Mono Fat 5 g, Poly Fat 2 g); Protein 16 g; Carb 52 g; Fiber 18 g; Cholesterol 0 mg; Sodium 700 mg; Total Sugar 11 g (Added Sugar 3 g)

EXCELLENT SOURCE OF: fiber, folate, iron, potassium, protein, vitamin A, vitamin C, vitamin K

GOOD SOURCE OF: calcium, manganese, vitamin B$_6$

russian salad plate

One of my favorite culinary adventures as a New York City kid was heading to Brighton Beach, Brooklyn, for Russian food. To this day, the restaurants there have a boisterous, party atmosphere with platters, vodka, and live music flowing—I still love to get out there whenever I have a chance. One of my must-haves on the menu is this crimson salad made with beets, potatoes, carrots, and pickled vegetables, seasoned with fresh dill in a tangy vinegar and olive oil dressing. Here, I have added boiled eggs to the mix to make it a meal in itself. It is an old-world dish, for sure, but it has the modern appeal of a rediscovered classic and the potential health benefits of probiotics to boot. Those good bacteria, which foster gut balance as well as overall immunity, are found in fermented sauerkraut and pickles (look for those found in the refrigerator case as opposed to on the shelf, since these good bacteria are denatured during the canning/jarring process). If you are a meal-prepper like I am who likes to cook in advance, you'll be happy to know all the roots and the eggs can be boiled and readied days ahead.

4 medium-size carrots (about 3½ ounces each), peeled, trimmed, and halved crosswise

4 large eggs

4 medium-size beets (about 4 ounces each), scrubbed, unpeeled

4 medium-size waxy potatoes, such as new red (about 5 ounces each), scrubbed, unpeeled

1 cup sauerkraut, drained

1 cup diced dill pickles

½ cup chopped red onion

¼ cup extra-virgin olive oil

2 tablespoons white vinegar, plus more to taste

Salt

12 Gem lettuce leaves or 8 romaine lettuce leaves

⅓ cup dill fronds

1. Place the carrots in a 3- to 4-quart pot and fill the pot about half full with cold water. Bring to a boil. Gently add the eggs to the pot, using a slotted spoon. Lower the heat to medium-low and simmer for 10 minutes, then use a slotted spoon to transfer the carrots and eggs to an ice water bath, leaving the water in the pot at a boil. Let cool until they have cooled completely, then transfer them to a dish.

2. Put the beets and potatoes into the boiling water in the pot, adding more water to cover the vegetables, if needed. Return to a boil, then simmer, partially covered, until the vegetables can be pierced with a skewer or paring knife, about 25 minutes for the potatoes and 35 minutes for the beets. (They are best cooked until slightly underdone, since they will continue to cook as they cool.) Drain and place in the refrigerator to cool.

3. Use your finger and/or a paring knife to remove the peel from the beets, then dice and set them aside. Then, peel the potato, the same way, and dice it. Dice the carrots. Peel the eggs and quarter them. Place the potatoes, carrots, sauerkraut, pickles, red onion, oil, and vinegar in a large bowl and toss to combine. Stir in the beets. Add salt and additional vinegar to taste, depending on the saltiness and tang of the pickles and kraut. The salad may be made ahead to this point and kept in an airtight container in the refrigerator for up to 4 days.

4. Serve over a bed of lettuce leaves, garnished with dill and the wedges of egg.

Makes 4 servings

SERVING SIZE: 2 cups salad and 1 egg

PER SERVING: Calories 350; Total Fat 19 g (Sat Fat 3.5 g, Mono Fat 12 g, Poly Fat 3 g); Protein 11 g; Carb 34 g; Fiber 8 g; Cholesterol 185 mg; Sodium 840 mg; Total Sugar 13 g (Added Sugar 0 g)

EXCELLENT SOURCE OF: fiber, folate, manganese, molybdenum, potassium, protein, riboflavin, selenium, vitamin A, vitamin C, vitamin K

GOOD SOURCE OF: iodine, iron, magnesium, pantothenic acid, phosphorous, vitamin B$_6$, vitamin D

chili bean apple jack stew

This recipe is my spin on a favorite from the very first cookbook I ever owned—*Moosewood Cookbook*, by Mollie Katzen. That book, which I still have—its cover sun-bleached and pages splattered—fed me throughout my college years and beyond. One dish from it I made again and again was the simply named Cheese-Beans, a savory, chili-seasoned bake of red beans, fresh tomatoes, chunks of sweet apple, and cheese—lots of cheese. That heavy cheesiness is one reason I had not made it in years. But I decided to take a fresh look at it and find a way to achieve its comforting, flavorful essence in a healthier way. I don't eliminate the cheese, but make it a supporting player rather than the lead. The resulting one-pot meal—the beans first and Monterey Jack at the finish—is a tasty tribute to the past with a sensibility that's just right for today. (To make this gluten-free, use hard cider in place of the beer and check to make sure your chili powder is wheat-free.)

2 tablespoons olive oil

1 large onion, diced

2 teaspoons chili powder

1½ teaspoons salt

1 teaspoon mustard powder

½ teaspoon freshly ground black pepper

⅓ cup pale lager beer

4 cups packed chopped baby kale leaves

3 (15-ounce) cans low-sodium red kidney or pinto beans, drained and rinsed

2 large Golden Delicious or Jonagold apples, unpeeled, cored, and diced

4 medium-size tomatoes, diced

1 cup packed grated Monterey Jack cheese

1. Preheat the oven to 350°F. Heat the oil in a large, ovenproof pot over medium heat. Add the onion and cook until it is translucent, 3 minutes. Stir in the chili powder, salt, mustard powder, and pepper. Add the beer, then the kale, and cook, stirring, until it is wilted, about 1 minute.

2. Remove from the heat; stir in the beans, apples, tomatoes, and cheese. Cover and bake until warmed through, the apple is tender, and the cheese is melted, 35 to 40 minutes.

The stew will keep in an airtight container in the refrigerator for up to 4 days.

Makes 6 servings

SERVING SIZE: 1⅓ cups

PER SERVING: Calories 350; Total Fat 11 g (Sat Fat 4.5 g, Mono Fat 8 g, Poly Fat 6 g); Protein 17 g; Carb 46 g; Fiber 15 g; Cholesterol 46 mg; Sodium 780 mg; Total Sugar 13 g (Added Sugar 0 g)

EXCELLENT SOURCE OF: calcium, fiber, manganese, phosphorous, potassium, protein, vitamin A, vitamin C, vitamin K

GOOD SOURCE OF: calcium, folate, iron, magnesium, riboflavin, thiamine, vitamin B_6, zinc

creamy caldo verde with mushrooms

There is something very modern about a soup made emerald with a blended whir of kale leaves. But hip as it may seem, green soup is an old-world staple. The most well-known is the traditional Portuguese caldo verde, made with potatoes and collards or kale, and often fortified with chunks of smoked sausage. Here, sautéed mushrooms coated in smoked paprika add a similar meaty smokiness in a plant-based way and white beans make it protein-rich, and once pureed give it a luxurious creaminess. The result is an on-trend, healthy comfort food that is destined to stand the test of time.

¼ cup olive oil, divided

10 ounces white button mushrooms, sliced

1½ teaspoons smoked paprika

Pinch of cayenne pepper

1¼ teaspoons salt, divided, plus more to taste

1 large onion, diced

2 garlic cloves, minced

2 large russet potatoes (about 10 ounces each), peeled and diced

2 (15-ounce) cans low-sodium white beans, such as cannellini or navy, drained and rinsed

6 cups low-sodium chicken or vegetable broth

1 small bunch kale (8 ounces), stemmed, leaves very thinly sliced, divided

½ teaspoon freshly ground black pepper

1. Heat 2 tablespoons of the oil in a large pot over medium-high heat. Add the mushrooms and cook, stirring occasionally, until they have released their liquid and become well browned and caramelized, 8 to 10 minutes. Remove the pot from the heat, stir in the paprika, cayenne, and ¼ teaspoon of the salt, then transfer the mushrooms to a plate.

2. Add the remaining 2 tablespoons of oil to the pot and heat it over medium heat. Add the onion and cook, stirring occasionally, until it has softened, 3 minutes; add the garlic and cook for 30 seconds more.

3. Add the potatoes, beans, and broth and bring to a boil. Lower the heat to medium-low and simmer, uncovered, until the potatoes are tender, about 15 minutes. Add about three quarters of the kale, increase the heat to medium-high, and cook until the kale is wilted but still vibrant green, about 3 minutes.

4. Remove from the heat and puree, using an immersion blender, until the soup is smooth with small flecks of kale. (Alternatively, allow to cool slightly, then puree it in several batches in a regular blender.) Return the pureed soup to a boil, then stir in the remaining kale, the mushrooms, the remaining teaspoon of salt, and the black pepper and cook until the kale is wilted, about 3 minutes. Season with additional salt to taste.

The soup will keep in an airtight container in the refrigerator for up to 3 days.

Makes 4 servings

SERVING SIZE: about 2¼ cups

PER SERVING: Calories 480; Total Fat 16 g (Sat Fat 2 g, Mono Fat 9 g, Poly Fat 2 g); Protein 19 g; Carb 70 g; Fiber 15 g; Cholesterol 0 mg; Sodium 850 mg; Total Sugar 7 g (Added Sugar 0 g)

EXCELLENT SOURCE OF: copper, fiber, folate, iron, magnesium, manganese, niacin, phosphorous, potassium, protein, riboflavin, thiamine, vitamin A, vitamin B₆, vitamin C, vitamin K, zinc

GOOD SOURCE OF: calcium, iodine, molybdenum, pantothenic acid, selenium

chickpea and farro stew

tasted a version of this dish at a neighborhood restaurant in Milan, Italy, and thought about it for weeks afterward. It was a warming, cozy bowl of goodness with a rustic-chic elegance that made it feel totally fresh and modern, an appeal I attributed to the pairing of chickpeas with farro, an ancient variety of wheat. I began to experiment with my own take on it when I got home. I soon realized it involved the same basic cooking technique as a familiar favorite, pasta e fagioli (pasta and beans). Here, though, the farro lends a delightful chew and subtly nutty flavor to the stew. This dish is designed for the pearled or quick-cooking variety, which cooks in fifteen to twenty minutes. But you can use the unpearled kind instead, if you soak or parcook it beforehand. I have to warn you though, once you try this dish, you might catch yourself daydreaming about it after.

2 (15-ounce) cans low-sodium chickpeas (3 cups), drained and rinsed, divided

3½ cups low-sodium chicken or vegetable broth, divided

2 tablespoons olive oil

1 medium-size onion, diced

1 medium-size carrot, diced

1 celery stalk, diced

2 garlic cloves, minced

1 (14.5-ounce) can no-salt-added diced tomatoes

1 rosemary sprig

½ teaspoon salt

¼ teaspoon freshly ground black pepper

½ cup pearled farro

2 cups lightly packed baby spinach leaves, coarsely chopped

⅓ cup freshly grated Parmesan cheese

1. Place 1 cup of the chickpeas and ½ cup of the broth in a blender and puree until smooth.

2. Heat the oil in a large pot over medium heat. Add the onion, carrot, and celery and cook, stirring occasionally, until softened, but not browned, 6 to 8 minutes. Add the garlic and cook for 1 minute more.

3. Add the remaining 2 cups of chickpeas, remaining 3 cups of broth, and the tomatoes with their juices, rosemary, salt, and pepper to the pot. Bring to a boil, then lower the heat to medium-low and simmer, covered, for 15 minutes.

4. Add the farro, return to a boil, then lower the heat to medium-low, cover, and cook, stirring occasionally, until the farro is tender, about 20 minutes. Remove the rosemary sprig. Add the chickpea puree, then stir in the spinach and cook until it is just wilted, 1 to 2 minutes. Serve garnished with the cheese.

The stew will keep in an airtight container in the refrigerator for up to 4 days.

Makes 4 servings

SERVING SIZE: 1½ cups

PER SERVING: Calories 380; Total Fat 12 g (Sat Fat 2.5 g, Mono Fat 6 g, Poly Fat 2 g); Protein 17 g; Carb 51 g; Fiber 12 g; Cholesterol 5 mg; Sodium 770 mg; Total Sugar 10 g (Added Sugar 0 g)

EXCELLENT SOURCE OF: fiber, iron, manganese, phosphorous, protein, vitamin A, vitamin B$_6$, vitamin C, vitamin K

GOOD SOURCE OF: calcium, copper, magnesium, potassium, zinc

split pea soup with sun-dried tomato "gremolata"

When I first made this soup, I was especially eager to witness the reactions of my loyal taste testers (Thom and Bella) because I expected them to be wowed by its deliciously different topping. But they managed to scarf down the entire soup, unadorned, before I even had a chance to tell them there was a topping. On the upside, that gave me confirmation that this classic, savory soup is plenty flavorful on its own. But trust me when I tell you, the topping takes it to another level. It is a simple condiment of finely chopped sun-dried tomatoes, parsley, and garlic, kissed with smoked paprika that gives the soup a savory, smoky umami-rich taste, similar to the way smoked ham would. Once Thom and Bella finally tried it with the gremolata their satisfied smiles and *mmmmmm*s told me they agreed 100 percent: the topping makes it.

2 tablespoons olive oil

1 large onion, diced

1 medium-size carrot, finely diced

2 celery stalks, finely diced

2 medium-size garlic cloves, minced, plus 1 small clove, very finely minced or grated, divided

1¼ cups dried green split peas

6 cups low-sodium chicken or vegetable broth

2 fresh thyme sprigs

1 bay leaf

1 teaspoon salt, divided, plus more to taste

¼ teaspoon freshly ground black pepper

½ cup finely chopped fresh parsley leaves

¼ cup sun-dried tomatoes, soaked in hot water for 10 minutes to reconstitute if very dry, finely chopped

¼ teaspoon smoked paprika

1. Heat the oil in a large pot over medium heat. Add the onion, carrot, and celery and cook until they have softened, about 6 minutes. Add the two cloves' worth of minced garlic and cook for 30 seconds more. Stir in the split peas, then add the broth, thyme, bay leaf, ¾ teaspoon of the salt, and the pepper and bring to a boil. Lower the heat to low and simmer, partially covered, until the peas are falling apart, about 1 hour 15 minutes.

2. Meanwhile, make the gremolata by combining the parsley, sun-dried tomatoes, paprika, the finely minced garlic, and the remaining ¼ teaspoon of salt in a small bowl.

3. Remove the thyme stems and the bay leaf from the soup. If you want it to be creamy, puree it with an immersion blender or in several batches in a regular blender; otherwise, keep it as it is. Add additional broth or water to thin as desired, and more salt to taste. Serve the soup topped with the gremolata.

The soup will keep in an airtight container in the refrigerator for up to 4 days, or frozen for 3 months. The gremolata may be made up to 4 days ahead and stored in a separate airtight container in the refrigerator.

Makes 4 servings

SERVING SIZE: 1½ cups soup and 2 tablespoons gremolata

PER SERVING: Calories 350; Total Fat 8 g (Sat Fat 1 g, Mono Fat 5 g, Poly Fat 1 g); Protein 19 g; Carb 51 g; Fiber 18 g; Cholesterol 0 mg; Sodium 750 mg; Total Sugar 10 g (Added Sugar 0 g)

EXCELLENT SOURCE OF: copper, folate, iron, manganese, phosphorous, potassium, thiamine, vitamin A, vitamin C, vitamin K

GOOD SOURCE OF: magnesium, niacin, pantothenic acid, zinc

ribollita

*R*ibollita—which means "reboiled" in Italian—is the ultimate in Mediterranean-style home cooking. It is like a vegetable-packed minestrone, seasoned with garlic and rosemary, that's made creamy with pureed beans and thickened into a spoonable stew with cubes of whole-grain bread added at the end of cooking so they break down just enough. If you love dunking bread or crushing crackers into your soup (and who doesn't, really), this belly-warming bowl of goodness is one step ahead of you. It not only provides a perfect antidote to a chilly night, but you can also take comfort in knowing it is easy to make, and incredibly healthy, too.

2 (15-ounce) cans low-sodium cannellini or navy beans, drained and rinsed, divided

4 cups low-sodium chicken or vegetable broth, divided

¼ cup olive oil

1 medium-size onion, diced

1 medium-size carrot, diced

1 celery stalk, diced

3 garlic cloves, minced

1 medium-size zucchini, diced

1 (28-ounce) can whole peeled tomatoes

1 rosemary sprig

¼ teaspoon salt, plus more to taste

¼ teaspoon freshly ground black pepper

Pinch of crushed red pepper flakes, or to taste

6 cups lightly packed chopped kale or escarole leaves (1 bunch)

1 cup cubed whole-grain Italian bread (ideally day old), crust removed

3 tablespoons freshly grated Parmesan cheese

1. Place about half of the beans in a food processor or blender with ½ cup of the broth and puree until smooth.

2. Heat the oil in a large pot over medium heat. Add the onion, carrot, and celery and cook, stirring occasionally, until the vegetables are softened but not browned, about 8 minutes. Stir in the garlic and zucchini and cook for 1 minute more.

3. Add the tomatoes one at a time, squeezing them over the pot to break them up as you add them, and pour in the remaining tomato juices. Add the bean puree, the whole beans, the remaining 3½ cups of broth, and the rosemary sprig, salt, black pepper, and red pepper flakes and stir to combine.

4. Bring to a boil, then lower the heat to low and simmer, uncovered, stirring occasionally, for 30 minutes.

5. Remove the rosemary sprig. (The dish may be made ahead up to this point and will keep in an airtight container in the refrigerator for up to 4 days.)

6. Stir in the kale, return to a boil, then simmer over low heat for 15 minutes. Add the bread cubes and cook until they are mostly broken down into the stew, 15 minutes more. Add additional salt to taste. Serve garnished with cheese.

Makes 4 servings

SERVING SIZE: 2½ cups

PER SERVING: Calories 410; Total Fat 17 g (Sat Fat 2.5 g, Mono Fat 10 g, Poly Fat 2 g); Protein 17 g; Carb 49 g; Fiber 12 g; Cholesterol 5 mg; Sodium 830 mg; Total Sugar 10 g (Added Sugar 0 g)

EXCELLENT SOURCE OF: copper, fiber, folate, iron, magnesium, manganese, phosphorous, potassium, protein, riboflavin, thiamine, vitamin A, vitamin C, vitamin K, zinc

GOOD SOURCE OF: calcium, iodine, molybdenum

butternut squash soup with tahini and crispy chickpeas

This glorious bowl of goodness is the epitome of modern comfort food. The soup itself is a golden, fragrantly spiced puree of butternut squash, made hearty and protein-rich with the addition of canned chickpeas blended right in. But it's the garnishes that seal the deal. A finishing drizzle of tahini adds a beautiful pale ribbon of creamy richness, punctuated by flecks of fresh parsley, and a new favorite from the snack aisle of the store—crispy chickpeas—make for a fun, healthy, croutonlike crunch. If you want to explore some other squash varieties, kabocha or honey nut would work well here too.

2 tablespoons olive oil

1 large onion, chopped

3 garlic cloves, chopped

7½ cups butternut squash, seeded and cut into 1-inch cubes (about 2 pounds)

1 cup canned no-salt-added chickpeas, drained and rinsed

¾ teaspoon salt

½ teaspoon ground cumin

¼ teaspoon freshly ground black pepper

⅛ teaspoons ground turmeric

Pinch of cayenne pepper

5 cups low-sodium chicken or vegetable broth

1 tablespoon honey

2 tablespoons tahini

½ cup packaged crispy chickpea snacks (plain or lightly salted)

2 tablespoons chopped fresh parsley

1. Heat the oil in a large pot over medium heat. Add the onion and cook until softened, about 4 minutes; add the garlic and cook for 30 seconds more. Stir in the squash, chickpeas, salt, cumin, black pepper, turmeric, and cayenne.

2. Add the broth and bring to a boil, then lower the heat to medium-low and simmer, covered, until the squash is very tender, about 20 minutes.

3. Use an immersion blender to puree until smooth. (Alternatively, allow to cool slightly, then puree it in several batches in a regular blender.) Stir in the honey.

4. Place the tahini in a bowl and stir in 2 tablespoons of cold water. Add more water by the teaspoon until the tahini is loose enough to be drizzled. Serve the soup drizzled with the tahini, garnished with the crispy chickpeas and parsley.

The soup will keep in an airtight container in the refrigerator for up to 4 days, or in the freezer for 3 months.

Makes 4 servings

SERVING SIZE: 2 cups

PER SERVING: Calories 390; Total Fat 12 g (Sat Fat 1.5 g, Mono Fat 6 g, Poly Fat 3 g); Protein 13 g; Carb 58 g; Fiber 8 g; Cholesterol 0 mg; Sodium 550 mg; Total Sugar 12 g (Added Sugar 4 g)

EXCELLENT SOURCE OF: copper, folate, magnesium, manganese, phosphorous, potassium, protein, thiamine, vitamin A, vitamin B₆, vitamin C, vitamin K

GOOD SOURCE OF: calcium, iron, molybdenum, niacin

red bean tortilla soup

Tortilla soup is one of those foods I am never not in the mood for. (For the record, both meatballs and pizza are on that list, too.) With its lively chili, bright lime flavor, and crunch of tortilla chips yielding to the warmth of the tomato-studded broth, the soup manages to hit the spot on a summer's night as much as takes the chill off in the wintertime. This recipe turns the soup into a complete and satisfying meal (vegan, if you use vegetable broth) with the addition of hearty pinto beans and golden kernels of sweet corn. Made as written, it comes out medium-spicy, with just enough heat to tingle your taste buds. Adjust the heat by adding or subtracting the jalapeño according to your taste.

2 tablespoons olive oil

1 small onion, chopped

3 garlic cloves, minced

1 jalapeño pepper, seeded and finely chopped, or to taste

1½ teaspoons chili powder

4 cups low-sodium chicken or vegetable broth

2 (15-ounce) cans low-sodium pinto beans, drained and rinsed

1 (14.5-ounce) can no-salt-added diced tomatoes

1½ cups fresh or frozen corn kernels

¾ teaspoon salt

½ teaspoon freshly ground black pepper

1 tablespoon freshly squeezed lime juice

2 cups crushed tortilla chips

¼ cup fresh cilantro leaves

1. Heat the oil in a large pot over medium heat. Add the onion and cook until it has softened, 4 minutes. Add the garlic, jalapeño, and chili powder and cook for 1 minute more. Add the broth, beans, tomatoes with their juices, corn, salt, and black pepper and bring to a boil, then lower the heat to low and simmer, covered, for 10 minutes. Stir in the lime juice.

2. To serve, place ¼ cup of the tortilla chips in each of four bowls. Ladle the soup into the bowls and serve topped with additional tortilla chips and a sprinkle of cilantro.

The soup will keep in an airtight container in the refrigerator for up to 4 days, or in the freezer for 3 months.

Makes 4 servings

SERVING SIZE: 2¼ cups

PER SERVING: Calories 470; Total Fat 15 g (Sat Fat 2 g, Mono Fat 7 g, Poly Fat 4 g); Protein 17 g; Carb 70 g; Fiber 14 g; Cholesterol 0 mg; Sodium 830 mg; Total Sugar 10 g (Added Sugar 0 g)

EXCELLENT SOURCE OF: copper, fiber, folate, iron, magnesium, manganese, phosphorous, potassium, protein, vitamin B₆, vitamin C

GOOD SOURCE OF: calcium, niacin, selenium, thiamine, vitamin A, vitamin K, zinc

polenta with "melted" beans and greens

Eating a bowl of this belly-warming dish is like wrapping yourself in a blanket of deliciousness. Freshly cooked polenta, golden and porridgelike, has that effect already built in, but this recipe takes it to new heights. It turns the whole grain into a complete, nourishing meal that's full of savory flavor by cooking it in the same pot as onion, carrots, cannellini beans, and escarole (or kale) that have been simmered with garlic and rosemary. The polenta (finely ground yellow cornmeal) is stirred right into the vegetable mixture and it is all softened and melted together. A drizzle of olive oil and heap of freshly grated Parmesan cheese seals the deal in making this a new favorite comfort food.

2 tablespoons plus 4 teaspoons olive oil, divided

1 small onion, diced

1 medium-size carrot, diced

2 garlic cloves, minced

1½ teaspoons chopped fresh rosemary, or ½ teaspoon dried

2 (15-ounce) cans low-sodium cannellini beans, drained and rinsed

5 cups chopped escarole or stemmed kale leaves

½ teaspoon salt, plus more to taste

¼ teaspoon freshly ground black pepper, plus more to taste

1 cup fine to medium ground yellow cornmeal (polenta, not instant or quick-cooking)

⅔ cup freshly grated Parmesan cheese

1. Heat 2 tablespoons of the oil in a large pot over medium heat. Add the onion and carrot and cook until they soften slightly, 3 minutes. Add the garlic and rosemary and cook for 1 minute more. Stir in the beans, escarole, salt, pepper, and 5 cups of water and bring to a boil. Then, lower the heat to medium-low and simmer, uncovered, until the vegetables are tender, 15 minutes.

2. Add the cornmeal gradually, in a slow stream, stirring constantly to prevent lumps from forming. Stir until the mixture comes to a simmer, then cook, uncovered, over medium-low heat, stirring frequently to prevent the mixture from sticking to the bottom of the pot, until the polenta is thick but pourable and the vegetables have melded with the polenta somewhat, but still have some texture, 15 to 20 minutes.

3. Serve in bowls, each drizzled with 1 teaspoon of oil and topped with cheese and additional salt and pepper to taste.

Makes 4 servings

SERVING SIZE: 1½ cups

PER SERVING: Calories 440; Total Fat 18 g (Sat Fat 4 g, Mono Fat 9 g, Poly Fat 1 g); Protein 17 g; Carb 55 g; Fiber 13 g; Cholesterol 0 mg; Sodium 630 mg; Total Sugar 3 g (Added Sugar 0 g)

EXCELLENT SOURCE OF: calcium, fiber, folate, iron, magnesium, phosphorous, potassium, protein, riboflavin, thiamine, vitamin A, vitamin K, zinc

GOOD SOURCE OF: iodine, manganese

loaded potato nachos

Eating bar food for dinner might seem like a good idea in the moment, but it's typically a greasy hodge-podge you regret after the fact. This festive sheet pan dinner captures all of the fun of happy hour munchies, but leaves the regret behind. It starts with rounds of thinly sliced potatoes roasted until crisp. Those are returned to the oven after being piled with a bounty of chili-spiced pinto beans and just the right amount of cheese to get the gooey, melty goodness you crave. A topping of fresh tomato-cilantro salsa and buttery avocado offer cool and creamy contrast. It's great to serve to a bunch of friends over to watch the game, or to make a regular weeknight feel like an extended happy hour.

1 tablespoon olive oil, plus more for brushing pan

2 medium-size russet potatoes (about 10 ounces each), unpeeled

½ plus ⅛ teaspoon salt, divided

1 (15-ounce) can low-sodium pinto beans, drained and rinsed

1 teaspoon chili powder

¼ teaspoon granulated garlic

¼ teaspoon ground cumin

¼ teaspoon ground coriander

¾ cup chopped fresh tomato

2 tablespoons chopped fresh cilantro leaves

1 tablespoon chopped red onion

1 tablespoon chopped fresh jalapeño pepper

½ teaspoon freshly squeezed lime juice

⅓ cup shredded extra-sharp Cheddar cheese

⅓ cup shredded Monterey Jack cheese

1 ripe avocado, pitted, peeled, and diced

¼ cup sour cream or plain Greek yogurt (optional)

1. Preheat the oven to 400°F. Brush a sheet pan with oil.

2. Cut the potatoes crosswise into ¼-inch-thick rounds. Place them on the sheet pan; drizzle with the oil, sprinkle with ¼ teaspoon of the salt, and toss to coat. Spread the potatoes in a single layer on the sheet pan and bake until they are crisp, browned on the bottom, and release easily from the pan, about 25 minutes. Flip the potatoes and cook 8 minutes more.

3. While the potatoes cook, toss the beans in a medium-size bowl with the chili powder, granulated garlic, cumin, coriander, and ¼ teaspoon of the salt. Combine the tomato, cilantro, red onion, jalapeño, lime juice, and the remaining ⅛ teaspoon of salt in a small bowl.

4. Use tongs to move the potatoes toward the center of the pan, fanning them out so they each overlap slightly. Top with the seasoned beans, then the Cheddar and Jack cheeses; return the pan to the oven, and cook until the cheese is melted, about 5 minutes.

5. Use a large spatula to transfer to a large serving platter or individual plates and serve topped with the tomato mixture, avocado and, if desired, a dollop of sour cream or yogurt.

Makes 4 servings

SERVING SIZE: about 7 pieces of loaded potato

PER SERVING: Calories 400; Total Fat 19 g (Sat Fat 6 g, Mono Fat 8 g, Poly Fat 5 g); Protein 15 g; Carb 48 g; Fiber 12 g; Cholesterol 20 mg; Sodium 650 mg

EXCELLENT SOURCE OF: calcium, fiber, iron, magnesium, phosphorous, potassium, protein, vitamin B_6, vitamin C, vitamin K

GOOD SOURCE OF: copper, manganese, pantothenic acid, riboflavin, thiamine, zinc

flatbread pizzas
with spinach and egg

The first time I saw egg cooked on a pizza, I was in Italy in my college days and although it was pretty ordinary there, it seemed revolutionary to me. Now, I don't know how I ever managed without it. It's such an easy way to turn pizza into a much more balanced, protein-rich meal. Here, I round out the plate further, adding color, texture, and health with fresh chopped spinach and sun-dried tomatoes and by using whole-grain flatbread for the crust. With their egg yolks sensuously runny, their golden melted cheese, and crispy, saucy bottoms, these pizzas offer loads of comfort-food flavor with minimal time or prep.

4 (6- to 7-inch) whole-grain flatbreads, such as pita or naan (2½ ounces each)

1 tablespoon olive oil

½ cup high-quality jarred marinara sauce

2 cups lightly packed chopped fresh baby spinach leaves

6 small sun-dried tomatoes, reconstituted in hot water for 10 minutes if very dry, sliced

½ cup shredded part-skim mozzarella cheese

4 large eggs

¼ cup freshly grated Parmesan cheese

Salt

Crushed red pepper flakes

1. Preheat the oven to 450°F. Place the flatbreads on a sheet pan and brush the tops with the olive oil. Spread 2 tablespoons of the marinara sauce on top of each bread, leaving a ½-inch sauce-free border around the edges. Top each with ½ cup of the spinach, a sprinkling of the sun-dried tomatoes, and 2 tablespoons of the mozzarella cheese.

2. Make a well in the center of the topping of each pizza. Crack an egg into a small bowl, then transfer the egg to one of the wells in the center of a pizza. Repeat with the remaining eggs. It's okay if some of the egg white drips off the bread a bit, but try to arrange the spinach so it keeps the egg in the center. Sprinkle each pizza all over with the Parmesan cheese.

3. Bake until the egg whites are mostly set but the yolks are still soft, 11 to 13 minutes. Let rest on the pan for 2 minutes before serving. (The egg will continue to set as it rests.) Season with salt and crushed red pepper to taste.

Makes 4 servings

SERVING SIZE: 1 pizza

PER SERVING: Calories 360; Total Fat 14 g (Sat Fat 4.5 g, Mono Fat 6 g, Poly Fat 2 g); Protein 19 g; Carb 43 g; Fiber 5 g; Cholesterol 210 mg; Sodium 760 mg; Total Sugar 5 g (Added Sugar 0 g)

EXCELLENT SOURCE OF: calcium, fiber, folate, iodine, iron, magnesium, manganese, phosphorous, protein, riboflavin, selenium, vitamin A, vitamin K

GOOD SOURCE OF: chloride, copper, niacin, pantothenic acid, potassium, thiamine, vitamin B_6, vitamin B_{12}, vitamin C, vitamin D, vitamin E

sesame marinated tofu with kale chips and sweet potato

This dish combines two favorite recipes—kale chips and marinated tofu—which you can make good use of individually besides as part of this scrumptious meal. The chips are made with only a touch of oil and salt, but they come out shatteringly crisp and flavorful. Make sure the kale you use is truly fresh—it won't get as crispy if you start with a wilted vegetable.

Beyond this dish, the marinated tofu is perfect for turning any salad or grain bowl into a vegetarian main dish. The secret to really tasty baked tofu is to get rid of all its water before marinating it, which is done here by blotting well with paper towels. Here, cubes of flavorful sesame-coated tofu are served perched atop mashed baked sweet potato, drizzled with a soy-orange-sesame dressing and finished with a topping of the crunchy kale. It's a hearty plate full of color, texture, and taste that is packed with good nutrition. You can make each element up to three days ahead, storing the chips in a bag at room temperature and the tofu and potato in the refrigerator.

¼ cup reduced-sodium soy sauce

3 tablespoons unseasoned rice vinegar

2 tablespoons toasted sesame oil

2 tablespoons honey

½ teaspoon chili garlic sauce, such as sriracha, plus more to taste

1 tablespoon finely grated fresh ginger

2 garlic cloves, minced

2 (14-ounce) packages extra-firm tofu

½ bunch kale (about 4 ounces)

2 teaspoons olive oil

⅛ teaspoon salt

4 small sweet potatoes (about 8 ounces each)

1½ tablespoons sesame seeds

1. Whisk together the soy sauce, rice vinegar, sesame oil, honey, and chili garlic sauce in a large bowl. Transfer 2 tablespoons of the mixture to a small bowl or pitcher to use as a finishing drizzle. Add the ginger and garlic to the marinade mixture in the large bowl and whisk to combine.

2. Drain the tofu, then slice each block into two slabs, each about ¾ inch thick. Lay the slabs on top of paper towels. Use more paper towels (altogether, you will need about six) to firmly pat the tofu, removing as much of the water as possible. Then, cut the slabs into ¾-inch cubes. Place the tofu in the bowl of marinade and toss gently to coat. Marinate for 1 hour at room temperature, or cover and refrigerate for up to 24 hours, giving it a gentle toss at the halfway point.

3. Preheat the oven to 375°F. Remove and discard the center rib and stems from each kale leaf. Tear or cut the leaves into bite-size pieces, 2 to 3 inches wide. Wash the kale and dry it very well, then place it onto a sheet pan. Drizzle the kale with the oil and sprinkle with the salt. Rub the oil into the kale with your hands to distribute it evenly. Arrange the kale in a single layer on a sheet pan and bake until it is crisp and the edges are slightly browned, about 10 minutes. Transfer the kale chips to a plate. The chips may be made up to 3 days ahead and kept in a paper bag at room temperature.

(Continued)

4. Carefully wipe off any bits of kale from the sheet pan, then line the pan with parchment. Pierce the sweet potatoes with a fork, place them on the prepared sheet pan, and roast for 40 minutes.

5. Flip the potatoes and move them to one side of the sheet pan. Arrange the marinated tofu in a single layer on the other side of the pan. Drizzle any remaining marinade over the tofu. Return the sheet pan to the oven and roast until the tofu begins to brown and the sweet potatoes are soft and easily pierced with the tip of a knife, about 20 minutes.

6. Transfer the sweet potatoes to a cutting board to cool slightly. Sprinkle the tops of the tofu with the sesame seeds and return the pan to the oven to bake until the tofu is nicely browned, 10 minutes more.

7. To serve, scoop out the flesh of the sweet potatoes, mounding it onto four individual plates and then mashing it slightly with a fork. Top each with about 1 cup of the tofu. Drizzle with the reserved soy mixture and then scatter the kale chips on top and around the plate, crushing them a little.

The tofu and potato will keep in an airtight container in the refrigerator for up to 4 days.

Makes 4 servings

SERVING SIZE: 1 cup potato, 1 cup tofu, 1 cup kale chips, and 1½ teaspoons dressing

PER SERVING: Calories 490; Total Fat 22 g (Sat Fat 3 g, Mono Fat 8 g, Poly Fat 10 g); Protein 26 g; Carb 51 g; Fiber 6 g; Cholesterol 0 mg; Sodium 940 mg; Total Sugar 20 g (Added Sugar 9 g)

EXCELLENT SOURCE OF: calcium, copper, fiber, folate, iron, manganese, potassium, protein, vitamin A, vitamin B_6, vitamin C, vitamin K

GOOD SOURCE OF: magnesium, pantothenic acid, phosphorous, thiamine

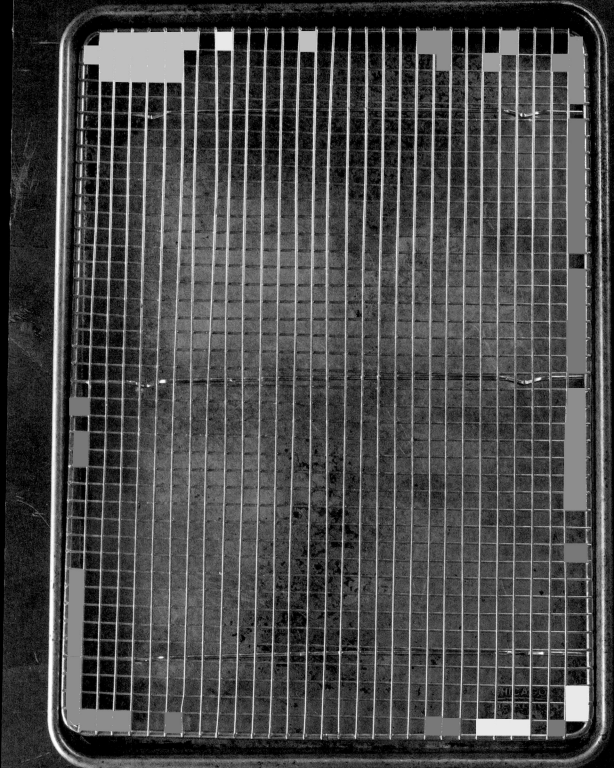

pesto spinach stuffed spaghetti squash

This dish turns roasted spaghetti squash into an edible bowl filled with a sumptuous, easy-to-make spinach-ricotta mixture that's seasoned with basil pesto and topped with mozzarella cheese. A key here is using good-quality prepared pesto—homemade if you have it on hand, but store-bought certainly works, too. When choosing pesto at the store, I suggest getting one from the refrigerator case, which is much fresher tasting than the kind in jars on the shelf. As you dig into the dish, the squash naturally reveals the noodlelike texture that gives it its name, and each forkful includes a generous bite of the creamy, herby spinach filling and melted mozzarella. The recipe serves four for a light meal, but if you are especially hungry, go for a double portion as my husband usually does.

1 medium-size spaghetti squash (about 3 pounds)

2 teaspoons olive oil

1 (16-ounce) package frozen, chopped spinach, thawed

½ cup prepared basil pesto

½ cup part-skim ricotta cheese

1 garlic clove, finely minced

½ teaspoon salt

¼ teaspoon freshly ground black pepper

½ cup shredded part-skim mozzarella cheese

1. Preheat the oven to 400°F. Cut the squash in half lengthwise (to make the squash easier to cut, heat it, whole, in a microwave for 1 minute to soften it), scoop out and discard the seeds, and brush the cut sides with the oil. Place, cut side down, on a sheet pan and cook until softened, about 40 minutes.

2. While the squash cooks, make the filling: Put the spinach into a fine-mesh strainer and press out as much of the liquid as possible. (You can discard the liquid or save it to use in soups or smoothies.) Put the spinach in a medium-size bowl along with the pesto, ricotta cheese, garlic, salt, and pepper and mix to combine.

3. When the squash is ready, flip it over on the sheet pan so it sits cut side up and fill both cavities with the spinach mixture. Sprinkle the mozzarella cheese on top of each squash half and return the pan to the oven. Bake until the cheese is melted and browned in spots, about 20 minutes more.

4. Allow to rest for 5 minutes, then cut each half lengthwise and serve. The cooked squash will keep in an airtight container in the refrigerator for up to 4 days.

Makes 4 servings

SERVING SIZE: ¼ squash

PER SERVING: Calories 340; Total Fat 21 g (Sat Fat 6 g, Mono Fat 10 g, Poly Fat 3 g); Protein 16 g; Carb 28 g; Fiber 7 g; Cholesterol 20 mg; Sodium 740 mg; Total Sugar 10 g (Added Sugar 0 g)

EXCELLENT SOURCE OF: calcium, fiber, folate, magnesium, manganese, phosphorous, potassium, protein, riboflavin, selenium, vitamin A, vitamin B_6, vitamin C, vitamin K

GOOD SOURCE OF: copper, iron, niacin, pantothenic acid, thiamine, zinc

southwest sweet potato bowl

This dish is a colorful and different spin on a grain bowl, with mashed sweet potato as its base and topped with exciting southwestern-inspired flavors and textures. Hearty black beans, charred scallions, crunchy jicama, juicy orange segments, buttery toasted pecans, and a chili-citrus dressing all come together for a satisfying and stunning meal. The scallions soften and mellow as they roast, taking on a beautiful brown char, making for an unexpected note that really elevates the dish.

4 medium-size sweet potatoes (about 12 ounces each)

2 bunches scallions

2 tablespoons plus 1 teaspoon extra-virgin olive oil, divided

½ teaspoon salt, plus a pinch, divided

Pinch of freshly ground black pepper

1 large navel orange

2 tablespoons freshly squeezed lime juice

2 teaspoons honey

½ teaspoon chili powder

Pinch of cayenne pepper, or to taste

⅓ cup pecan pieces

1 (15-ounce) can black beans, drained and rinsed

¼ medium-size jicama, cut into matchsticks (about 1 cup)

1. Preheat the oven to 400°F. Line a sheet pan with parchment paper. Pierce the sweet potatoes in several places with a fork, then place them on one side of the pan.

2. Trim the roots off the scallions, then cut them crosswise to remove the dark green part, leaving about 3-inch-long pieces of the white and light green part. Thinly slice about ¼ cup of the dark greens and set aside for garnish. Place the 3-inch scallion pieces on the other side of the sheet pan and toss with 1 teaspoon of the oil, a pinch of salt, and the black pepper.

3. Roast in the oven until the scallions have softened and are nicely charred, about 20 minutes, giving them a toss after the first 10 minutes. Remove the scallions from the pan, then flip the sweet potatoes over and return them to the oven. Roast until they are soft to the touch and easily pierced with a knife, about 40 minutes more.

4. Meanwhile, cut the orange into segments by slicing off the top and bottom of the fruit, then, standing it on one end, cut down following the curve of the fruit to remove the peel and white pith. Then, with a paring knife, working over a bowl, remove the fruit segments from their membrane. Squeeze any juice from the remaining membrane into the bowl and discard the membrane.

5. Whisk together 2 tablespoons of the orange juice, the remaining 2 tablespoons of oil, the lime juice, honey, and chili powder, and the remaining ½ teaspoon of salt and the cayenne.

6. When the sweet potatoes are done, remove from the oven and set aside to cool until they are comfortable to handle. Remove the parchment from the sheet pan, place the pecans directly on the pan, and toast until they are fragrant and a shade darker, 2 to 3 minutes. Remove from the oven and allow to cool.

7. To serve, cut each sweet potato in half and scoop the flesh of each into four individual serving bowls, mashing it slightly with a fork. Arrange about ⅓ cup of the beans, two or three orange segments, ¼ cup of jicama, and a few roasted scallions on top of the sweet potato. Sprinkle each with the pecan pieces and scallion greens and drizzle with the dressing.

Each element may be made ahead and stored separately in the refrigerator for up to 4 days.

Makes 4 servings

SERVING SIZE: 1 bowl

PER SERVING: Calories 440; Total Fat 15 g (Sat Fat 2 g, Mono Fat 10 g, Poly Fat 3 g); Protein 11 g; Carb 70 g; Fiber 22 g; Cholesterol 0 mg; Sodium 590 mg; Total Sugar 16 g (Added Sugar 3 g)

EXCELLENT SOURCE OF: copper, fiber, folate, iron, magnesium, manganese, molybdenum, phosphorous, potassium, protein, thiamine, vitamin A, vitamin B₆, vitamin C, vitamin K

GOOD SOURCE OF: calcium, niacin, pantothenic acid, riboflavin, vitamin E, zinc

roasted beets with oranges and savory granola

Many foods sit teasingly on the border of sweet and savory and can be tipped in either direction depending on what they are paired with. This unforgettable dish of roasted beets with savory granola showcases that quality perfectly. The nut-free granola is a mixture of oats and seeds seasoned with fennel seed, ginger, cinnamon, and fresh thyme. It is served atop a generous smear of Greek yogurt, scattered with the roasted beets, bright orange segments, and watercress, then drizzled with a quick lemon-olive oil dressing that's spiked with orange zest. It's easy and impressive, and you can do the cooking and prep days ahead so you can pull it together on a moment's notice.

4 medium-size beets (about 3½ ounces each)

¼ cup plus 1 teaspoon olive oil, divided

½ cup rolled oats

2 tablespoons unsalted hulled pumpkin seeds

1 tablespoon unsalted hulled sunflower seeds

1 teaspoon fennel seeds

½ teaspoon ground cinnamon

¼ teaspoon ground ginger

¼ teaspoon salt, divided

2 tablespoons plus 1 teaspoon honey, divided

2 tablespoons egg white

2 teaspoons fresh thyme leaves

3 small or 2 medium-size oranges (blood oranges, Cara Cara, or navel)

1 tablespoon freshly squeezed lemon juice

⅛ teaspoon freshly ground black pepper

2 cups plain low-fat or whole-milk Greek yogurt

1 cup lightly packed watercress leaves and small sprigs, or baby arugula leaves

1. Preheat the oven to 300°F. Trim away the stems and roots from the beets, then rub each with the oil, using 1 teaspoon in total. Wrap each beet in foil and place on one side of a sheet pan. Line the other side of the sheet pan with parchment.

2. Toss together the oats, pumpkin seeds, sunflower seeds, fennel seeds, cinnamon, ginger and ⅛ teaspoon of the salt in a medium-size bowl. Whisk together 2 tablespoons of the oil, 2 tablespoons of the honey, and the egg white in a small bowl. Pour the oil mixture over the oat mixture and toss to coat evenly. Spread the granola on the parchment side of the sheet pan.

3. Bake until the granola is nicely browned and nearly crisped, about 20 minutes, stirring once or twice as it cooks to ensure even browning. Stir in the thyme and cook for 3 minutes more. Remove the parchment along with the granola from the sheet pan and set aside to cool. The granola will crisp further as it cools.

4. Return the sheet pan with the beets to the oven, increase the temperature to 400°F, and continue to cook until they are easily pierced with a fork, about 30 minutes more. Remove from the oven, unwrap and allow to cool, then remove the peel with a paring knife and/or by rubbing the peel away with your fingers. Slice the beets into ½-inch-thick half-moons.

5. When ready to serve, zest one of the oranges until you have ¼ teaspoon of zest. Then, cut the peel and the white pith off the oranges and slice them into ½-inch half-moons.

6. Whisk together the remaining 2 tablespoons of olive oil, the lemon juice, the remaining teaspoon of honey, the orange zest, and the remaining ⅛ teaspoon of salt and the pepper in a small bowl.

7. To plate, spread ½ cup of the yogurt on each of four plates. Top each with 3 tablespoons of the granola, then ¼ cup of the greens. Scatter the beet and orange slices on top of that. Drizzle each plate with a scant tablespoon of the dressing and sprinkle with the remaining granola.

The granola and beets may be made ahead and stored in separate airtight containers, the beets for up to 4 days and the granola for 2 weeks.

Makes 4 servings

SERVING SIZE: 1 plate

PER SERVING: Calories 410; Total Fat 19 g (Sat Fat 3 g, Mono Fat 12 g, Poly Fat 3 g); Protein 18 g; Carb 46 g; Fiber 7 g; Cholesterol 5 mg; Sodium 280 mg; Total Sugar 30 g (Added Sugar 10 g)

EXCELLENT SOURCE OF: calcium, fiber, folate, magnesium, manganese, phosphorous, potassium, protein, riboflavin, vitamin C, vitamin K

GOOD SOURCE OF: iron, selenium, vitamin B_6, vitamin B_{12}

roasted eggplant with tahini, tomatoes, and pine nuts

The roasted eggplant in this dish is delectably custardlike inside, while on the exterior it is nicely browned with slightly crisped, absolutely edible skin. Starting with smaller eggplants helps ensure a lovely, mild flavor in the first place, but scoring and salting the vegetable before cooking it allows any possible bitterness to drain away. The eggplant needs a thirty-minute salting and sixty minutes in the oven, so the dish takes some time, but very little effort. The eggplant is served as the centerpiece it deserves to be, plated atop a spread of thick yogurt (ideally the ultra-creamy Middle Eastern version called labneh, if available, otherwise plain Greek yogurt), then drizzled with lemony tahini sauce and surrounded by a scattering of tomatoes, parsley, and toasted pine nuts with warm pita alongside.

2 pounds eggplant (4 Italian, a.k.a. "baby" eggplants, or 2 globe)

1 teaspoon salt

¼ cup pine nuts

2 tablespoons olive oil

¼ cup tahini

1½ tablespoons freshly squeezed lemon juice

4 whole wheat pita breads

1 cup labneh or Greek yogurt

2 medium-size tomatoes, diced

¼ cup fresh parsley leaves

Crushed red pepper flakes

1. Slice the eggplants in half lengthwise. Use the tip of a knife to score the eggplant, making three diagonal slits into the flesh of each in one direction, then again in the opposite direction to make a crosshatch pattern. Spread the eggplant halves open a bit and sprinkle the salt on the cut side, on top, and inside the slits. Let the eggplant sit, cut side up, for 30 minutes.

2. Preheat the oven to 400°F. Place the pine nuts on a dry sheet pan and toast until golden and fragrant, 3 to 4 minutes. Remove from the oven and allow to cool completely, then transfer the nuts to a dish and line the sheet pan with parchment.

3. Squeeze the eggplant lightly to remove any accumulated juice, then wipe dry with a paper towel. Brush the eggplants all over, but mostly on the cut sides, with the oil. Place facedown on the sheet pan and roast until they have collapsed, the cut sides are browned, and the flesh is tender, about 60 minutes.

4. Meanwhile, make the tahini sauce: Stir together the tahini and lemon juice, then, using about ¼ cup total, stir in 1 tablespoon of water at a time until the sauce is the consistency of a thin pancake batter. (The mixture will seize up at first, but don't worry—it will become smooth again as you add the water.)

5. Warm the pita in the oven as you plate the rest of the ingredients. To serve, spread ¼ cup of the labneh or yogurt onto each of four individual plates. Then, use a spatula to transfer two Italian eggplant halves or one globe eggplant half, cut side up, onto each plate on top of the labneh. Drizzle each with about 2 tablespoons of the tahini sauce, on top of the eggplant and all over the plate, then scatter the tomatoes, parsley, and pine nuts on top of that. Sprinkle with red pepper flakes to taste and serve with the warmed pita.

Makes 4 servings

SERVING SIZE: 2 Italian eggplant halves or 1 globe eggplant half, and 1 pita

PER SERVING: Calories 470; Total Fat 23 g (Sat Fat 3.5 g, Mono Fat 10 g, Poly Fat 7 g); Protein 18 g; Carb 55 g; Fiber 10 g; Cholesterol 5 mg; Sodium 660 mg; Total Sugar 11 g (Added Sugar 0 g)

EXCELLENT SOURCE OF: copper, fiber, folate, iron, magnesium, manganese, niacin, phosphorous, potassium, protein, thiamine, vitamin C, vitamin K

GOOD SOURCE OF: calcium, molybdenum, pantothenic acid, vitamin A, vitamin B_6, zinc

spiced roasted carrot
and avocado lettuce wraps

Here, bright leaves of Bibb lettuce become cups cradling a treasure of colorful, flavorful, and nourishing ingredients. They are piled on one by one: first, a luxurious bed of creamy yogurt and then tender, roasted carrots with a deep natural sweetness that is spiked with an aromatic medley of spices—cumin, coriander, and ginger. Next, slices of avocado and crunchy toasted sunflower seeds are strewn on top; and finally some salt, lemon, a squirt of hot sauce, and a few green leaves reserved from the carrot tops. These wraps are fun to eat, with each bite revealing layers of surprising tastes and textures, and they are fun to serve taco style with all the ingredients spread out on the table so everyone can build their own.

½ cup unsalted hulled sunflower seeds

2 pounds small (not baby) carrots (2 to 3 bunches), ¼ cup of leafy tops reserved

2 tablespoons olive oil

1 tablespoon honey

¾ teaspoon ground cumin

½ teaspoon ground coriander

½ teaspoon ground ginger

½ teaspoon salt, plus more to taste

¼ teaspoon freshly ground black pepper

Pinch of cayenne pepper

1 large head Bibb lettuce, separated into leaves

1 cup plain full-fat or low-fat Greek yogurt or labneh

2 large ripe avocados, pitted, peeled, and sliced

Lemon wedges, for serving

Hot sauce, such as harissa or sriracha, for serving

1. Preheat the oven to 400°F. Place the sunflower seeds on a dry sheet pan and toast until fragrant and a shade darker, 4 to 5 minutes. Remove from the oven and transfer the seeds to a dish to cool.

2. Peel and trim the carrots, then cut them crosswise on the diagonal into pieces about 3 inches long. If there are any thicker pieces, cut them in half lengthwise. Stir together the olive oil, honey, cumin, coriander, ginger, salt, black pepper, and cayenne in a large bowl. Add the carrots to the bowl and toss to coat evenly.

3. Transfer the carrots to the sheet pan and drizzle with any of the spice mixture lingering at the bottom of the bowl. Spread out the carrots evenly on the sheet pan and cook until they are firm-tender and browned, stirring once or twice, 15 to 20 minutes. The carrots may be served in the wraps warm or at room temperature, and they may be made ahead and kept in an airtight container in the refrigerator for up to 4 days.

4. To serve, set out the carrots, lettuce leaves, yogurt, sunflower seeds, avocado slices, lemon wedges, carrot greens, salt, and hot sauce on the table and let everyone fix their own lettuce wraps, taco style. To assemble, spread 1 tablespoon of the yogurt on a lettuce leaf, top with

a few carrots, then avocado, and then a sprinkle of sunflower seeds and carrot greens. Season with salt to taste, and add a squeeze of lemon and a few drops of hot sauce, if desired.

Makes 4 servings

SERVING SIZE: about 4 lettuce wraps

PER SERVING: Calories 470; Total Fat 32 g (Sat Fat 5 g, Mono Fat 17 g, Poly Fat 8 g); Protein 15 g; Carb 39 g; Fiber 16 g; Cholesterol 5 mg; Sodium 490 mg; Total Sugar 15 g (Added Sugar 0 g)

EXCELLENT SOURCE OF: copper, folate, magnesium, manganese, niacin, pantothenic acid, phosphorous, potassium, riboflavin, selenium, vitamin A, vitamin B_6, vitamin C, vitamin K

GOOD SOURCE OF: calcium, iron, molybdenum, thiamine, zinc

pizza primavera

This pizza achieves 360 degrees of tastiness without any tomato or mozzarella cheese. Instead, it starts with a spread of creamy ricotta cheese, which is enlivened by a touch of lemon zest, atop a whole-grain crust. The ricotta melts luxuriously in the oven under a shower of colorful spring vegetables. A generous sprinkle of Parmesan cheese browns and crisps on top of it all, and it is served garnished with fragrant fresh basil. Roasting the asparagus first on the same pan you ultimately use to bake the pizza preheats the pan, helping the crust crisp up beautifully. If you don't want to bother with stretching the pizza dough, feel free to substitute a prepared, thin whole-grain crust.

½ **bunch asparagus (about 12 medium-size spears)**

1 **tablespoon olive oil**

¼ **teaspoon salt, divided**

1 **tablespoon cornmeal**

12 **ounces whole wheat pizza dough, thawed if frozen**

1 **cup part-skim ricotta cheese**

1 **teaspoon finely grated lemon zest**

¼ **cup fresh or frozen peas**

¼ **cup thin ribbons of carrot (sliced using a vegetable peeler)**

¼ **cup very thinly sliced red onion**

⅓ **cup packed, freshly grated Parmesan cheese**

Freshly ground black pepper

6 **large or 12 small fresh basil leaves**

1. Preheat the oven to 400°F. Trim the woody ends off the asparagus spears. Place them on a sheet pan, drizzle with the oil, and toss to coat, then sprinkle with ⅛ teaspoon of the salt. Roast until the asparagus is just tender, about 6 minutes. Remove from the oven and transfer to a cutting board to cool slightly, then cut the asparagus into ¾-inch lengths. Set the sheet pan aside, with the oil still on it, to use for the pizza. Increase the oven temperature to 500°F.

2. Sprinkle a work surface with the cornmeal and use a rolling pin and/or your hands to stretch the dough into a 12-inch circle. Place the dough on the sheet pan that you used to roast the asparagus.

3. Stir together the ricotta cheese, lemon zest, and remaining ⅛ teaspoon of salt in a small bowl. Then, use the back of a spoon to smear the ricotta cheese over the dough, leaving a ¾-inch cheese-free border for the crust. Arrange the asparagus, peas, carrot, and onion on top, then sprinkle with the Parmesan cheese and a few turns of black pepper. Bake until the cheese is melted and lightly browned and the crust is browned, 10 to 12 minutes. While the pizza is baking, slice the basil into ribbons. Remove the pizza from the oven, garnish with the basil, and slice into eight wedges.

Makes 4 servings

SERVING SIZE: 2 slices

PER SERVING: Calories 380; Total Fat 14 g (Sat Fat 4.5 g, Mono Fat 4 g, Poly Fat 1 g); Protein 17 g; Carb 48 g; Fiber 8 g; Cholesterol 25 mg; Sodium 830 mg; Total Sugar 4 g (Added Sugar 0 g)

EXCELLENT SOURCE OF: calcium, fiber, phosphorous, protein, selenium, vitamin A, vitamin K

GOOD SOURCE OF: folate, iron, riboflavin, zinc

rice and bean stuffed poblano peppers

On a heat scale of 1 to 10, these stuffed peppers are about a 7, so if you love spicy food, they will be right up your alley. The heat is tempered, though, by a generous dousing of yogurt crema, so even my husband who calls himself a spice-wimp (he's a medium-salsa kind of guy) heartily enjoys them. That said, if you want to make this recipe without the heat, you can substitute small green bell peppers.

8 large poblano or Anaheim peppers

1 tablespoon olive oil

2 cups frozen, cooked brown rice (to yield 1½ cups thawed)

1 (15-ounce) can low-sodium pinto beans, drained and rinsed

1 cup no-salt-added canned diced fire-roasted tomatoes

¾ cup shredded Monterey Jack cheese

¾ teaspoon ground cumin

¾ teaspoon chili powder

½ teaspoon granulated garlic

½ teaspoon salt

½ cup plain whole-milk Greek yogurt

2 teaspoons freshly squeezed lime juice

Makes 4 servings

SERVING SIZE: 2 stuffed peppers and about 2½ tablespoons crema

PER SERVING: Calories 370; Total Fat 13 g (Sat Fat 6 g, Mono Fat 4 g, Poly Fat 1 g); Protein 17 g; Carb 48 g; Fiber 10 g; Cholesterol 25 mg; Sodium 500 mg; Total Sugar 9 g (Added Sugar 0 g)

EXCELLENT SOURCE OF: calcium, fiber, protein, vitamin A, vitamin C

GOOD SOURCE OF: iron, magnesium, manganese, phosphorous, selenium

1. Preheat the oven to 475°F. Place the peppers on a sheet pan. Rub them all over with the oil and roast until they are somewhat softened and blistered, about 8 minutes. Remove from the oven and transfer the peppers to a plate; cover the plate tightly with foil. Lower the oven temperature to 350°F.

2. Once they are cool enough to handle (after about 15 minutes), use your fingers to remove and discard any blistered skin on the peppers. Then, keeping the stem intact, cut a slice lengthwise into one side of each pepper and use a spoon to remove the seeds. Place the peppers, cut side up, back on the sheet pan.

3. While the peppers are cooking and cooling, prepare the filling: Place the rice in a microwave-safe dish with a vented cover and microwave on HIGH until it is warmed through, about 3 minutes. Remove the cover from the rice (be careful of the steam!), then add the beans, tomatoes, cheese, cumin, chili powder, granulated garlic, and salt, and stir to combine.

4. Stuff the peppers generously with the filling (the pepper will not close around the stuffing completely), then return them to the oven to bake until warmed through, 15 minutes.

5. While the stuffed peppers bake, stir together the yogurt, lime juice, and 3 tablespoons of cold water in a small bowl. Serve the stuffed peppers drizzled with the yogurt "crema."

The stuffed peppers will keep for up to 4 days, stored in an airtight container in the refrigerator.

crispy crushed potatoes and roasted broccoli with peanut sauce

A recent trip to Ecuador had all of my culinary pistons firing. Among the many delightful dishes I experienced there was a plate of potato cakes drizzled generously with savory peanut sauce; this sheet pan dinner captures the essence of that dish in a healthier way. The potatoes here are made crispy by cooking them twice: first, in a microwave to render them soft so they can be smashed flat with the heel of your hand; then, once slathered with olive oil, they are roasted in the oven, with spears of broccoli alongside, until the potatoes are crisp and golden brown outside and creamy inside, and the broccoli becomes tender with a scrumptious char. Both roasted vegetables are compellingly delicious in their own right, but the flavorful peanut sauce—made easily by whirring peanut butter, lime juice, garlic, scallion, cumin, coriander, and red pepper flakes in a food processor—transforms them into a unique, richly satisfying meal.

8 small Yukon gold potatoes (about 1½ pounds total)

1 small head broccoli, trimmed and cut into 2-inch-wide spears

¼ cup olive oil, divided

¾ teaspoon salt, divided

½ cup natural smooth peanut butter

2 tablespoons freshly squeezed lime juice

1 small garlic clove, minced

½ teaspoon ground cumin

¼ teaspoon ground coriander

¼ teaspoon freshly ground black pepper

Pinch of crushed red pepper flakes, plus more to taste

1 scallion, chopped

1. Preheat the oven to 450°F. Pierce the potatoes in several places with a fork, then place them on a microwave-safe plate and microwave on HIGH for 6 minutes. Then, use tongs to turn the potatoes over and microwave for 6 to 7 minutes more, until they are firm, yet easily pierced with the tip of a knife. Alternatively, put the pierced potatoes on a sheet pan and bake them for about 45 minutes, then use the same sheet pan later to prepare the rest of the dish. Allow the potatoes to cool for 20 minutes. They may also be cooked up to 4 days ahead and stored in an airtight container in the refrigerator.

2. Place the broccoli on a sheet pan and toss it with 2 tablespoons of the oil and sprinkle with ¼ teaspoon of the salt. Push the broccoli to one side of the pan. Place the potatoes on the other side of the sheet pan. Crush each potato with the heel of your hand to flatten it into a patty about ½ inch thick. Crush them just enough so they spread and come apart somewhat, while much of their skin remains intact.

3. Brush the tops of the potatoes with 1 tablespoon of the oil, then use a flat spatula to flip the potatoes and brush the other side with the remaining tablespoon of oil. Sprinkle the tops with ¼ teaspoon of the salt. Bake for 15 minutes, then remove the pan from the oven, toss the broccoli, and return the pan to the oven. Bake until the broccoli is softened and nicely

(Continued)

charred and the potatoes are crisp and golden brown, about 10 minutes more. If the broccoli is done before the potatoes, transfer the broccoli to a serving plate and allow the potatoes to cook further.

4. While the vegetables are cooking, make the peanut sauce: Place the peanut butter, lime juice, garlic, cumin, coriander, black pepper, red pepper flakes, and the remaining ¼ teaspoon of salt in the small bowl of a food processor with 6 tablespoons of cold water and process until smooth. Add more water, 1 tablespoon at a time, until the sauce is the consistency of a loose pancake batter. Add the scallion and pulse to combine. Serve the crispy potatoes and broccoli with the sauce alongside for drizzling.

Makes 4 servings

SERVING SIZE: 2 potatoes, 1 cup broccoli, and ¼ cup sauce

PER SERVING: Calories 510; Total Fat 30 g (Sat Fat 4.5 g, Mono Fat 19 g, Poly Fat 6 g); Protein 15 g; Carb 48 g; Fiber 9 g; Cholesterol 0 mg; Sodium 650 mg; Total Sugar 5 g (Added Sugar 0 g)

EXCELLENT SOURCE OF: calcium, folate, protein, vitamin A, vitamin C, vitamin K

GOOD SOURCE OF: iron, manganese, molybdenum, phosphorous, potassium, riboflavin, vitamin B$_6$

roasted vegetable bowl with white beans and roasted garlic balsamic dressing

This recipe turns a sheet pan of simply roasted potatoes and zucchini into a boldly flavorful plant-powered meal with hardly any effort at all. The vegetables are roasted with whole cloves of garlic that soften and caramelize and ultimately serve as the foundation of a fabulous dressing. White beans and toasted pine nuts bring the protein, and fresh tomatoes and arugula add a springlike brightness to the bowl for a meal that is definitely destined to be put on repeat.

¼ cup pine nuts

3 medium-size Yukon gold potatoes, diced into ½-inch pieces (1¼ pounds)

4 garlic cloves, unpeeled

¼ cup olive oil, divided

¾ teaspoon salt, divided

½ teaspoon freshly ground black pepper, divided

2 medium-size zucchini, quartered

lengthwise then cut into ½-inch pieces

1½ teaspoons chopped fresh rosemary, or ½ teaspoon dried

1 tablespoon balsamic vinegar

1 (15-ounce) can cannellini beans, drained and rinsed

3 cups baby arugula

1 cup grape tomatoes, halved

Makes 4 servings

SERVING SIZE: 2 cups

PER SERVING: Calories 380; Total Fat 20 g (Sat Fat 2.5 g, Mono Fat 12 g, Poly Fat 4 g); Protein 10 g; Carb 45 g; Fiber 8 g; Cholesterol 0 mg; Sodium 530 mg; Total Sugar 5 g (Added Sugar 0 g)

EXCELLENT SOURCE OF: calcium, fiber, iron, manganese, protein, thiamine, vitamin A, vitamin C

GOOD SOURCE OF: magnesium, phosphorous, potassium, vitamin K, zinc

1. Preheat the oven to 400°F. Place the pine nuts on a dry sheet pan and toast in the oven until they are golden and fragrant, about 3 minutes. Remove from the oven and transfer to a plate to cool.

2. Place the potatoes and garlic on the sheet pan. Drizzle with 1 tablespoon of the oil and sprinkle with ¼ teaspoon of the salt and ⅛ teaspoon of the pepper. Cook for 20 minutes. Use a metal spatula to move the potatoes and garlic to one side of the pan. On the other side of the pan toss the zucchini with 1 tablespoon of the oil, ¼ teaspoon of the salt, ⅛ teaspoon of the pepper, and the rosemary. Return to the oven until browned, about 25 minutes more.

3. Squeeze the roasted garlic out of its skin into a small bowl, mashing it slightly with a fork. Add the remaining 2 tablespoons of oil, the balsamic vinegar, and the remaining ¼ teaspoon each of salt and pepper and whisk to combine. The potatoes, zucchini, and dressing may be made up to 3 days ahead and stored in separate airtight containers in the refrigerator.

4. Toss the roasted potatoes and zucchini in a large bowl with the beans, arugula, tomatoes, and the dressing. Serve in bowls sprinkled with the toasted pine nuts.

seafood

cauliflower "risotto" with shrimp and peas

This dish is a satisfying mash-up of two comfort-food classics—cauliflower with cheese sauce and risotto with shrimp and peas—which makes for a healthy, modern, and doubly comforting skillet dinner. The cauliflower, which has been grated so it resembles rice, is simmered briefly with flour-thickened milk and Parmesan cheese, forming a creamy sauce to coat the vegetable and create a risotto-like base. Shrimp and peas are added to the skillet, and minutes later the dish is ready to be served, garnished beautifully with ribbons of fresh basil and a shower of Parmesan. (To make this gluten-free, dissolve 1 tablespoon plus ½ teaspoon of cornstarch into the milk instead of using the flour.)

Note: To make cauliflower rice, grate the tops of cauliflower florets on the wide holes of a box grater, or in a food processor using the grater attachment. Cauliflower rice may also be purchased in the refrigerated produce section of many stores, or you can buy it frozen. If using frozen cauliflower rice, cook it in the skillet for a bit longer (about six minutes), until it is thawed and its water has evaporated before adding the flour.

1. Heat the oil in a large, nonstick skillet over medium heat. Add the shallot and cook until softened, 2 minutes. Stir in the cauliflower rice, salt, and pepper and cook for 2 minutes.

2. Sprinkle the flour over the cauliflower and stir to incorporate, then add the milk and cook, stirring occasionally, until it comes to a gentle boil. Stir in ½ cup of the Parmesan cheese until incorporated, then add the shrimp and the peas.

3. Return to a simmer, then continue to cook, stirring occasionally, until the shrimp are pink and no longer translucent and the sauce has thickened, about 5 minutes more. Season with additional salt to taste, then serve immediately, garnished with basil and the remaining Parmesan.

Makes 4 servings

SERVING SIZE: about 1¼ cups

PER SERVING: Calories 360; Total Fat 13 g (Sat Fat 4.5 g, Mono Fat 6 g, Poly Fat 1 g); Protein 36 g; Carb 26 g; Fiber 5 g; Cholesterol 200 mg; Sodium 680 mg; Total Sugar 11 g (Added Sugar 0 g)

EXCELLENT SOURCE OF: calcium, copper, folate, magnesium, manganese, phosphorous, potassium, protein, riboflavin, vitamin A, vitamin C, vitamin K

GOOD SOURCE OF: fiber, iron, pantothenic acid, selenium, thiamine, vitamin B_6, vitamin B_{12}

---

2 tablespoons olive oil

½ cup chopped shallot

3 cups cauliflower rice

¼ teaspoon salt, plus more to taste

¼ teaspoon freshly ground black pepper

2 tablespoons plus 1 teaspoon all-purpose flour

1¾ cups 1% low-fat milk

¾ cup freshly grated Parmesan cheese, divided

1 pound medium-size shrimp (26–30 count per pound), cleaned, tail-off

1½ cups fresh or frozen peas

2 tablespoons fresh basil leaves, cut into ribbons

crab quesadillas

This fresh, sea-inspired quesadilla has just enough queso to bring the filling together, but not so much that it outshines the real star ingredient here: crab. It is a surprising filling that is completely winning, especially since it is tossed with lime, cilantro, red bell pepper, scallions, and pickled jalapeño for colorfully contrasting flavor and texture, along with mild, melty Monterey Jack cheese. A handful of fresh spinach adds another layer of goodness to the whole wheat flour package (you could certainly substitute corn to make them gluten-free), and each is warm, toasted, and ready to gobble up after about four minutes in a skillet. Served with a quick and simple guacamole for dipping, they make for a light and lovely meal. They could also be served in smaller wedges for a fun pool or beach party appetizer.

8 ounces claw or lump crabmeat, picked over and pressed to remove as much water as possible

½ medium-size red bell pepper, seeded and finely chopped

½ cup packed shredded Monterey Jack cheese

2 scallions, thinly sliced (about ⅓ cup)

¼ cup plus 1 tablespoon chopped fresh cilantro leaves, divided

1 tablespoon plus 2 teaspoons chopped pickled jalapeño pepper, or to taste, divided

2 tablespoons freshly squeezed lime juice, divided

1 large avocado, pitted and peeled

¼ teaspoon salt

4 (8-inch) whole wheat tortillas

2 cups chopped fresh baby spinach leaves

1 teaspoon olive oil, divided

1. Combine the crab, bell pepper, cheese, scallions, ¼ cup of the cilantro, 1 tablespoon of the jalapeño, and 1 tablespoon of the lime juice in a medium-size bowl. In another medium-size bowl, mash the avocado with the remaining tablespoon of lime juice and the salt, then stir in the remaining tablespoon of cilantro and 2 teaspoons of jalapeño.

2. Lay the tortillas on a work surface and place a quarter of the crab mixture on half of each tortilla. Pile ½ cup of spinach on top of each. Fold the other half of the tortilla over the filling to create a half-moon.

3. Brush a large, nonstick skillet with half of the oil and heat over medium-high heat. Put two quesadillas into the skillet and weigh them down with a kettle or heatproof plate with a heavy can on top. Cook until the quesadillas are golden brown on both sides and the cheese is melting, 1 to 2 minutes per side. Repeat with remaining quesadillas in same manner.

4. Cut the warm quesadillas into wedges and serve with a dollop of the guacamole alongside.

Makes 4 servings

SERVING SIZE: 1 quesadilla and ¼ cup guacamole

PER SERVING: Calories 340; Total Fat 17 g (Sat Fat 5 g, Mono Fat 7 g, Poly Fat 1 g); Protein 20 g; Carb 30 g; Fiber 7 g; Cholesterol 70 mg; Sodium 850 mg; Total Sugar 1 g (Added Sugar 0 g)

EXCELLENT SOURCE OF: calcium, copper, fiber, folate, manganese, phosphorous, protein, selenium, vitamin A, vitamin B_{12}, vitamin C, vitamin K, zinc

GOOD SOURCE OF: iron, magnesium, niacin, pantothenic acid, potassium, riboflavin, vitamin B_6

lemony shrimp and zucchini skillet with feta

am enamored with the way the acidity of lemon juice wakes a dish with bright sunniness and how the zest imbues it with fragrant freshness. Here, a skillet brimming with tender whole-grain orzo pasta, succulent shrimp, and summer squash seasoned with garlic and fresh parsley gets the luscious lemon treatment. First, the orzo is partially cooked in the skillet with garlic and broth. As the liquid reduces and thickens, it forms a light and luxurious sauce. Then, the shrimp, zucchini, and lemon are added and cooked nearly through before a final sprinkle of tangy feta cheese is added on top to melt sumptuously into the dish. It is a perfect meal to enjoy in the summer, but you can make it anytime for a year-round taste of a sunny day.

2 tablespoons olive oil

3 garlic cloves, thinly sliced

1½ cups uncooked whole-grain orzo pasta

2 cups low-sodium chicken broth (seafood or vegetable broth will work, too)

2 small zucchini (6 ounces each), cut into ¼-inch-thick half-moons (3½ cups)

1¼ pounds medium-size shrimp (26–30 count per pound), cleaned, tail-off

¼ cup finely chopped fresh flat-leaf parsley, plus more for garnish

1 teaspoon finely grated lemon zest

3 tablespoons freshly squeezed lemon juice

¼ teaspoon salt

¼ teaspoon freshly ground black pepper

⅔ cup crumbled feta cheese

1. Heat the oil in a large, deep skillet over medium heat, add the garlic, and cook, stirring often, until it is a pale golden color, 1 minute. Stir in the orzo and cook, stirring, until it is well coated with oil and lightly toasted, 1 to 2 minutes more. Add the broth and bring to a boil, then lower the heat to medium-low, cover, and simmer until the orzo is about halfway cooked, 5 minutes.

2. Stir in the zucchini, shrimp, ¼ cup of the parsley, the lemon zest and juice, and the salt and pepper. Cover and cook, stirring two or three times, until the shrimp is cooked on the outside but still a bit translucent inside, and the zucchini is crisp-tender, about 4 minutes. Sprinkle with the feta, then cover again and continue cooking until the cheese has melted slightly and the shrimp are cooked through, 2 minutes more. Serve garnished with the remaining chopped parsley.

Makes 4 servings

SERVING SIZE: about 2 cups

PER SERVING: Calories 490; Total Fat 15 g (Sat Fat 5 g, Mono Fat 6 g, Poly Fat 2 g); Protein 43 g; Carb 50 g; Fiber 7 g; Cholesterol 250 mg; Sodium 590 mg; Total Sugar 5 g (Added Sugar 0 g)

EXCELLENT SOURCE OF: calcium, copper, fiber, iron, magnesium, manganese, niacin, phosphorous, potassium, protein, riboflavin, selenium, thiamine, vitamin B_6, vitamin C, vitamin K, zinc

GOOD SOURCE OF: folate, molybdenum, vitamin A

cod in saffron broth with white beans

Here, flaky, firm white cod fillets are simmered in a sumptuous broth that's made magically golden and aromatic with a generous pinch of saffron, along with onion, carrot, fennel, white beans, and thyme. A subtle touch of tomato paste adds sweet, earthy depth. The dish has the elegant essence of a bouillabaisse, but with a heartiness from the beans and an under-thirty-minute cooking time that makes it ideal for a busy weeknight. Serve with crusty whole-grain bread for sopping up the broth, if you'd like.

2 tablespoons olive oil

1 small onion, diced

1 large carrot, peeled and diced

1 small bulb fennel, diced, some fronds reserved for garnish

1 garlic clove, minced

1 tablespoon tomato paste

2½ cups seafood or fish stock

1 (15-ounce) can low-sodium white beans, such as cannellini or small white beans, drained and rinsed

1 large thyme sprig

¾ teaspoon salt, divided, plus more to taste

¼ teaspoon freshly ground black pepper

⅛ teaspoon saffron threads

4 (6-ounce) cod fillets, or other white, firm fish, such as halibut or monkfish

1. Heat the oil in a large, high-sided skillet over medium heat. Add the onion and cook until it is softened, 3 minutes. Add the carrot and fennel and cook for 4 minutes more. Stir in the garlic and cook for 30 seconds, then stir in the tomato paste. Add the fish stock, beans, thyme, ½ teaspoon of the salt, ⅛ teaspoon of the pepper, and the saffron and bring to a boil. Cook, uncovered, over medium-high heat, until the stock is reduced slightly, 5 minutes. The base may be made up to 2 days ahead and refrigerated or frozen for up to 3 months.

2. Season the fish with the remaining ¼ teaspoon of salt and ⅛ teaspoon of pepper. Arrange the fish in the pan, nestling it into the liquid as much as possible (it is okay if it isn't covered completely). Return the liquid to a boil, then lower the heat to medium-low, cover the pan, and cook until the fish flakes easily with a fork, about 7 minutes. Remove the thyme sprig and season with additional salt to taste, depending on the saltiness of the stock.

3. To serve, use a large slotted spatula to transfer a piece of fish into each of four shallow bowls, ladle the broth and vegetables into each bowl, and garnish with the fennel fronds.

Makes 4 servings

SERVING SIZE: 1 piece fish and 1 cup vegetables and broth

PER SERVING: Calories 320; Total Fat 9 g (Sat Fat 1 g, Mono Fat 5 g, Poly Fat 1 g); Protein 37 g; Carb 23 g; Fiber 7 g; Cholesterol 80 mg; Sodium 760 mg; Total Sugar 5 g (Added Sugar 0 g)

EXCELLENT SOURCE OF: fiber, magnesium, niacin, phosphorous, potassium, protein, riboflavin, selenium, thiamine, vitamin A, vitamin B_6, vitamin B_{12}, vitamin C, vitamin K

GOOD SOURCE OF: calcium, copper, folate, manganese, vitamin D, zinc

jamaican-style snapper escovitch

This take on Jamaican escovitch lassos all of the traditional dish's exciting flavors and colors into a healthful, one-pan meal. The traditional dish usually involves a whole, crispy fried fish that is doused with a tangy quick-pickling sauce bountiful with bell peppers, onions, and carrots and spiked with hot pepper. Here, fish is pan-seared to make the dish weeknight-easy. Skin-on red snapper fillets are optimal since the white-fleshed fish's skin crisps beautifully in the pan, but if you can't find that, any firm white fish fillet will work instead. Once the fish is cooked, the mélange of colorful sweet vegetables hits the pan along with the quintessential Jamaican combo of Scotch bonnet pepper (don't worry, you can use any hot pepper to taste), thyme, and warm-savory allspice. The resulting medley is a tongue-tingling party of sweet, spicy, savory, and tangy that makes for an unforgettable dinner.

4 cups frozen, cooked brown rice (to yield 3 cups)

4 (5- to 6-ounce) skin-on red snapper fillets, or skinless tilapia, mahimahi, or other firm, white fish fillets

½ teaspoon paprika

¼ teaspoon granulated garlic

½ teaspoon salt, divided

½ teaspoon freshly ground black pepper, divided

¼ cup olive oil, divided

1 garlic clove, minced

1 medium-size white onion, thinly sliced into half-moons

1 red bell pepper, seeded and thinly sliced

1 yellow bell pepper, seeded and thinly sliced

1 large carrot, cut into thin matchsticks

½ Scotch bonnet pepper, or another variety of hot pepper, thinly sliced, or to taste

2 teaspoons chopped fresh thyme leaves

¼ teaspoon ground allspice

½ cup unseasoned rice vinegar

1. Place the rice in a microwave-safe dish with a vented cover and microwave on HIGH until it is steaming, about 6 minutes. Then, allow the rice to rest, covered, as you cook the fish and vegetables.

2. Pat the fish dry with a paper towel. Combine the paprika, granulated garlic, and ¼ teaspoon each of the salt and black pepper in a small bowl and sprinkle over both sides of the fish.

3. Heat 2 tablespoons of the oil in a large skillet over medium-high heat. When the oil is shimmering, place two of the fish fillets into the skillet (skin side down, if using snapper) and cook until the bottom is crispy and the fish releases easily from the pan, 3 to 4 minutes. Use a fish spatula to flip the fish and cook for 1 minute more, until the fish is barely cooked though (it will continue to cook as it rests). Transfer the cooked fish to a plate. Add another tablespoon of the oil to the pan and repeat with the remaining fish fillets, transferring them to the plate.

4. Add the remaining tablespoon of oil to the pan, then add the garlic, onion, bell peppers, carrot, Scotch bonnet pepper, thyme, allspice, and the remaining ¼ teaspoon each of salt and black pepper and cook, stirring occasionally, until the vegetables soften slightly but are still crisp, 2 to 3 minutes. Add the vinegar to the pan, lower the heat to medium, and simmer until the vegetables have softened a bit further but still retain some crispness, 2 minutes more.

5. To serve, place ¾ cup of rice on each serving plate, then top each with a fish fillet and vegetables.

Makes 4 servings

SERVING SIZE: 1 fish fillet, 1 cup vegetables, and ¾ cup rice

PER SERVING: Calories 520; Total Fat 17 g (Sat Fat 2.5 g, Mono Fat 10 g, Poly Fat 2 g); Protein 34 g; Carb 56 g; Fiber 5 g; Cholesterol 50 mg; Sodium 880 mg; Total Sugar 15 g (Added Sugar 0 g)

EXCELLENT SOURCE OF: phosphorous, potassium, protein, selenium, vitamin A, vitamin B_6, vitamin B_{12}, vitamin C, vitamin D

GOOD SOURCE OF: fiber, folate, magnesium, manganese, pantothenic acid, vitamin K

lox and cream cheese frittata

For this recipe, I spun the classic New York cream cheese and smoked salmon breakfast into a skillet egg dish that is nice either hot or at room temperature and works for pretty much any meal you can think of from breakfast/brunch to a light lunch or dinner, to, when cut into smaller pieces, a cocktail party nibble. I especially love the way the nuggets of cream cheese melt decadently on top of the frittata, so the fact that it is so healthfully balanced never occurs to you as you are eating it. To round it out as a complete meal, serve it with sliced ripe tomato and half of a (whole-grain) toasted bagel or dark rye bread.

7 large eggs

¼ cup 1% low-fat milk

½ teaspoon salt

⅛ teaspoon freshly ground black pepper

1 tablespoon olive oil

1 small onion, diced

4 ounces sliced smoked salmon, chopped

¼ cup chopped fresh chives

2 tablespoons chopped fresh dill

1 ounce cream cheese, cut into ½-inch chunks (¼ cup)

1. Whisk together the eggs, milk, salt, and pepper in a medium-size bowl.

2. Heat the oil in a 10-inch cast-iron or oven-proof, nonstick skillet over medium heat. Add the onion and cook, stirring occasionally, until it is tender and beginning to brown, about 4 minutes. Lower the heat to medium-low. Stir in the salmon, chopped chives, and dill, then pour the egg mixture over the salmon mixture, covering it evenly. Cook until the egg mixture has set around the edges but is still liquidy in the middle, about 8 minutes. Put an oven rack in the top position and preheat the broiler.

3. Distribute the cream cheese over the top of the eggs. Place the skillet on the rack under the broiler and cook until the surface is set and golden brown, 1½ to 2 minutes. Allow the frittata to rest for a minute or two before slicing into wedges. Serve warm or at room temperature.

The frittata will keep for up to 4 days in an airtight container in the refrigerator.

Makes 4 servings

SERVING SIZE: ¼ frittata

PER SERVING: Calories 290; Total Fat 18 g (Sat Fat 5 g, Mono Fat 7 g, Poly Fat 3 g); Protein 29 g; Carb 4 g; Fiber 0 g; Cholesterol 375 mg; Sodium 460 mg; Total Sugar 2 g (Added Sugar 0 g)

EXCELLENT SOURCE OF: iodine, molybdenum, niacin, phosphorous, protein, riboflavin, selenium, vitamin B$_6$, vitamin B$_{12}$

GOOD SOURCE OF: folate, iron, potassium, thiamine, vitamin D, vitamin K

scallops with corn, zucchini, and miso butter

Scallops, corn, zucchini, and onion are a standard summertime farmers' market haul for me, and are lovely simply sautéed together. But the easy addition of a dollop of miso paste, a dash of soy sauce, some honey, and a touch of butter makes for a light sauce that brings those market ingredients together in an unforgettably sumptuous and savory way. It's a dish that is dreamy when fresh corn is in high season, but you can also use frozen corn to make it any time of the year when you want a taste of summer.

1 tablespoon white miso paste

1 tablespoon unsalted butter, softened

2 teaspoons honey

1½ teaspoons reduced-sodium soy sauce

1¼ pounds large sea scallops (about 16)

3 tablespoons neutral-tasting high-heat oil, such as canola, divided

1 small onion, diced (about 1 cup)

2 medium-size zucchini (about 8 ounces each), diced

3 cups corn kernels, from 4 large ears fresh corn, or frozen, thawed

1 scallion, thinly sliced

1. Combine the miso, butter, honey, and soy sauce in a small bowl, mashing them together with a fork, then whisking until smooth.

2. Pat the scallops as dry as possible, using a paper towel. Heat 1 tablespoon of the oil in a large skillet over high heat until it is shimmering. Add half of the scallops, flat side down, and cook without moving them until they are well browned on the underside, 1½ to 2 minutes, transferring them to a plate once they are seared on one side. Repeat with another tablespoon of the oil and the remaining scallops (lower the heat to medium-high if the oil begins to smoke), and transfer them to the plate.

3. Lower the heat to medium, add the remaining tablespoon of oil to the pan, then add the onion and cook, stirring a few times, for 1 minute. Stir in the zucchini and corn and cook, stirring occasionally, until the vegetables are nearly tender, about 3 minutes. Stir the miso butter into the vegetables to combine, then return the scallops to the pan, nestling them into the vegetables, and cook, uncovered, stirring gently once or twice, until the scallops are opaque throughout and the vegetables are tender, 2 to 3 minutes more. Garnish with the sliced scallion and serve.

Makes 4 servings

SERVING SIZE: 4 scallops and 1 heaping cup vegetables

PER SERVING: Calories 360; Total Fat 16 g (Sat Fat 3 g, Mono Fat 8 g, Poly Fat 4 g); Protein 23 g; Carb 35 g; Fiber 4 g; Cholesterol 40 mg; Sodium 750 mg; Total Sugar 14 g (Added Sugar 3 g)

EXCELLENT SOURCE OF: folate, magnesium, manganese, molybdenum, phosphorous, potassium, protein, selenium, vitamin B$_{12}$, vitamin C, vitamin K

GOOD SOURCE OF: fiber, niacin, pantothenic acid, riboflavin, thiamine, vitamin B$_6$, zinc

shrimp stir-fry with tomato-ginger-garlic sauce and snow peas

Not only do I write a weekly column in the *Washington Post* food section, I am an avid reader of it as well, always finding inspiration on its pages. One recipe that caught my attention not long ago was a shrimp stir-fry that used ketchup as a primary ingredient. Besides that surprising add-in, I was just as intrigued by what the recipe didn't have—there was none of the soy sauce or sesame oil that I usually use in my stir-fries. Although I actually love ketchup (don't judge), I decided to make a version of the recipe using a combination of tomato paste, vinegar, and honey so I could easily modify the amount of sugar. I also added a few big handfuls of snow peas to make it a well-rounded meal. The result is absolutely delicious. Making use of frozen brown rice keeps it a true one-pot wonder.

1 large egg white

2 teaspoons cornstarch, divided

1¼ pounds large shrimp (16–20 count per pound), cleaned, tail-off

1½ tablespoons minced fresh ginger

3 garlic cloves, thinly sliced

1 teaspoon crushed red pepper flakes

⅔ cup low-sodium chicken broth

¼ cup tomato paste

¼ cup unseasoned rice vinegar

3 tablespoons honey

¾ teaspoon salt

4 cups frozen, cooked brown rice (to yield 3 cups)

3 tablespoons canola or peanut oil

12 ounces snow peas, trimmed

3 large scallions, thinly sliced

1. Beat the egg white in a large bowl. Whisk in 1 teaspoon of the cornstarch, then add the shrimp to the bowl and toss to coat. Add the ginger, garlic, and red pepper flakes and toss to combine.

2. Whisk together the broth, tomato paste, vinegar, honey, salt, and the remaining teaspoon of cornstarch in a medium-size bowl or pitcher until the cornstarch dissolves.

3. Place the rice in a microwave-safe bowl with a vented cover and microwave on HIGH until it is steaming, about 6 minutes. Then, allow the rice to rest, covered, as you cook the stir-fry.

4. Heat the oil in a large, nonstick skillet over high heat. Add the shrimp and cook, stirring frequently for 1 minute. Add the snow peas, then pour in the tomato mixture and cook, stirring often, until the shrimp is just cooked through and the snow peas are crisp-tender, about 3 minutes. Stir in the scallions and serve over the rice.

Makes 4 servings

SERVING SIZE: 1½ cups stir-fry and ¾ cup rice

PER SERVING: Calories 520; Total Fat 13 g (Sat Fat 1.5 g, Mono Fat 7 g, Poly Fat 3 g); Protein 37 g; Carb 65 g; Fiber 6 g; Cholesterol 230 mg; Sodium 690 mg; Total Sugar 20 g (Added Sugar 13 g)

EXCELLENT SOURCE OF: copper, fiber, phosphorous, protein, vitamin C, vitamin K

GOOD SOURCE OF: calcium, iron, magnesium, potassium, zinc

salmon with kimchi and warm broccoli slaw

Kimchi does double duty in this recipe, first adding a layer of flavor to a quick marinade for the salmon, and second awakening the accompanying sautéed slaw with its spicy, mouthwatering pungency. A traditional Korean fermented vegetable, kimchi is rich in probiotics, good bacteria that promote not only digestive health but overall well-being. It can be found in the refrigerator section at many regular supermarkets and it is made in all different styles. The most common, made with cabbage, is what I used here, but feel free to experiment if another type calls your name. Besides using it in this recipe (which I know you will want to make again), use the rest of the jar wherever you imagine pickles would work—on sandwiches, burgers, and grain bowls.

½ cup kimchi, chopped, divided

¼ cup reduced-sodium soy sauce, divided

1 tablespoon plus 1 teaspoon toasted sesame oil, divided

4 (6-ounce) center-cut salmon fillets, skin removed

2 tablespoons honey

2 tablespoons sesame seeds

2 tablespoons canola or other neutral-tasting oil, divided

1 small onion, sliced into half-moons

2 large garlic cloves, minced

1 tablespoon minced fresh ginger

5 cups broccoli slaw (from 1 [12- to 14-ounce] bag, or 1¼ pounds broccoli stalks and 1 medium-size carrot, peeled and shredded)

1. Combine ¼ cup of the kimchi, 2 tablespoons of the soy sauce, and 1 tablespoon of the sesame oil in a small bowl. Place the salmon on a large, rimmed plate, spoon the kimchi mixture over the salmon, and allow to marinate for 20 minutes. In the same small bowl, whisk together the remaining 2 tablespoons of soy sauce, the remaining teaspoon of sesame oil, the honey, and 2 tablespoons of water.

2. Toast the sesame seeds in a large, dry nonstick skillet over medium-high heat, stirring frequently, until they are golden, 2 minutes. Transfer them to a dish.

3. Heat 1 tablespoon of the canola oil in the same skillet over medium-high heat. Place the salmon in the skillet, top side down, and cook for 3 minutes without disturbing. Then, flip and cook to desired doneness, about 3 minutes more for medium. Transfer the fish to a clean plate. Drain any oil from the pan and carefully wipe it with a paper towel.

4. Add the remaining tablespoon of oil to the skillet. Add the onion and cook until softened and beginning to brown, 3 minutes. Add the garlic and ginger and cook, stirring, for 30 seconds more. Add the slaw and the honey mixture and cook, stirring frequently until the vegetables are tender, 3 minutes. Remove from the heat and stir in the remaining kimchi.

5. Serve the salmon on top of a mound of the vegetables, with sesame seeds sprinkled all over.

The salmon and vegetables will keep in an airtight container in the refrigerator for up to 2 days and may be served warm or at room temperature.

Makes 4 servings

SERVING SIZE: ¾ cup vegetables and 1 piece salmon

PER SERVING: Calories 430; Total Fat 21 g (Sat Fat 3 g, Mono Fat 10 g, Poly Fat 6 g); Protein 40 g; Carb 21 g; Fiber 4 g; Cholesterol 80 mg; Sodium 690 mg; Total Sugar 13 g (Added Sugar 9 g)

EXCELLENT SOURCE OF: niacin, phosphorous, potassium, protein, selenium, vitamin A, vitamin B_6, vitamin B_{12}, vitamin C, vitamin D

GOOD SOURCE OF: calcium, copper, fiber, iron, magnesium, manganese, pantothenic acid, riboflavin, thiamine, vitamin K

brazilian-style seafood stew

The ingredients here are nothing unusual, but pulled together in this remarkably flavorful and stunning stew they take on an entirely new and exciting life. The dish is a festival of flavor and color, with chunks of flaky fish and shrimp simmered in a golden-hued coconut sauce enlivened with lime, chili, and garlic, and chock-full of peppers, tomatoes, scallions, and cilantro. It is one of those meals that have a tremendous impressiveness-to-effort ratio, meaning it will wow whomever you serve it to, but you can easily pull it together in less than thirty minutes, start to finish.

1½ pounds skinless white fish fillets, such as halibut, tilapia, mahimahi, or cod, cut into 2-inch pieces

8 ounces large shrimp (16–20 count per pound), cleaned

3 tablespoons freshly squeezed lime juice

3 tablespoons olive oil, divided

4 garlic cloves, minced, divided

¾ teaspoon salt, divided

¼ teaspoon freshly ground black pepper

1 medium-size onion, diced

1 medium-size red bell pepper, seeded and thinly sliced

1 medium-size yellow bell pepper, seeded and thinly sliced

2 teaspoons sweet paprika

½ teaspoon crushed red pepper flakes, plus more to taste

1 cup chopped fresh tomatoes

2 scallions, thinly sliced

1 cup light coconut milk

½ cup seafood or fish stock, or water

¼ cup fresh cilantro leaves

1. Place the fish and the shrimp in a medium-size bowl and toss with the lime juice, 1 tablespoon of the olive oil, half of the garlic, ¼ teaspoon of the salt, and the black pepper. Allow to marinate as you prepare the remaining ingredients.

2. Heat the remaining 2 tablespoons of oil in a large pot over medium heat. Add the onion and the bell peppers and cook until they have softened, about 5 minutes. Add the remaining garlic, the paprika, and the red pepper flakes, and cook, stirring, for 30 seconds. Then, stir in the tomatoes and the scallions and the remaining ½ teaspoon of salt.

3. Nestle the fish into the vegetable mixture, then pour the coconut milk and stock over it. Bring to a simmer, then lower the heat to medium-low and simmer, covered, until the shrimp is cooked through and the fish flakes easily with a fork, about 6 minutes. Stir in the cilantro and add more red pepper flakes, if desired.

The stew will keep in an airtight container in the refrigerator for up to 2 days.

Makes 4 servings

SERVING SIZE: 1¾ cups

PER SERVING: Calories 390; Total Fat 16 g (Sat Fat 4.5 g, Mono Fat 8 g, Poly Fat 2 g); Protein 45 g; Carb 16 g; Fiber 3 g; Cholesterol 175 mg; Sodium 670 mg; Total Sugar 6 g (Added Sugar 0 g)

EXCELLENT SOURCE OF: niacin, phosphorous, potassium, protein, selenium, vitamin A, vitamin B_6, vitamin B_{12}, vitamin C, vitamin D, vitamin K

GOOD SOURCE OF: copper, folate, magnesium, manganese, pantothenic acid, thiamine, zinc

green chowder with salmon and scallops

This recipe brings the green juice trend into the soup realm by blending fresh spinach leaves into a pot of potatoes, leeks, garlic, celery, and thyme that have been simmered in a seafood broth. Pureed until smooth, the potatoes make the soup thick and creamy; the aromatics and herbs give it a full, rounded flavor; and the spinach makes it a gorgeous emerald green. Chunks of salmon and scallops are added to that sumptuous base (you could swap any combo of fish and shellfish you like), along with a brightening splash of lemon juice. The result is a fresh take on seafood chowder that is as stunning and satisfying as it is good for you.

2 tablespoons olive oil

1 large or 2 small leeks, white and light green parts, chopped (2 cups)

2 celery stalks, chopped

2 garlic cloves, minced

1 tablespoon chopped fresh thyme, or 1 teaspoon dried

1½ pounds Yukon gold potatoes (6 medium-size), cut into ½-inch dice

½ teaspoon salt, plus more to taste

⅛ teaspoon ground white pepper

2 cups seafood or fish stock

2 cups lightly packed spinach leaves

1 pound salmon fillet, cut into ¾-inch chunks

8 ounces bay scallops

1 tablespoon freshly squeezed lemon juice

1 teaspoon finely grated lemon zest

1. Heat the oil in a soup pot over medium heat. Add the leek and celery and cook, stirring occasionally, until they have softened, 3 minutes. Add the garlic and thyme and cook for 30 seconds more. Stir in the potatoes, salt, and white pepper, then add the stock and 1½ cups of water and bring to a boil. Lower the heat to medium-low and simmer, covered, until the potatoes are tender, 10 minutes.

2. Use a slotted spoon to remove about 1 cup of the vegetables from the pot and set that aside. Add the spinach to the pot and cook until wilted, 30 seconds. Remove the pot from the heat and puree until smooth, using an immersion blender. (Alternatively, allow to cool slightly, then puree it in several batches in a regular blender.) The chowder may be made ahead up to this stage and refrigerated for up to 2 days, or frozen for up to 3 months.

3. Return the puree to a boil, add the salmon and scallops, and simmer until they are just barely translucent in the center, 3 minutes. Stir in the reserved vegetables and the lemon juice and season with additional salt to taste, depending on the saltiness of the stock. Serve in shallow bowls, garnished with lemon zest.

Makes 4 servings

SERVING SIZE: 2 cups

PER SERVING: Calories 460; Total Fat 19 g (Sat Fat 4.5 g, Mono Fat 10 g, Poly Fat 4 g); Protein 34 g; Carb 39 g; Fiber 5 g; Cholesterol 75 mg; Sodium 770 mg; Total Sugar 3 g (Added Sugar 0 g)

EXCELLENT SOURCE OF: phosphorous, protein, vitamin A, vitamin B$_{12}$, vitamin C, vitamin K

GOOD SOURCE OF: calcium, fiber, folate, iron, magnesium, manganese, potassium, selenium

mussels with white wine dijon mustard sauce and greens

A pot of mussels had always seemed like fancy restaurant fare to me as opposed to something I could make at home. That was until I learned how ridiculously easy they are to make, not to mention affordable and kid friendly (eating out of a shell is just plain fun). To cook mussels, you simply put them in a big pot with some boiling liquid, cover, and let them steam until they open, which takes all of five minutes. That's it. In this recipe, after you transfer the shellfish to serving bowls, you take the flavor up a level by whisking some mustard and butter into the liquid in the pot to form a flavorful, emulsified sauce. And you heighten the dish's elegance by serving the mussels piled high with a mound of frisée salad. Served with a crusty baguette for sopping up the sauce, it's an impressively upscale meal that is everyday easy.

4 pounds mussels (in shell)

¼ cup olive oil, divided

2 medium-size shallots, finely chopped (about ½ cup)

2 garlic cloves, very thinly sliced

¾ cup dry white wine

2 teaspoons sherry vinegar

2 tablespoons plus 1 teaspoon Dijon mustard, divided

Pinch of salt, plus more to taste, divided

¼ teaspoon freshly ground black pepper, plus a pinch, divided

4 cups torn frisée, baby arugula, or watercress

2 tablespoons unsalted butter

2 tablespoons chopped fresh parsley

1. Rinse the mussels in cold water, remove any hairy clumps with a paring knife, and scrub the shells with a vegetable brush. Discard any mussels that are open and do not close tightly when tapped.

2. Heat 2 tablespoons of the oil in a large pot with a tight-fitting lid over medium heat. Add the shallots and cook, stirring occasionally, until softened, about 2 minutes. Add the garlic and cook, stirring, until it is fragrant, 1 minute longer. Add the wine and bring to a boil over high heat.

3. Add the mussels to the pot, cover, and cook over high heat just until they have opened, about 5 minutes. While the mussels are cooking, whisk together the remaining 2 tablespoons of oil, the sherry vinegar, 1 teaspoon of the Dijon mustard, and a pinch each of the salt and pepper in a medium-size bowl. Add the frisée and toss to coat.

4. When the mussels are done, lower the heat to low and transfer them, using a large slotted scooper, to shallow serving bowls, discarding any that have not opened and leaving the liquid in the pot. Whisk the remaining 2 tablespoons of mustard and the butter into the broth to form an emulsified sauce. Stir in the parsley

and the remaining ¼ teaspoon of pepper plus salt to taste. Pour the sauce over the mussels in the bowls, top each with a mound of the greens, and serve immediately.

Makes 4 servings

SERVING SIZE: about 30 small mussels, ½ cup sauce, and 1 cup greens

PER SERVING: Calories 320; Total Fat 21 g (Sat Fat 6 g, Mono Fat 12 g, Poly Fat 2 g); Protein 12 g; Carb 10 g; Fiber 1 g; Cholesterol 40 mg; Sodium 440 mg; Total Sugar 3 g (Added Sugar 0 g)

EXCELLENT SOURCE OF: iron, manganese, protein, selenium, vitamin A, vitamin B_{12}, vitamin C, vitamin K

GOOD SOURCE OF: folate, phosphorous, potassium, riboflavin, thiamine

miso noodle soup with shrimp

There is nothing like a belly full of hot soup and noodles as an antidote for a cold, dreary day. But with all the salt and refined grain in the typical ramen bowls, I hungered to have the pleasure more often, in a healthier way. The base of this recipe is a soothing miso broth fortified with ginger and garlic and chock-full of meaty shiitake mushrooms, shrimp, fresh spinach leaves, and just the right amount of noodles. I opt for brown rice noodles, but if you can't find those, regular thin rice noodles will do.

Not only does miso add savory flavor to dishes, it is also rich in probiotics, good bacteria—like those in yogurt—that are good for digestive and overall health. The bit of fresh ginger stirred in at the end of cooking gives this big steaming bowl of goodness a bright touch and makes it extra-soothing so it hits the spot just right. Grab a pair of chopsticks (or a fork) along with a soup spoon to eat it—you'll want them both to enjoy every drop.

2 tablespoons canola or other neutral-tasting oil, divided

4 ounces shiitake mushroom caps (8 medium-size caps), sliced

4 scallions, thinly sliced, dark green part reserved for garnish

3 medium-size garlic cloves, minced

1 tablespoon plus 2 teaspoons finely minced fresh ginger, divided

6 cups low-sodium chicken broth

¼ cup white (blond) miso paste

12 ounces medium-size shrimp (26–30 count per pound), cleaned

5 ounces thin brown rice noodles (vermicelli)

2 cups lightly packed baby spinach leaves

Salt

1. Heat 1 tablespoon of the oil in a soup pot over medium-high heat. Add the mushrooms and cook, stirring occasionally until they are browned, about 3 minutes. Transfer the mushrooms to a plate. Add the remaining tablespoon of oil to the pot, lower the heat to medium, then add the scallions, garlic, and 1 tablespoon of the ginger and cook, stirring, until fragrant, about 30 seconds.

2. Add the broth to the pot and bring to a boil. Transfer ½ cup of the hot broth to a small bowl or pitcher, add the miso, and whisk until smooth.

3. Add the shrimp and noodles to the soup pot, return to a boil, then simmer over medium-low heat until the shrimp is cooked through and the noodles are tender, about 3 minutes. Remove from the heat. Stir the dissolved miso into the pot, return the mushrooms to the pot, and stir in the spinach and remaining 2 teaspoons of ginger. Season with salt to taste. Serve in large soup bowls, garnished with the reserved scallion greens.

Makes 4 servings

SERVING SIZE: 2 cups

PER SERVING: Calories 330; Total Fat 8 g (Sat Fat 1 g, Mono Fat 5 g, Poly Fat 2 g); Protein 27 g; Carb 39 g; Fiber 2 g; Cholesterol 135 mg; Sodium 760 mg; Total Sugar 5 g (Added Sugar 0 g)

EXCELLENT SOURCE OF: copper, folate, manganese, niacin, phosphorous, protein, vitamin A, vitamin C, vitamin K

GOOD SOURCE OF: calcium, fiber, iron, magnesium, potassium, zinc

roasted cod niçoise

I am not sure whether much sheet pan cooking is done in the South of France, but the classic Niçoise flavors (meaning "in the style of Nice") of olives, garlic, tomatoes, herbs, vegetables, and seafood combine beautifully on one pan for a healthy and sumptuously tasty meal. A key short-cut here is to buy prepared olive tapenade. That is spread onto cod fillets (any white flaky fillet will work) and nestled on the pan with new potatoes that have been given a head start in the oven, and haricots verts (thin green beans) that have been tossed with grainy Dijon mustard. Once plated, everything is given a bright, fresh sprinkle of color and flavor with lemon wedges, fresh tomatoes, and a sprinkle of parsley. Serve it with a baguette, if you'd like, just as they'd do in France.

1½ pounds small new red potatoes, cut into 1-inch chunks

2 tablespoons olive oil, divided

¼ plus ⅛ teaspoon salt, divided

8 ounces haricots verts, or thin green beans

1½ teaspoons grainy Dijon mustard

⅛ teaspoon freshly ground black pepper

4 (6-ounce) cod fillets

3 tablespoons prepared black olive tapenade

Lemon wedges

1 cup grape tomatoes, halved

2 tablespoons chopped fresh parsley

1. Preheat the oven to 400°F. Place the potatoes in a medium-size bowl. Toss with 1½ table-spoons of the oil and ¼ teaspoon of the salt. Transfer to the sheet pan and roast in the oven for 20 minutes.

2. Put the haricots verts in the bowl and toss to coat with the remaining 1½ teaspoons of oil, the mustard, the remaining ⅛ teaspoon of salt, and the pepper. Push the potatoes to one side of the pan, add the green beans to the pan next to the potatoes, leaving room for the fish, and then place the cod on the sheet pan. Spread ¾ tablespoon of the tapenade on top of each piece of cod. Return the pan to the oven and roast until the fish is no longer translucent and flakes easily with a fork, 12 to 15 minutes. Once the cod is cooked, if the vegetables need more cooking time, transfer the cod to a plate and cover with foil to keep warm while you roast the vegetables for 5 to 10 minutes more.

3. To serve, place a piece of cod on each plate and arrange the potatoes, green beans, and a lemon wedge or two on each side. Scatter the tomatoes around each plate and sprinkle with the parsley.

The fish and vegetables will keep in an airtight container in the refrigerator for up to 2 days and may be served warm or at room temperature.

Makes 4 servings

SERVING SIZE: 1 piece fish, about 12 green beans, and ¾ cup potatoes

PER SERVING: Calories 370; Total Fat 11 g (Sat Fat 1.5 g, Mono Fat 5 g, Poly Fat 1 g); Protein 35 g; Carb 34 g; Fiber 5 g; Cholesterol 75 mg; Sodium 460 mg; Total Sugar 5 g (Added Sugar 0 g)

EXCELLENT SOURCE OF: fiber, magnesium, manganese, niacin, phosphorous, potassium, protein, selenium, thiamine, vitamin B₆, vitamin B₁₂, vitamin C, vitamin K

GOOD SOURCE OF: copper, folate, iron, riboflavin, vitamin A, vitamin D, zinc

maryland crab soup

This soup feels retro to me in the best possible way. Its tomato-y base is riddled with a confetti of colorful cut vegetables that brings to mind pictures of soup you might see in a 1960s women's magazine. It has all the essentials of the midatlantic coast classic, including lots of crab and Old Bay seasoning, of course, but here that quintessential flavor is offered with considerably less saltiness than is common. The result is a comforting, family-favorite meal in a bowl that you will want to put in regular rotation. If you don't have Old Bay seasoning in your cupboard, it is worth picking some up not only for this recipe but to use to season seafood in general, or egg salad or avocado toast, for example. If need be, you can also substitute Creole seasoning here for a somewhat different, but also delicious flavor profile.

1 tablespoon olive oil

1 medium-size onion, diced

2 medium-size carrots, diced

2 celery stalks, diced

2 medium-size Yukon Gold potatoes, unpeeled, diced

1¼ cups fresh or frozen corn kernels

1¼ cups fresh or frozen lima beans

8 ounces green beans, fresh, trimmed and cut into ½-inch pieces, or frozen

1 tablespoon Old Bay seasoning

1½ teaspoons mustard powder

⅛ teaspoon red pepper flakes

1 (28-ounce) can crushed tomatoes

2 tablespoons Worcestershire sauce

1 pound lump crabmeat, drained and picked over to remove any shells

1. Heat the oil in a large pot over medium heat. Add the onion, carrots, and celery and cook until softened but not browned, about 4 minutes. Add the potatoes, corn, lima beans, green beans, Old Bay, mustard powder, and red pepper flakes and stir to combine. Add the tomatoes, Worcestershire, and 6 cups of water and bring to a boil. Lower the heat to medium-low and simmer, covered, until the vegetables are tender, about 30 minutes. The soup base may be made ahead to this point and kept in an airtight container in the refrigerator for up to 4 days, or frozen for up to 3 months.

2. Add the crab, return to a gentle boil, and simmer for 5 minutes more.

Makes 6 servings

SERVING SIZE: 2½ cups

PER SERVING: Calories 300; Total Fat 4 g (Sat Fat 0 g, Mono Fat 2 g, Poly Fat 1 g); Protein 26 g; Carb 43 g; Fiber 8 g; Cholesterol 90 mg; Sodium 710 mg; Total Sugar 10 g (Added Sugar 0 g)

EXCELLENT SOURCE OF: calcium, fiber, iron, manganese, potassium, protein, vitamin A, vitamin B_6, vitamin C, vitamin K

GOOD SOURCE OF: copper, folate, magnesium, niacin, phosphorous, riboflavin, thiamine

roasted salmon with ginger-soy broccolini, mushrooms, and edamame

This meal is both sumptuously fulfilling and light at the same time, with buttery salmon, meaty shiitake mushrooms, crisp broccolini, and hearty edamame all married on one sheet pan with a flavorful soy-ginger-garlic sauce. When roasted with the sauce, the mushrooms develop a deeply savory flavor and firm texture. The broccolini catches tasty bits of ginger and garlic in its tops, while along with the edamame, it becomes lightly charred in the oven. It's a perfect example of how it's not just ingredients that bring the flavor, the oven plays an important role in that, too.

2 tablespoons canola or peanut oil

2 tablespoons reduced-sodium soy sauce

1 tablespoon honey

1½ teaspoons grated fresh ginger

2 garlic cloves, minced

1 teaspoon toasted sesame oil

½ teaspoon sriracha

8 ounces shiitake mushrooms, sliced

4 (6-ounce) center-cut, skinless salmon fillets

⅛ teaspoon salt

⅛ teaspoon freshly ground black pepper

1 head broccolini (about 6 ounces), trimmed

1 cup frozen, shelled edamame

SERVING SIZE: 1 piece fish and about 1 cup vegetables

PER SERVING: Calories 420; Total Fat 21 g (Sat Fat 2.5 g, Mono Fat 9 g, Poly Fat 7 g); Protein 41 g; Carb 17 g; Fiber 5 g; Cholesterol 95 mg; Sodium 490 mg; Total Sugar 7 g (Added Sugar 4 g)

EXCELLENT SOURCE OF: copper, niacin, pantothenic acid, phosphorous, potassium, protein, riboflavin, selenium, thiamine, vitamin B_6, vitamin B_{12}, vitamin C, vitamin D, vitamin K

GOOD SOURCE OF: fiber, folate, iron, magnesium, manganese, vitamin A, zinc

1. Preheat the oven to 425°F. Whisk together the oil, soy sauce, honey, ginger, garlic, sesame oil, and sriracha in a medium-size bowl.

2. Place the mushrooms on a sheet pan, drizzle with a little less than half of the sauce, and toss to coat. Spread them out evenly on the pan, then roast for 5 minutes.

3. While the mushrooms roast, pat the fish dry with a paper towel; brush the tops with some of the soy mixture and season with the salt and pepper. Place the broccolini in the bowl with the remaining soy mixture and toss to coat.

4. Remove the sheet pan from the oven, give the mushrooms a toss, and push them to one side of the pan. Place the fish in the center of the pan, and place the broccolini and edamame together on the other side of the pan. Return the pan to the oven and roast until the fish flakes easily with a fork and the broccolini is firm-tender and charred a bit, about 15 minutes. Serve the fish with the vegetables alongside.

The salmon and vegetables will keep in an airtight container in the refrigerator for up to 2 days and may be served warm or at room temperature.

Makes 4 servings

shrimp and white bean bruschetta

These Italian-inspired toasts—piled high with plump shrimp and cannellini beans in a savory, garlic-laced tomato sauce, then showered with fragrant basil leaves—are a dreamy weeknight dinner requiring just one bowl, one sheet pan, minimal chopping, and only about forty minutes from start to finish. If you toast the bread ahead, you can have dinner on the table in twenty minutes. The dish won raves from my at-home focus group of two (Thom and Bella) and has since been in regular rotation on our menu. The toasts also make a crowd-pleasing appetizer for stress-free entertaining.

8 medium-size or 16 small, ½-inch-thick slices of crusty whole-grain bread (8 ounces)

3 tablespoons plus 4 teaspoons olive oil, divided

2 tablespoons tomato paste

1 teaspoon anchovy paste

½ teaspoon salt

¼ teaspoon crushed red pepper flakes, plus more to taste

1 pound medium-size shrimp (26–30 count per pound), cleaned, tail-off

1 (15-ounce) can low-sodium cannellini beans, drained and rinsed

4 medium-size garlic cloves, very thinly sliced

1 (28-ounce) can no-salt-added diced tomatoes

½ cup fresh basil leaves, cut into ribbons

1. Preheat the oven to 375°F. Place the bread slices on a sheet pan and brush the tops with 1½ tablespoons of the olive oil. Bake until crisp and browned, 15 to 20 minutes. Transfer the bread to serving plates. (The toasts may be made a day ahead and stored in an airtight container.)

2. Put 1½ tablespoons of the oil, the tomato paste, and the anchovy paste, salt, and red pepper flakes in a medium-size bowl and stir to combine. Add the shrimp, beans, and garlic to the bowl and toss to coat. Then, stir in the tomatoes with their juices. Spread the mixture evenly on the sheet pan and bake, stirring once at the midway point, until bubbling and the shrimp is pink and no longer translucent, about 15 minutes.

3. To serve, spoon the shrimp mixture generously onto the toasts; drizzle each plate with a teaspoon of olive oil, and garnish with basil leaves and additional red pepper flakes to taste.

Makes 4 servings

SERVING SIZE: 2 medium or 4 small toasts and 1 heaping cup shrimp mixture

PER SERVING: Calories 520; Total Fat 19 g (Sat Fat 3 g, Mono Fat 11 g, Poly Fat 5 g); Protein 38 g; Carb 50 g; Fiber 10 g; Cholesterol 185 mg; Sodium 790 mg; Total Sugar 11 g (Added Sugar 0 g)

EXCELLENT SOURCE OF: calcium, copper, fiber, iron, magnesium, manganese, phosphorous, protein, selenium, thiamine, vitamin A, vitamin C, vitamin K, zinc

GOOD SOURCE OF: folate, niacin, potassium, riboflavin

red snapper with greek-style baked vegetables

This recipe turns a classic Greek summer vegetable bake into a complete sheet-pan dinner with the addition of beautiful fillets of red snapper. The vegetable medley of potatoes, zucchini, and tomatoes with garlic and oregano is so simple you almost can't believe how incredibly flavorful and savory tasting it turns out. (If you'd like, you can swap out one or two of the zucchini for sliced eggplant and/or bell pepper.) The fish is placed right on top of the vegetables to cook and dinner—which has the essence of a home-cooked meal on a Greek island—is on the table fifteen minutes later.

3 medium-size Yukon gold potatoes (about 6 ounces each), unpeeled, sliced into ¼-inch-thick rounds

5 tablespoons olive oil, divided

1 teaspoon salt, divided

¾ teaspoon freshly ground black pepper, divided

3 medium-size zucchini, sliced into ½-inch rounds

½ large onion, sliced into half-moons

1 (14.5-ounce) can no-salt-added crushed tomatoes

3 garlic cloves, thinly sliced

2 teaspoons dried oregano

4 (6-ounce) skin-on red snapper fillets or similar fish fillet, such as trout or tilapia

2 tablespoons freshly squeezed lemon juice

3 tablespoons chopped fresh parsley leaves

1. Preheat the oven to 450°F. Place the potatoes onto a sheet pan and toss with 2 tablespoons of the oil and ¼ teaspoon each of the salt and pepper. Lay them out evenly on the pan and roast in the oven for 20 minutes, until they are lightly browned and release easily from the pan with a metal spatula.

2. While the potatoes cook, toss the zucchini, onion, tomatoes, garlic, oregano, 2 tablespoons of the oil, ½ teaspoon of the salt, and ¼ teaspoon of the pepper in a large bowl. Pour the zucchini mixture onto the pan with the potatoes and toss to combine everything, then spread out the mixture evenly over the pan. Cover with foil and bake for 20 minutes.

3. Remove the foil from the pan. Place the fish fillets on top of the vegetables, skin side down. Drizzle the fillets with the remaining tablespoon of oil and ¼ teaspoon each of the salt and pepper. Return the pan to the oven and cook, uncovered, until the fish flakes easily with a fork, about 15 minutes.

4. Drizzle the fish with lemon juice, sprinkle the parsley over everything, and serve.

The fish and vegetables will keep in an airtight container in the refrigerator for up to 2 days and may be served warm or at room temperature.

Makes 4 servings

SERVING SIZE: 1 fish fillet and about 1½ cups vegetables

PER SERVING: Calories 490; Total Fat 20 g (Sat Fat 3 g, Mono Fat 12 g, Poly Fat 3 g); Protein 41 g; Carb 37 g; Fiber 6 g; Cholesterol 65 mg; Sodium 750 mg; Total Sugar 9 g (Added Sugar 0 g)

EXCELLENT SOURCE OF: calcium, fiber, iron, magnesium, manganese, molybdenum, phosphorous, potassium, protein, selenium, vitamin B_6, vitamin B_{12}, vitamin C, vitamin D, vitamin K

GOOD SOURCE OF: folate, niacin, pantothenic acid, riboflavin, thiamine

spice-rubbed salmon with ginger carrots and green beans

This recipe proves that healthy cooking doesn't take a lot of time and effort: salmon fillets and tender vegetables on a sheet pan—salt, pepper, olive oil, lemon juice, twenty minutes in the oven, done. You cannot go wrong with that simple preparation, but here a few easy add-ons rocket the idea to another level entirely. First, there's the spice rub for the salmon—chili powder, coriander, garlic, turmeric, and black pepper—which adds not only tremendous flavor but also health benefits to the good fat–rich fish. The vegetables, too, are treated to a kick of delightful, healthful seasonings. The result is a supremely flavorful, easy cleanup, weeknight meal that proves the possibility of cooking and eating well even when time and energy are in short supply.

1 pound medium-size carrots, halved lengthwise and then crosswise

2 tablespoons olive oil, divided

1 tablespoon honey

1 tablespoon minced fresh ginger

¾ teaspoon salt, divided

½ teaspoon chili powder

¼ teaspoon ground turmeric

¼ teaspoon ground coriander

¼ teaspoon granulated garlic

¼ teaspoon freshly ground black pepper

4 (6-ounce) center-cut salmon fillets (skinless)

8 ounces thin green beans or haricots verts, trimmed

Zest of 1 lemon, finely grated

2 tablespoons freshly squeezed lemon juice (from same lemon)

1. Preheat the oven to 400°F. Place the carrots on one half of a sheet pan. Drizzle with 1 tablespoon of the oil and the honey, then sprinkle with the ginger and ¼ teaspoon of the salt. Toss to combine, keeping the carrots on one side of the pan. Roast in the oven for 20 minutes, tossing them once or twice but keeping them on the same side of the pan to prevent the honey from burning.

2. Meanwhile, combine the chili powder, turmeric, coriander, garlic, pepper, and ¼ teaspoon of the salt in a small bowl. Sprinkle the spice mixture over the salmon and rub it in a little with your fingers. Place the green beans in a medium-size bowl and toss with the remaining tablespoon of oil and ¼ teaspoon of salt.

3. Place the salmon on the sheet pan and then the green beans and bake for 15 minutes more, until the salmon flakes easily with a fork, the carrots are softened and browned in spots, and the green beans are crisp-tender. Sprinkle the green beans with the lemon zest and drizzle the lemon juice over the green beans and the salmon.

The salmon and vegetables will keep in an airtight container in the refrigerator for up to 2 days and may be served warm or at room temperature.

Makes 4 servings

SERVING SIZE: 1 piece salmon and 1 cup vegetables

PER SERVING: Calories 360; Total Fat 15 g (Sat Fat 2.5 g, Mono Fat 7 g, Poly Fat 2 g); Protein 37 g; Carb 20 g; Fiber 5 g; Cholesterol 80 mg; Sodium 650 mg; Total Sugar 12 g (Added Sugar 4 g)

EXCELLENT SOURCE OF: niacin, pantothenic acid, phosphorous, potassium, selenium, vitamin A, vitamin B$_6$, vitamin B$_{12}$, vitamin C, vitamin D, vitamin K

GOOD SOURCE OF: copper, fiber, folate, magnesium, manganese, molybdenum, riboflavin, thiamine

spinach-stuffed sole roll-ups with lemon herb couscous

After some experimenting, I was delighted to discover that you can cook certain grains on a sheet pan along with the rest of the meal's ingredients, eliminating the need for an extra pot. Here, it's whole-grain couscous, which is stirred on the pan with boiling water, wine, thyme, and lemon. That's topped with fillets of sole (or flounder) that are stuffed with lemon, capers, and scallion-seasoned spinach. Fresh grape tomatoes are scattered over the top, then the pan is covered and placed in the oven where everything—protein, vegetable, and grain—steams together and winds up tender, fragrant with lemon and herbs, colorful, and perfectly cooked.

3 cups lightly packed fresh spinach leaves, coarsely chopped

1 scallion, finely chopped, dark green separated and reserved for garnish

1 tablespoon capers, drained

2 teaspoons olive oil

2 lemons: 1 finely zested and juiced, the other cut into wedges

¾ teaspoon salt, divided

¼ teaspoon freshly ground black pepper

4 sole or flounder fillets (about 5 ounces each)

1½ cups uncooked whole wheat couscous

2 teaspoons fresh thyme leaves

2 cups boiling water

½ cup dry white wine, such as pinot grigio

2 teaspoons unsalted butter

1 cup grape tomatoes, halved

1½ tablespoons finely chopped parsley

1. Preheat the oven to 400°F. Place the spinach in a medium-size microwave-safe bowl, and microwave on HIGH for 1 minute, until just wilted. Drain off any excess liquid, then stir in the white and light green parts of the scallion, and the capers, olive oil, 2 teaspoons of the lemon juice, and ⅛ teaspoon each of the salt and the pepper.

2. Lay the fish fillets on a work surface, more attractive side down, mound the spinach mixture on the narrow end of each fillet, then roll up so the spinach is enclosed.

3. Place the couscous on the sheet pan. Sprinkle with the lemon zest (about 1 teaspoon), thyme, and ½ teaspoon of the salt. Add the boiling water, wine, and 2 tablespoons of the lemon juice to the pan and stir lightly to combine. Spread the couscous evenly around the sheet pan, using the back of a large spoon. Place the fish rolls on top of the couscous, seam side down, and sprinkle the tops of them with the remaining ⅛ teaspoon each of the salt and pepper. Top each piece of fish with a ½-teaspoon pat of butter. Distribute the tomatoes on top of the couscous, then cover the pan with foil, crimping the edges of the foil around the sides of the pan, and bake until the fish is no longer translucent and the couscous is tender, about 15 minutes.

4. Sprinkle the couscous with the parsley and reserved scallion greens and fluff it well with a fork. Drizzle any remaining lemon juice onto the fish. Serve with the lemon wedges.

The fish and couscous will keep in an airtight container in the refrigerator for up to 2 days.

Makes 4 servings

SERVING SIZE: 1 piece fish and 1½ cups couscous

PER SERVING: Calories 410; Total Fat 8 g (Sat Fat 2 g, Mono Fat 3 g, Poly Fat 1 g); Protein 25 g; Carb 54 g; Fiber 9 g; Cholesterol 60 mg; Sodium 840 mg; Total Sugar 6 g (Added Sugar 0 g)

EXCELLENT SOURCE OF: fiber, phosphorous, protein, selenium, vitamin A, vitamin B_{12}, vitamin C, vitamin D, vitamin K

GOOD SOURCE OF: calcium, folate, iron, magnesium, manganese, niacin, potassium, vitamin B_6

halibut with roasted fennel, orange, and olives

In the middle of winter when I inevitably tire of root vegetables, I am grateful for the sunny bright spot that shows up in the produce aisle: citrus. I relish it all, but one variety I can never pass up is blood oranges. I often combine their segments in a salad with thinly sliced raw fennel, olives, and red onion, to serve as a side or starter. Happily, I discovered that these ingredients, with the addition of a steaklike fillet of halibut (or cod), also work beautifully as a sheet pan dinner. Here, the fennel bulb is roasted, which mellows its flavor and brings out its natural sweetness. The fish cooks on the pan alongside it, simply seasoned with oil, salt, and pepper. They are plated together with orange segments, olives, and onion scattered around them and married with a lemon-parsley dressing drizzled over everything. If you can't find blood oranges, any type of navel orange will work well. I like to serve this with some warm, crusty whole-grain bread and olive oil for dipping.

2 medium-size fennel bulbs

3 blood oranges or 2 medium-size navel oranges

3½ tablespoons olive oil, divided

½ teaspoon salt, divided

4 (6-ounce) halibut or cod fillets

¼ teaspoon freshly ground black pepper, divided

1 tablespoon freshly squeezed lemon juice

1 tablespoon finely chopped fresh parsley leaves

12 pitted green olives

2 tablespoons very thinly sliced red onion

1. Preheat the oven to 400°F. Trim the stems and fronds off of the fennel bulbs, reserving a tablespoon or two of fronds for garnish. Peel away any bruised or tough outer layers of the bulbs, then cut the bulbs in half lengthwise. Cut each half lengthwise into six wedges, leaving part of the core attached to each wedge so it stays together.

2. Cut the oranges into segments by slicing off the top and bottom of the fruit, then, standing it on one end, cut down following the curve of the fruit to remove the peel and white pith. Then, with a paring knife, working over a bowl, remove the fruit segments from their membranes.

3. Put the fennel wedges on a sheet pan. Toss with 1 tablespoon of the oil and ¼ teaspoon of the salt and roast for 20 minutes. Then, flip the wedges over and push them over a bit to make room for the fish. Brush the fish on both sides with 1½ teaspoons of the oil and sprinkle with ⅛ teaspoon each of the salt and pepper. Return the pan to the oven and bake until the fish flakes easily with a fork and the fennel is tender and lightly browned, 12 to 15 minutes. If the fish is done before the fennel, transfer it to a plate and tent with foil to keep warm as the fennel continues to cook.

4. Meanwhile, combine the remaining 2 tablespoons of oil, the lemon juice and the parsley, and the remaining ⅛ teaspoon each of salt and pepper in a small bowl.

5. To serve, place a piece of fish and some fennel on individual plates or a serving platter. Drizzle everything with the parsley mixture, then scatter with the orange segments, olives, red onion slices, and fennel fronds.

Leftovers will keep in an airtight container in the refrigerator for up to 2 days and may be served warm or at room temperature.

Makes 4 servings

SERVING SIZE: 1 piece fish and 6 pieces fennel

PER SERVING: Calories 410; Total Fat 19 g (Sat Fat 3 g, Mono Fat 12 g, Poly Fat 4 g); Protein 37 g; Carb 24 g; Fiber 6 g; Cholesterol 120 mg; Sodium 610 mg; Total Sugar 14 g (Added Sugar 0 g)

EXCELLENT SOURCE OF: fiber, niacin, phosphorous, potassium, protein, selenium, vitamin B_6, vitamin B_{12}, vitamin C, vitamin K

GOOD SOURCE OF: calcium, folate, magnesium, manganese, vitamin K

smoky shrimp with corn, zucchini, and tomatoes

This quick dinner is an oven version of a summer seafood bake, but one with an alluring Spanish flair, thanks to the dusting of aromatic smoked paprika. The meal is as brilliantly colorful as it is delicious and healthful, with rounds of golden corn on the cob, tomatoes that soften and intensify in flavor with cooking, and chunks of tender zucchini. The plump shrimp take on the brick hue of the paprika and the dish is seasoned further with fresh garlic and bites of smoky chorizo sausage. It's a smile-inducing dinner that begs to be made at the end of summer when corn, tomatoes, and zucchini are at their peak and you want to get in and out of the kitchen fast. Feel free to leave out the sausage, if you prefer.

1 pint grape or cherry tomatoes, halved

1 medium-size zucchini, diced

3 tablespoons olive oil, divided

½ plus ⅛ teaspoon salt, divided

½ teaspoon freshly ground black pepper, divided

2 ears fresh corn, husked and sliced crosswise into 1-inch-thick rings

1¼ pounds medium-size shrimp (26–30 count per pound), cleaned, tail-off

1½ teaspoons smoked paprika

3 garlic cloves, minced

Pinch of cayenne pepper

2½ ounces dried (cooked) chorizo sausage, finely diced (heaping ½ cup)

1. Preheat the oven to 425°F. Place the tomatoes and zucchini on a sheet pan. Drizzle with 1 tablespoon of the oil, sprinkle with ¼ teaspoon each of the salt and black pepper, and roast in the oven until the vegetables have softened somewhat, 10 minutes.

2. Place the corn in a medium-size bowl and toss with 1 tablespoon of the oil and ¼ teaspoon of the salt. Place the shrimp in another medium-size bowl and toss with the remaining tablespoon of oil, the paprika, garlic, and cayenne, and the remaining ⅛ teaspoon of salt and ¼ teaspoon of black pepper. Add the corn, shrimp, and chorizo to the sheet pan, scattering them around evenly. Return the pan to the oven to cook until the corn is tender-firm and the shrimp is cooked through, 10 minutes more.

The shrimp and vegetables will keep in an airtight container in the refrigerator for up to 2 days and may be served warm or at room temperature.

Makes 4 servings

SERVING SIZE: about 2 cups

PER SERVING: Calories 380; Total Fat 19 g (Sat Fat 4.5 g, Mono Fat 11 g, Poly Fat 3 g); Protein 36 g; Carb 19 g; Fiber 3 g; Cholesterol 245 mg; Sodium 770 mg; Total Sugar 8 g (Added Sugar 0 g)

EXCELLENT SOURCE OF: copper, magnesium, phosphorous, potassium, protein, vitamin C, zinc

GOOD SOURCE OF: calcium, folate, magnesium, manganese, molybdenum, niacin, thiamine, vitamin A, vitamin B$_6$, vitamin K

sole with roasted spring vegetables and lemon herb drizzle

This dish is what happens in my kitchen after a visit to my local farmers' market. Once my bags of just-picked goodies are unloaded, I quickly rinse and prep them, then tumble the vegetables onto a sheet pan to roast. The potatoes get a bit of a head start, then radishes, and finally, asparagus, ribbons of carrots, and peas, along with fresh-caught flounder. Everything on the sheet pan is simply seasoned with olive oil, salt, and pepper as it awaits a finishing drizzle on the plate with a glorious pestolike sauce made by whirring herbs, lemon juice, and oil in a food processor. (I used parsley and basil, but you could use any combination of tender herbs you like—cilantro would be a nice addition.) The result is an easy meal, brimming with color and flavor, that's ready in less than forty minutes and is a real celebration of spring.

½ cup lightly packed flat-leaf parsley leaves and tender stems

½ cup lightly packed fresh basil leaves

1 scallion, white and light green part only, coarsely chopped

1½ tablespoons freshly squeezed lemon juice

½ teaspoon salt, divided

¼ teaspoon freshly ground black pepper, divided

4½ tablespoons olive oil, divided

1 pound new baby potatoes, halved (1-inch pieces)

1 bunch radishes, quartered, or cut into eighths if large

1 bunch asparagus, trimmed and cut on the bias into 2-inch pieces

1 cup fresh or frozen peas

1 medium-size carrot, sliced into thin ribbons using a vegetable peeler

4 sole or flounder fillets (about 5 ounces each)

2 teaspoons unsalted butter (optional)

1. Preheat the oven to 425°F. Make an herb drizzle by putting the parsley, basil, scallion, lemon juice, ¼ teaspoon of the salt, and ⅛ teaspoon of the pepper into the small bowl of a food processor or a mini-chopper and process until finely chopped. With the processor running, drizzle in 3 tablespoons of the oil.

2. Toss the potatoes with 1½ teaspoons of the oil and ⅛ teaspoon of the salt on a sheet pan and roast in the oven for 15 minutes. Place the radishes in a medium-size bowl and toss with 1½ teaspoons of the oil and the remaining ⅛ teaspoon of salt. Add them to the sheet pan with the potatoes and roast for 6 minutes more. (Don't bother trying to stir the potatoes at this stage—they will not easily release from the pan yet.)

3. Place the asparagus, peas, and carrot in the same bowl along with the remaining 1½ teaspoons of oil. Add them to the sheet pan, giving all the vegetables a toss together, using a metal spatula to turn the potatoes.

4. Season the fish with the remaining ⅛ teaspoon of pepper. With the more attractive side of the fish facing down, roll each fish fillet starting with the thinner end. As you roll each piece, place it on the sheet pan, seam side down, nestling it into the vegetables. Dot each fillet with ½ teaspoon of butter, if using. Return the sheet pan to the oven and cook until the fish flakes easily with a fork and the vegetables are firm-tender, 15 to 20 minutes more.

5. Serve the fish and vegetables drizzled with the herb sauce.

| whole in one |

The herb drizzle will keep for 4 days in the refrigerator. The fish and vegetables will keep in an airtight container in the refrigerator for up to 2 days and may be served warm or at room temperature.

Makes 4 servings

SERVING SIZE: 1 fish fillet, about 1 cup vegetables, and 1 tablespoon sauce

PER SERVING: Calories 380; Total Fat 18 g (Sat Fat 2.5 g, Mono Fat 12 g, Poly Fat 2 g); Protein 22 g; Carb 35 g; Fiber 8 g; Cholesterol 55 mg; Sodium 720 mg; Total Sugar 6 g (Added Sugar 0 g)

EXCELLENT SOURCE OF: fiber, folate, iron, manganese, phosphorous, potassium, protein, selenium, thiamine, vitamin A, vitamin B_{12}, vitamin C, vitamin D, vitamin K

GOOD SOURCE OF: calcium, copper, magnesium, molybdenum, niacin, riboflavin, vitamin B_6, zinc

poultry

chili-lime chicken
with corn and black beans

Here, tender chicken breast is seasoned with a flavorful chili-lime rub, then skillet cooked and served atop a sauté of hearty black beans, sweet corn, and fresh tomatoes warmed until barely bursting. It is made savory and given a gentle heat with onion, garlic, and a kiss of jalapeño. (If you like a lot of heat, feel free to add more jalapeño and/or more cayenne in the rub for the chicken.) Finished with a bright note of lime juice, fresh cilantro, and creamy avocado, this is a colorful, satisfying meal that is on point any season of the year, and destined to become a go-to favorite.

1 teaspoon
chili powder

½ teaspoon finely
grated lime zest

¼ teaspoon ground
cumin

¼ teaspoon
granulated garlic

½ teaspoon salt,
divided

Pinch of cayenne
pepper

1½ pounds boneless,
skinless chicken
breast, pounded to
½-inch thickness

2 tablespoons olive oil,
divided

½ small onion,
chopped

1 tablespoon seeded
and minced jalapeño
pepper

1 garlic clove, minced

1 (15-ounce) can low-
sodium black beans,
drained and rinsed

1 pint grape tomatoes,
halved

1½ cups corn kernels,
from 1 large or 2 small
ears fresh corn, or
frozen

1 ripe avocado, pitted,
peeled, and diced

3 tablespoons freshly
squeezed lime juice

3 tablespoons fresh
cilantro leaves

1. Combine the chili powder, lime zest, cumin, granulated garlic, ¼ teaspoon of the salt, and the cayenne in a small bowl. Sprinkle the spice mixture on both sides of the chicken, rubbing it in a little with your fingers.

2. Heat 1 tablespoon of the oil in a large, non-stick skillet over medium-high heat. Add the chicken to the pan, lower the heat to medium, and cook until it is browned and cooked through, about 5 minutes per side. Transfer the chicken to a cutting board.

3. Add the remaining tablespoon of oil to the pan and heat over medium-high heat. Add the onion and jalapeño and cook until they soften, 2 minutes. Add the garlic and cook for 30 seconds more, then stir in the beans, tomatoes, and corn and cook until all the vegetables are softened but still retain their shape, about 3 minutes. Season with the remaining ¼ teaspoon of salt.

4. Divide the vegetable mixture among four plates. Slice the chicken and divide it among the plates along with some avocado. Sprinkle each with lime juice and cilantro and serve.

The chicken and vegetables will keep in an airtight container in the refrigerator for up to 4 days.

Makes 4 servings

SERVING SIZE: 1 cup vegetable mixture, 6 or 7 slices chicken, and ¼ avocado

PER SERVING: Calories 510; Total Fat 20 g (Sat Fat 3 g, Mono Fat 11 g, Poly Fat 3 g); Protein 48 g; Carb 38 g; Fiber 4 g; Cholesterol 125 mg; Sodium 550 mg; Total Sugar 5 g (Added Sugar 0 g)

EXCELLENT SOURCE OF: copper, fiber, folate, magnesium, manganese, niacin, riboflavin, thiamine, pantothenic acid, phosphorous, potassium, protein, selenium, vitamin B_6, vitamin C, vitamin K

GOOD SOURCE OF: iron, vitamin A, zinc

lemon chicken with artichokes, capers, and arugula

If there were an award for "most elegant, tastiest skillet meal made in less than thirty minutes" (and I think there should be), this dish would be the clear winner. With tender chicken breast in a lemony caper and white wine sauce that's studded with artichokes served atop a mound of fresh arugula, it is beautiful on the plate, packed with flavor, and requires almost no chopping. The chicken is coated lightly in flour, which allows it to brown nicely and serves to thicken the pan sauce. (You can substitute a cup-for-cup gluten-free flour.) A tablespoon of butter takes the tangy sauce to the next level into luxuriously velvety territory. It's just the recipe to hit refresh on your busy weeknight dinner routine and definitely good enough for company. I like to serve it with some crusty whole-grain Italian bread.

3 tablespoons all-purpose flour

½ teaspoon salt, plus more to taste

½ teaspoon freshly ground black pepper, plus more to taste

4 boneless, skinless chicken breasts (about 6 ounces each), pounded to ½-inch thickness

¼ cup olive oil, divided

2 garlic cloves, thinly sliced

6 ounces frozen artichoke hearts, thawed

1 cup dry white wine

½ cup low-sodium chicken broth or water

3 tablespoons freshly squeezed lemon juice

2 tablespoons capers, drained and rinsed

1 tablespoon unsalted butter

4 cups lightly packed baby arugula

1. Place the flour on a plate and toss it with the salt and pepper. Dredge the chicken in the flour mixture so it is lightly coated, shaking off the excess. Heat 1½ tablespoons of the oil in a large skillet over medium-high heat. Place two pieces of chicken in the pan and cook until they are browned, about 2 minutes per side, then transfer them to a plate. Repeat with another 1½ tablespoons of oil and the remaining chicken, transferring it to the plate.

2. Add the remaining tablespoon of oil to the skillet, lower the heat to medium, then add the garlic and artichoke hearts and cook until the garlic has softened a bit, 1 minute. Add the wine, increase the heat to high, and reduce by about half, about 3 minutes. Add the chicken broth, lemon juice, and capers to the skillet, bring to a boil, then cook until the sauce has thickened somewhat, 2 to 3 minutes. Stir in the butter until it is melted.

3. Return the chicken, with any accumulated juices, to the pan, nestling it into the sauce. Lower the heat to medium-low and simmer until the chicken is cooked through, about 3 minutes.

4. To serve, place a cup of the arugula on each of four serving plates. Top each with a chicken breast and spoon the sauce and artichokes on top. Season with salt and pepper to taste.

The chicken and artichoke sauce will keep in an airtight container in the refrigerator for up to 4 days.

Makes 4 servings

SERVING SIZE: 1 cup arugula, 1 piece chicken breast, and about ⅓ cup artichokes and sauce

PER SERVING: Calories 450; Total Fat 21 g (Sat Fat 4.5 g, Mono Fat 12 g, Poly Fat 2 g); Protein 41 g; Carb 10 g; Fiber 4 g; Cholesterol 130 mg; Sodium 300 mg; Total Sugar 2 g (Added Sugar 0 g)

EXCELLENT SOURCE OF: niacin, pantothenic acid, phosphorous, protein, selenium, vitamin A, vitamin B$_6$

GOOD SOURCE OF: calcium, fiber, magnesium, potassium, riboflavin, thiamine, vitamin C, vitamin K

thai curry chicken and vegetables

If you don't yet have a jar of Thai red curry paste and a bottle of Thai fish sauce in your kitchen, this recipe is your call to action to pick some up. The pair of seasonings can effortlessly flip the switch on a basic stir-fry, soup, or stew, immediately imparting a bold, mouthwatering, distinctly Thai taste. Here, they work their magic on a simple sauté of chicken and vegetables, imbuing the dish's rich coconut milk sauce with their deep, tongue-tingling flavor and a glorious red color. It's a quick, easy meal you will want to make again and again, which means you're sure to make good use of those condiments.

1¼ pounds boneless, skinless chicken breast, sliced into ½-inch-thick strips

¼ teaspoon salt

2 tablespoons canola or other neutral-tasting oil, divided

½ cup thinly sliced shallot

8 ounces thin green beans or haricots verts, trimmed

1 red bell pepper, seeded and sliced into thin strips

1 cup low-sodium chicken broth

1 cup canned light coconut milk

1 tablespoon Thai red curry paste

1 tablespoon Thai fish sauce

4 cups frozen, cooked brown rice (to yield 3 cups thawed)

2 cups baby spinach leaves, coarsely chopped

2 tablespoons freshly squeezed lime juice

¼ cup fresh cilantro leaves

1. Season the chicken with the salt. Heat 1 tablespoon of the oil in a large skillet over medium-high heat. Add the chicken and cook, stirring occasionally, until it is just cooked through, about 5 minutes. Transfer the chicken to a large bowl.

2. Add the remaining tablespoon of oil to the pan, then add the shallot, green beans, and red pepper and cook, stirring, until the vegetables are crisp-tender, about 3 minutes. If the pan seems dry while cooking the vegetables, add a splash of the chicken broth. Transfer the vegetables to the bowl with the chicken.

3. Add the chicken broth, coconut milk, curry paste, and the fish sauce to the skillet and bring to a gentle boil, whisking until the curry paste is dissolved. Simmer over medium heat until the sauce is reduced to about 1¼ cups, about 6 minutes. While the sauce is reducing, place the rice in a microwave-safe dish with a vented cover and microwave on HIGH until it is steaming, 6 minutes, then let sit, covered, until the curry is ready.

4. Once the sauce is reduced, return the chicken and vegetables to the skillet and cook until warmed through, about 2 minutes. Stir in the spinach and lime juice and cook until the spinach is just wilted, 30 seconds. Serve in bowls over the rice, garnished with the cilantro.

This dish will keep in an airtight container in the refrigerator for up to 4 days.

Makes 4 servings

SERVING SIZE: 1½ cups

PER SERVING: Calories 510; Total Fat 15 g (Sat Fat 4 g, Mono Fat 5 g, Poly Fat 3 g); Protein 39 g; Carb 52 g; Fiber 6 g; Cholesterol 105 mg; Sodium 830 mg; Total Sugar 7 g (Added Sugar 0 g)

EXCELLENT SOURCE OF: fiber, folate, magnesium, manganese, niacin, pantothenic acid, phosphorous, potassium, protein, riboflavin, selenium, vitamin A, vitamin B$_6$, vitamin C, vitamin K

GOOD SOURCE OF: iron, thiamine

kale salad with warm caesar dressing and chicken

f you have yet to meet a kale salad that has won you over, let me introduce you to the one that will. It is nothing like those leathery, overly vegetal-tasting salads you may have been subject to in the past. Here, the hearty green leaves are sliced thinly and tamed into tender submission with a dressing that is packed with bold, umami flavor from the classic blend of Parmesan cheese, mustard, Worcestershire sauce, and anchovy paste. (Don't worry, you can't even tell the anchovy paste is in there, it just majorly amps up the flavor.) All the elements come together for a richly satisfying meal that will actually have you raving to your friends about how much you love kale salad.

2 cups cubed crusty whole-grain bread, ideally day-old (½-inch cubes)

5 tablespoons olive oil, divided

¼ plus ⅛ teaspoon salt, divided

¼ plus ⅛ teaspoon freshly ground black pepper, divided

4 boneless, skinless chicken breasts (about 6 ounces each), pounded to an even ½-inch thickness

3 tablespoons freshly squeezed lemon juice, divided

2 garlic cloves, thinly sliced

½ cup low-sodium chicken broth or water

1 teaspoon Dijon mustard

1 teaspoon anchovy paste

½ teaspoon Worcestershire sauce

6 cups lightly packed thinly sliced kale leaves

¼ cup freshly grated Parmesan cheese, divided

1. Toss the bread in a large skillet with 1 tablespoon of the olive oil and ⅛ teaspoon each of the salt and pepper, then toast over medium heat, stirring occasionally, until it is crisp and browned, about 7 minutes. Transfer to a plate and carefully wipe any crumbs out of the pan.

2. Season the chicken on both sides with the remaining ¼ teaspoon each of the salt and pepper. Add 1 tablespoon of the olive oil to the skillet and heat it over medium heat. Place two pieces of the chicken into the pan and cook until they are browned and cooked through, 3 to 4 minutes per side, then transfer them to a plate. Add another tablespoon of the oil to the skillet and repeat with the remaining chicken, transferring it to the plate. Drizzle the chicken with 1 tablespoon of the lemon juice.

3. Add the garlic to the skillet and cook for 30 seconds, then add the chicken broth and the remaining 2 tablespoons of lemon juice to the skillet and bring to a simmer, scraping up any browned bits of chicken so they dissolve into the liquid. Stir in the mustard, anchovy paste, and Worcestershire and remove from the heat. Whisk in the remaining 2 tablespoons of olive oil.

4. Place the kale in a bowl, pour the dressing over it, and toss well to coat. Sprinkle with 3 tablespoons of the Parmesan cheese and toss to incorporate. Serve the salad with the chicken and croutons on top, sprinkled with the remaining Parmesan cheese.

(Continued)

The chicken and the dressing will keep in separate airtight containers in the refrigerator for up to 4 days. The croutons may be made a day ahead and stored at room temperature.

Makes 4 servings

SERVING SIZE: about 1½ cups salad, 1 piece chicken, and ½ cup croutons

PER SERVING: Calories 470; Total Fat 25 g (Sat Fat 4.5 g, Mono Fat 14 g, Poly Fat 3 g); Protein 46 g; Carb 17 g; Fiber 3 g; Cholesterol 130 mg; Sodium 640 mg; Total Sugar 3 g (Added Sugar 0 g)

EXCELLENT SOURCE OF: copper, folate, magnesium, manganese, niacin, pantothenic acid, phosphorous, potassium, protein, riboflavin, selenium, vitamin A, vitamin B_6, vitamin C, vitamin K

GOOD SOURCE OF: calcium, fiber, iron, thiamine, zinc

chicken with provençal white bean and vegetable ragout

I think everyone should have at least five rush-hour dinner recipes up their sleeve at all times—dishes that can easily be make in less than thirty minutes with easy-access ingredients. Knowing you can whip up a meal like that can tip the scales toward cooking instead of grabbing takeout, which, over time, could make a real difference in your health and well-being. This dish of tender chicken breast atop a sumptuous, herb-infused simmer of vegetables and white beans that rings of the flavors of the French Mediterranean fits the bill and then some, since it all comes together fast and in a single skillet. Definitely a keeper.

4 boneless, skinless chicken breasts (about 6 ounces each), pounded to ½-inch thickness

½ teaspoon salt, divided

½ teaspoon freshly ground black pepper, divided

3 tablespoons olive oil, divided

1 small onion, chopped

1 large carrot, peeled and finely diced

1 small zucchini, diced

4 ounces thin green beans or haricots verts, trimmed and cut into 1-inch pieces

2 garlic cloves, minced

2 teaspoons chopped, fresh thyme, or ½ teaspoon dried

2 tablespoons tomato paste

1½ cups low-sodium chicken broth

1 (15-ounce) can low-sodium white beans, such as cannellini, drained and rinsed

½ cup packed fresh basil leaves, sliced into ribbons, divided

1 tablespoon freshly squeezed lemon juice

1. Season the chicken with ¼ teaspoon each of the salt and pepper. Heat 1 tablespoon of the oil in a large skillet over medium-high heat, add two pieces of the chicken, lower the heat to medium, and cook until they are browned on both sides and cooked through, 3 to 4 minutes per side. Transfer the cooked chicken to a plate and cover it with foil to keep warm. Repeat with another tablespoon of oil and the remaining two pieces of chicken, transferring the chicken to the plate and covering with foil.

2. Add the remaining tablespoon of oil to the pan, then add the onion and carrot and cook, stirring frequently, to dissolve any browned bits from the chicken still in the pan, until the onion is softened, about 3 minutes. Add the zucchini, green beans, garlic, thyme, and remaining ¼ teaspoon each of the salt and pepper and cook, stirring for 1 minute. Stir in the tomato paste to incorporate, then add the broth and beans and bring to a boil. Lower the heat to medium and cook, stirring occasionally, until the vegetables are tender and the sauce has thickened, about 5 minutes. Stir in ¼ cup of the basil and the lemon juice.

3. To serve, spoon the vegetable mixture onto serving plates and top each with a piece of chicken. Garnish with fresh basil.

The chicken and vegetable mixture will keep in an airtight container in the refrigerator for up to 4 days.

SERVING SIZE: 1 piece chicken and 1 cup vegetable mixture

PER SERVING: Calories 420; Total Fat 16 g (Sat Fat 2.5 g, Mono Fat 9 g, Poly Fat 2 g); Protein 46 g; Carb 23 g; Fiber 6 g; Cholesterol 125 mg; Sodium 510 mg; Total Sugar 5 g (Added Sugar 0 g)

EXCELLENT SOURCE OF: fiber, magnesium, niacin, pantothenic acid, phosphorous, potassium, protein, riboflavin, selenium, vitamin A, vitamin B_6, vitamin C, vitamin K

GOOD SOURCE OF: folate, iron, manganese, zinc

orzo puttanesca with chicken

This recipe spins a classic puttanesca sauce of tomatoes, garlic, olives, and capers into a single-skillet meal by cooking chicken breasts in the pan to start, then making the sauce and cooking the orzo pasta together in the same pan. Convenience is not the only benefit—the method adds flavor, too, as the fond (the brown bits left in the pan) from the chicken flavors the sauce and the pasta both absorbs and thickens it. Served sprinkled with Parmesan and fresh basil, it gives new life to an old favorite.

4 boneless, skinless chicken breasts (about 6 ounces each), pounded to ½-inch thickness

½ teaspoon salt, divided

¼ teaspoon freshly ground black pepper

3 tablespoons olive oil, divided

1 small onion, diced

3 garlic cloves, thinly sliced

1 (28-ounce) can no-salt-added diced tomatoes

⅓ cup pitted kalamata olives, chopped

2 tablespoons capers, drained and rinsed

1½ teaspoons dried oregano

¼ teaspoon crushed red pepper flakes

1¼ cups uncooked whole wheat orzo pasta

¼ cup grated Parmesan cheese

½ cup fresh basil leaves, cut into ribbons

1. Season the chicken with ¼ teaspoon each of the salt and black pepper.

2. Heat 1 tablespoon of the oil in a large, deep skillet over medium-high heat. Add two pieces of the chicken to the skillet, then lower the heat to medium and cook until they are browned and nearly cooked through, 3 minutes per side, then transfer them to a plate. Repeat with another tablespoon of the oil and the remaining chicken, transferring it to the plate.

3. Add the remaining tablespoon of oil to the skillet and lower the heat to medium. Add the onion and cook, stirring, until softened, 2 minutes. Add the garlic and cook for 30 seconds more. Add the tomatoes, olives, capers, oregano, red pepper flakes, and the remaining ¼ teaspoon of salt and cook until the mixture thickens slightly, 4 minutes.

4. Add 2¼ cups of water to the pan and bring to a boil, then stir in the orzo. Return to a boil, then lower the heat to medium-low and simmer, uncovered, stirring frequently, until the orzo is nearly cooked, 10 minutes. Return the chicken and any accumulated juices to the pan, nestling it into the orzo mixture. Cover and cook, stirring occasionally, until the orzo is cooked al dente and the chicken is cooked through, 2 to 3 minutes more.

5. Serve the orzo topped with the chicken, a sprinkle of Parmesan cheese, and fresh basil leaves.

The chicken and orzo will keep in an airtight container in the refrigerator for up to 4 days.

Makes 4 servings

SERVING SIZE: 1¼ cups pasta and sauce and 1 piece chicken

PER SERVING: Calories 540; Total Fat 18 g (Sat Fat 3 g, Mono Fat 9 g, Poly Fat 2 g); Protein 43 g; Carb 52 g; Fiber 6 g; Cholesterol 110 mg; Sodium 680 mg; Total Sugar 15 g (Added Sugar 0 g)

EXCELLENT SOURCE OF: fiber, iron, magnesium, manganese, niacin, pantothenic acid, phosphorous, potassium, protein, riboflavin, selenium, thiamine, vitamin A, vitamin B$_6$, vitamin C, vitamin K

GOOD SOURCE OF: calcium, copper, folate, zinc

one-skillet grain bowl with chicken, spinach, and tahini dressing

Grain bowls deliver all the elements of a balanced grain plus protein plus vegetable—in a modern, customizable, plant-focused way. Their elements can be prepared in advance and pulled together at the last minute. Often though, cooking up each ingredient means a sink full of dirty dishes, but not here. In this recipe the protein (chicken breast seasoned with lemon and pepper), one of the vegetables (garlicky sautéed spinach), and the grain (tender, nutty bulgur) are all cooked in the same skillet in less than thirty minutes. They are piled in serving bowls with a crunch of fresh cucumber, plus olives, chopped tomatoes, and parsley, and drizzled with a rich, creamy lemon-tahini sauce. If you want to make it vegetarian, use chickpeas instead of the chicken and vegetable broth or water to cook the bulgur.

1 pound boneless, skinless chicken breast, pounded to ½-inch thickness

½ teaspoon salt, divided

½ teaspoon freshly ground black pepper, divided

2 tablespoons olive oil, divided

2 tablespoons freshly squeezed lemon juice, divided, plus lemon wedges for serving

2 garlic cloves, thinly sliced

4 cups fresh baby spinach

2 cups low-sodium chicken broth

1¼ cups quick-cooking (fine) bulgur wheat

¼ cup tahini

1 cup diced cucumber

1 cup chopped fresh tomato

⅓ cup pitted kalamata olives

¼ cup fresh parsley leaves

1. Season the chicken with ¼ teaspoon each of the salt and pepper. Heat 1 tablespoon of the oil in a large, deep skillet over medium-high heat. Add the chicken to the skillet, then lower the heat to medium and cook the chicken until it is browned and cooked through, 3 to 4 minutes per side, and transfer it to a cutting board to rest for 5 minutes. Then, slice it against the grain and drizzle with 1½ teaspoons of the lemon juice.

2. Heat the remaining tablespoon of oil in the same skillet over medium heat. Add the garlic and cook, stirring, for 30 seconds. Then, stir in the spinach and cook until it is just wilted, 1 minute more. Transfer the spinach mixture to a bowl. Season it with ⅛ teaspoon each of the salt and pepper.

3. Add the broth to the skillet and bring to a boil, then stir in the bulgur. Lower the heat to low, cover, and simmer for 8 minutes, then remove from the heat and allow to steam, covered, until the bulgur is tender, 5 to 7 minutes more. Fluff with a fork.

4. Meanwhile, make the tahini sauce: Stir together the tahini and the remaining 1½ tablespoons of lemon juice with 2 tablespoons of water, then add more water, 1 tablespoon at a time, until the sauce is the consistency of a thin pancake batter. (The mixture will seize up at first, but don't worry—it will become smooth again as you add the water.) Stir in the remaining ⅛ teaspoon each of the salt and pepper.

(Continued)

5. To serve, put 1 cup of the bulgur into each of four bowls and top with a few slices of chicken, some spinach, cucumber, tomato, and olives. Drizzle with the tahini sauce and top with the parsley leaves.

Each of the elements will keep in the refrigerator in separate containers for up to 4 days.

Makes 4 servings

SERVING SIZE: 1 bowl

PER SERVING: Calories 490; Total Fat 20 g (Sat Fat 3 g, Mono Fat 16 g, Poly Fat 6 g); Protein 37 g; Carb 43 g; Fiber 8 g; Cholesterol 85 mg; Sodium 520 mg; Total Sugar 2 g (Added Sugar 0 g)

EXCELLENT SOURCE OF: copper, fiber, folate, iron, magnesium, manganese, niacin, pantothenic acid, phosphorous, potassium, protein, selenium, thiamine, vitamin A, vitamin B_6, vitamin C, vitamin K

GOOD SOURCE OF: calcium, riboflavin, zinc

chipotle chicken with pineapple pomegranate guacamole

Once, over margaritas with friends at a neighborhood restaurant, I was served guacamole that was jeweled with fresh pomegranate and pineapple and had just the right spicy kick to offset the sweetness of the fruit. It was served as a starter, but I couldn't help but ponder how those fabulous flavors would translate into a main dish. After playing a bit in my kitchen, I came up with this refreshing recipe that turns that fruit-studded guacamole into a meal by topping it with chipotle-rubbed chicken breast and cool crunchy jicama. While the chicken itself is pretty spicy, the fruit and avocado in the dish balance it so each bite is pure pleasure. If you prefer things on the milder side, though, feel free to substitute smoky ancho chili or regular chili powder for the chipotle.

1 teaspoon chipotle chile powder

1 teaspoon paprika

½ teaspoon ground cumin

¼ teaspoon granulated garlic

¾ teaspoon salt, divided

1½ pounds boneless, skinless chicken breast, pounded to ½-inch thickness

2 tablespoons olive oil, divided

2 ripe avocados, pitted and peeled

1 tablespoon plus 4 teaspoons freshly squeezed lime juice, divided

½ cup diced fresh pineapple

½ cup matchstick-cut jicama or radish

⅓ cup pomegranate arils

¼ cup fresh cilantro leaves

1. Combine the chile powder, paprika, cumin, granulated garlic, and ¼ teaspoon of the salt in a small bowl. Sprinkle the spice mixture on both sides of the chicken, rubbing it in a little with your fingers.

2. Heat 1 tablespoon of the oil in a large skillet over medium heat. Add half of the chicken to the pan, then lower the heat to medium and cook until it is browned and cooked through, 3 to 4 minutes per side. Transfer the chicken to a clean cutting board. Repeat with the remaining tablespoon of oil and the remaining chicken, transferring it to the board once it is cooked. Allow the chicken to rest while you make the guacamole.

3. Mash the avocado with 1 tablespoon of the lime juice and the remaining ½ teaspoon of salt. Slice the chicken.

4. To serve, spread about ½ cup of the avocado onto each of four plates and arrange chicken slices, pineapple, jicama, and pomegranate arils on top. Sprinkle with the cilantro leaves and 1 teaspoon each of the remaining lime juice.

The chicken may be made up to 4 days ahead and kept in an airtight container in the refrigerator. It may be served warm or at room temperature.

Makes 4 servings

SERVING SIZE: 1 plate

PER SERVING: Calories 460; Total Fat 26 g (Sat Fat 4 g, Mono Fat 16 g, Poly Fat 3 g); Protein 41 g; Carb 16 g; Fiber 9 g; Cholesterol 125 mg; Sodium 540 mg; Total Sugar 5 g (Added Sugar 0 g)

EXCELLENT SOURCE OF: folate, magnesium, niacin, pantothenic acid, phosphorous, potassium, protein, riboflavin, selenium, vitamin B$_6$, vitamin C, vitamin K

GOOD SOURCE OF: copper, manganese, thiamine, zinc

chicken larb lettuce wraps

This dish brings exciting Thai flavor to taco night in a superfresh and healthy way. Tender leaves of Bibb lettuce cradle the savory-sweet-tangy-spicy (but not too spicy) ground chicken mixture. That's topped with quick-pickled red onion, crunchy cabbage, cucumber, and a fragrant burst of fresh herbs, then finished with a squeeze of lime and, if you like, an extra shot of hot sauce. They are as fun and easy as they are tasty—just put all the ingredients in bowls out on the table and let everyone build their own. Serve with rice (heated from frozen or pouched) for a heartier meal.

⅓ cup thinly sliced red onion

⅓ cup unseasoned rice vinegar

2 tablespoons canola or other neutral-tasting oil

1½ pounds ground dark meat chicken

3 garlic cloves, minced

4 large scallions, green and white parts, thinly sliced

1 Thai, serrano, or jalapeño chile pepper, seeded and thinly sliced lengthwise

2 tablespoons reduced-sodium soy sauce

1 tablespoon Thai fish sauce, or an additional tablespoon reduced-sodium soy sauce

1 tablespoon sambal oelek or sriracha sauce, plus more to taste

1 tablespoon light or dark brown sugar

½ English cucumber, quartered lengthwise, then thinly sliced

2 cups thinly sliced green cabbage

1 cup fresh cilantro leaves

½ cup fresh mint and/or basil leaves

1 large head Bibb or Boston lettuce, leaves separated

8 lime wedges

1. Toss together the red onion and vinegar in a small bowl and allow to sit as you prepare the other ingredients.

2. Heat the oil in a large skillet over medium-high heat, then add the chicken and the garlic and cook, stirring and breaking the chicken up into small pieces with the spoon, until the chicken is no longer pink, about 5 minutes. Stir in the scallions and the chile pepper, then add the soy sauce, fish sauce, sambal oelek, and brown sugar and stir until combined. Add additional hot sauce to taste.

3. Drain the onion mixture. To serve, put the chicken, pickled onion, cucumber slices, cabbage, herbs, lettuce leaves, lime wedges, and additional hot sauce in separate serving dishes on the table and let everyone build their own wraps, taco style.

4. To assemble, put about ¼ cup of the chicken in a lettuce leaf. Top with pickled onion, cucumber, cabbage, and herbs, then sprinkle with lime juice and additional hot sauce, if desired.

The chicken may be made up to 4 days ahead and kept in an airtight container in the refrigerator.

Makes 4 servings

SERVING SIZE: 4 lettuce wraps

PER SERVING: Calories 320; Total Fat 13 g (Sat Fat 2 g, Mono Fat 4 g, Poly Fat 2 g); Protein 38 g; Carb 11 g; Fiber 3 g; Cholesterol 135 mg; Sodium 830 mg; Total Sugar 6 g (Added Sugar 3 g)

EXCELLENT SOURCE OF: iron, protein, vitamin A, vitamin C, vitamin K

GOOD SOURCE OF: folate, manganese, potassium

chicken ratatouille skillet

This recipe turns the beloved French vegetable medley into a complete skillet meal that can be pulled together fast. It is a comforting stew of eggplant, zucchini, tomato, and onion that's perfumed with garlic and thyme and simmered until the vegetables are softened and melded. The juicy, tender chicken thighs are browned in the skillet before the vegetables go in, leaving a layer of meaty flavor in the pan, and are ultimately nestled into the vegetable mixture so everything finishes cooking together. The result is a tasty, cozy meal that's a testament to the power of simple pleasure. It's nice to serve it with some crusty bread for sopping up the tomato-y liquid.

1 medium-size eggplant (about 12 ounces) trimmed, peeled, and cut into ½-inch dice

1 teaspoon salt, divided, plus more to taste

1½ pounds boneless, skinless chicken thighs

½ teaspoon freshly ground black pepper, divided, plus more to taste

¼ cup olive oil, divided

1 medium-size onion, diced

2 medium-size zucchini (1 pound total), trimmed and cut into ½-inch dice

3 garlic cloves, thinly sliced

1 tablespoon fresh thyme leaves, or 1 teaspoon dried

1½ teaspoons chopped fresh rosemary, or ½ teaspoon dried

1 tablespoon tomato paste

1 (14.5-ounce) can no-salt-added diced tomatoes

¼ cup fresh parsley leaves

1. Place the eggplant into a colander in the sink or over a bowl. Sprinkle with ¼ teaspoon of the salt and let sit for 30 minutes to drain as you prepare the remaining ingredients, then pat dry with a paper towel.

2. Season the chicken on both sides with ¼ teaspoon each of the salt and pepper. Heat 1 tablespoon of the olive oil in a large, high-sided skillet over medium-high heat. Place half of the chicken in the skillet and cook until it is browned on both sides, 1½ to 2 minutes per side. Transfer the cooked chicken to a plate. Repeat with another tablespoon of the oil and the remaining chicken, transferring it to the plate.

3. Add 1 tablespoon of the olive oil to the skillet. Lower the heat to medium, then add the onion and cook, stirring, until softened and translucent, about 3 minutes. Add the remaining tablespoon of oil, then add the eggplant and cook, stirring occasionally, until it has softened somewhat, about 4 minutes, then add the zucchini, garlic, thyme, rosemary, and the remaining ¾ teaspoon of salt and ¼ teaspoon of pepper and cook, stirring occasionally, until the zucchini is softened slightly, 3 minutes more.

4. Stir in the tomato paste, then add the tomatoes with their juices. Return the chicken to the pan along with any accumulated juices, nestling the chicken into the vegetables. Bring

to a boil, then lower the heat to medium-low, cover, and simmer until the vegetables are softened and melded and the chicken is tender and cooked through, about 15 minutes. Season with additional salt and pepper to taste.

5. Serve in shallow bowls or rimmed plates, garnished with parsley.

The dish will keep in an airtight container in the refrigerator for up to 4 days.

Makes 4 servings

SERVING SIZE: about 1¼ cups ratatouille and 1 or 2 pieces chicken

PER SERVING: Calories 410; Total Fat 21 g (Sat Fat 4 g, Mono Fat 12 g, Poly Fat 3 g); Protein 37 g; Carb 19 g; Fiber 7 g; Cholesterol 160 mg; Sodium 760 mg; Total Sugar 11 g (Added Sugar 0 g)

EXCELLENT SOURCE OF: fiber, magnesium, manganese, molybdenum, niacin, pantothenic acid, phosphorous, potassium, protein, riboflavin, selenium, thiamine, vitamin A, vitamin B_6, vitamin C, vitamin K, zinc

GOOD SOURCE OF: copper, folate, iron, vitamin B_{12}

chicken tinga tacos

Two shortcuts make these smoky, tangy, tomato-saucy tacos a ridiculously easy weeknight dinner. First, using shredded rotisserie chicken not only spares you the extra cooking step, it also makes this recipe a great vehicle for using up leftover chicken (or turkey). Second, taking advantage of jarred tomatillo salsa provides a mouthwatering layer of tanginess without having to boil and puree tomatillos. Once the sauce is simmered and thickened in the skillet, you simply add the chicken and heat it long enough for the ingredients to meld. Don't forget to warm the tortillas before serving; you can do this in a microwave, but if you have a gas stove, I strongly encourage you to do it directly on the grates—it's a game changer.

1 tablespoon olive oil

1 small onion, diced

2 garlic cloves, minced

1 (14-ounce) can pureed or crushed tomatoes

⅓ cup jarred tomatillo salsa (salsa verde)

1 canned chipotle chile in adobo, finely chopped, plus 1 tablespoon adobo sauce, plus more to taste

½ teaspoon dried oregano

3 cups shredded chicken (from ½ medium-size rotisserie chicken)

¾ cup low-sodium chicken broth

¼ teaspoon salt, plus more to taste

12 (6-inch) corn tortillas

3 cups shredded romaine hearts

3 medium-size tomatoes, diced

1 medium-size avocado, pitted, peeled, and diced

1 small red onion, finely diced

½ cup fresh cilantro leaves

1. Heat the oil in a large, high-sided skillet over medium heat. Add the onion and cook until it has softened, 3 minutes. Add the garlic and cook for 30 seconds more. Add the tomatoes, salsa, chipotle, adobo sauce, and oregano and bring to a boil, then lower the heat to low and simmer, partially covered, until the mixture has thickened and is a darker shade of red, 8 to 10 minutes.

2. Stir in the chicken, broth, and salt and return to a boil, then lower the heat to medium-low and simmer, uncovered, until the liquid has absorbed and the chicken is warmed through, 5 minutes. Add more chipotle pepper and/or more salt to taste. The chicken may be made up to 4 days ahead and kept in an airtight container in the refrigerator.

3. Warm the tortillas directly on the grates of a gas stovetop over medium heat, using tongs, for about 10 seconds per side, or wrap them in a damp paper towel and microwave in 30-second bursts until warmed through.

4. To serve, place all the ingredients on the table in serving dishes for everyone to build their own tacos. To assemble, place ⅓ cup of the chicken mixture on a tortilla, then top with lettuce, tomato, avocado, red onion, and cilantro.

Makes 4 to 6 servings

SERVING SIZE: 2 or 3 tacos

PER SERVING (BASED ON 6 SERVINGS): Calories 350; Total Fat 14 g (Sat Fat 2.5 g, Mono Fat 7 g, Poly Fat 2 g); Protein 22 g; Carb 39 g; Fiber 5 g; Cholesterol 55 mg; Sodium 530 mg; Total Sugar 7 g (Added Sugar 0 g)

EXCELLENT SOURCE OF: fiber, folate, magnesium, manganese, niacin, phosphorous, potassium, protein, selenium, vitamin A, vitamin B$_6$, vitamin C, vitamin K

GOOD SOURCE OF: calcium, copper, iron, pantothenic acid, riboflavin, thiamine, zinc

savory chicken skillet with mushrooms, potato, and kale

This satisfying recipe brings together a medley of deep, earthy flavors and hearty textures, with tender, paprika-dusted chicken breast and a garlic-thyme scented sauté of wild mushrooms, golden potatoes, and kale in a silky Dijon sauce. It all comes together in one skillet for a wonderful, week-night-friendly meal. A cup-for-cup gluten-free flour may be used instead of the all-purpose flour.

3 tablespoons all-purpose flour

1½ teaspoons paprika

1 teaspoon salt, divided

¾ teaspoon freshly ground black pepper, divided

4 boneless, skinless chicken breasts (about 6 ounces each), pounded to ½-inch thickness

¼ cup olive oil, divided

1 small onion, diced

10 ounces mixed wild mushrooms, coarsely chopped

2 medium-size Yukon gold potatoes, skin on, diced into ¼-inch pieces (10 ounces)

2 cups lightly packed coarsely chopped kale leaves

2 teaspoons fresh thyme leaves

1 large garlic clove, minced

1 cup low-sodium chicken broth

1 tablespoon Dijon mustard

Makes 4 servings

SERVING SIZE: 1 piece chicken breast and about 1 cup vegetables and sauce

PER SERVING: Calories 420; Total Fat 18 g (Sat Fat 3 g, Mono Fat 11 g, Poly Fat 2 g); Protein 43 g; Carb 20 g; Fiber 3 g; Cholesterol 125 mg; Sodium 580 mg; Total Sugar 2 g (Added Sugar 0 g)

EXCELLENT SOURCE OF: niacin, pantothenic acid, protein, riboflavin, vitamin A, vitamin B$_6$, vitamin C, vitamin K

GOOD SOURCE OF: fiber, folate, iron, magnesium, manganese, thiamine, zinc

1. Place the flour on a plate and toss it with the paprika and ½ teaspoon each of the salt and pepper. Dredge the chicken in the flour mixture so it is lightly coated, shaking off the excess. Heat 1½ tablespoons of the oil in a large skillet over medium-high heat. Place two pieces of chicken in the pan and cook until they are browned, about 2 minutes per side, transferring the browned chicken to a plate. Repeat with another 1½ tablespoons of oil and the remaining chicken, transferring it to the plate.

2. Add the remaining tablespoon of oil to the skillet, then add the onion, mushrooms, and potatoes and cook, stirring occasionally, until the mushrooms have released their liquid and are beginning to brown and the potatoes have begun to soften, about 8 minutes. Stir in the kale, thyme, garlic, and the remaining ½ teaspoon of salt and ¼ teaspoon of pepper and cook, stirring, until the kale is wilted, about 1 minute more.

3. Whisk the broth and mustard together in a small measuring pitcher. Add the broth mixture to the skillet, then return the chicken, with any accumulated juices, to the skillet, nestling it into the vegetable mixture. Bring to a boil, then lower the heat to medium and simmer, uncovered, for 2 minutes, then flip the chicken and continue to cook until the chicken is cooked through, the potatoes are tender, and the liquid has reduced to a sauce, 1 to 3 minutes more, and serve.

The dish will keep in an airtight container in the refrigerator for up to 4 days.

one-pot spaghetti and turkey meatballs

If loving this recipe is wrong I don't want to be right. I realize a true Italian chef might wince at the idea of cooking spaghetti in the same pot right along with the sauce and meatballs, but I'm not claiming this is traditionally correct form. I'm just saying it is darn good! The secret ingredient in the meatballs is quick-cooking oats, which lock in the meat's juices and add a whole grain instead of the usual refined bread crumbs. A few handfuls of fresh arugula up the vegetable ante and add another flavor element. The result is an extraordinary family-favorite comfort food meal that is easy and healthy enough for a regular weeknight.

⅓ cup quick-cooking oats

3 tablespoons 1% low-fat milk

½ cup freshly grated Parmesan cheese, divided

1 large egg, lightly beaten

2 tablespoons very finely minced onion

2 tablespoons minced fresh parsley

4 medium-size garlic cloves, divided (2 cloves finely minced and 2 cloves sliced)

¾ teaspoon salt, divided

¼ plus ⅛ teaspoon freshly ground black pepper, divided

1 pound 90% lean ground turkey (or a mix of light and dark meat)

¼ cup olive oil, divided

1 (28-ounce) can crushed tomatoes

1½ tablespoons tomato paste

12 ounces whole wheat spaghetti

3 cups baby arugula

1. Place the oats and milk in a medium-size bowl, stir, and let sit for a minute or two until the liquid is absorbed. Add ¼ cup of the Parmesan cheese, the egg, onion, parsley, the finely minced garlic, ½ teaspoon of the salt, and ¼ teaspoon of the pepper and stir to combine. Add the turkey and mix with your hands to combine, but avoid overmixing. Form the turkey mixture into twelve balls, wetting your hands if they become sticky as you work. The meatballs may be made a day ahead and stored in an airtight container in the refrigerator.

2. Heat 2 tablespoons of the oil in a large, wide soup pot over medium-high heat. Add the meatballs and cook, turning them two or three times, until they are browned all over, about 5 minutes. Transfer the meatballs to a plate.

3. Add the remaining 2 tablespoons of oil to the pot and lower the heat to medium. Stir in the sliced garlic, then add the tomatoes, tomato paste, 3½ cups of water, the remaining ¼ teaspoon of salt and ⅛ teaspoon of pepper, and bring to a boil.

4. Add the pasta, pressing it down as it yields to the heat, until it is completely submerged in the liquid. Place the meatballs in the pot, submerging them in the sauce as much as possible. Lower the heat to medium-low and cook, uncovered, stirring occasionally, until the pasta is cooked al dente, the meatballs are cooked

through, and the sauce has thickened, about 15 minutes. Remove the pot from the heat, stir in the arugula until it is wilted, and serve garnished with the remaining Parmesan cheese.

Makes 6 servings

SERVING SIZE: 1 cup pasta and sauce and 2 meatballs

PER SERVING: Calories 510; Total Fat 20 g (Sat Fat 4.5 g, Mono Fat 10 g, Poly Fat 4 g); Protein 29 g; Carb 59 g; Fiber 9 g; Cholesterol 95 mg; Sodium 750 mg; Total Sugar 9 g (Added Sugar 0 g)

EXCELLENT SOURCE OF: copper, fiber, iron, magnesium, manganese, niacin, phosphorous, potassium, protein, riboflavin, selenium, thiamine, vitamin B_6, vitamin C, vitamin K, zinc

GOOD SOURCE OF: calcium, pantothenic acid, vitamin B_{12}

chicken, vegetable, and quinoa soup

An image of this big, comforting meal-in-a-bowl could rightly be next to the word *nourishing* in the dictionary. It is brimming with colorful vegetables, loaded with chunks of chicken breast, and made thick and hearty with tender quinoa. It not only provides a serious dose of nutrition, its rosemary-scented broth is supremely tasty, and it's the kind of meal you want to huddle over to take the chill off of the coldest day. It's a lot like the chicken and vegetable soup you know and love, but with a twist that offers something different, making it an excellent way to introduce new foods to finicky eaters. The soup will keep in the refrigerator for several days and can also be frozen—just add some more broth or water when reheating because it thickens up as it sits.

2 tablespoons olive oil

1 medium-size onion, chopped

3 celery stalks, chopped

2 medium-size carrots, cut into coins

2 garlic cloves, minced

2 teaspoons chopped fresh rosemary, or ¾ teaspoon dried

¾ teaspoon salt

¼ teaspoon freshly ground pepper

8 cups low-sodium chicken broth

2 pounds bone-in chicken breast, skin removed

2 (14.5-ounce) cans no-salt-added diced tomatoes

2 cups peeled, seeded, and diced butternut squash

½ cup uncooked quinoa (prerinsed)

3 cups chopped kale leaves

1. Heat the oil in a large pot over medium heat. Add the onion, celery, and carrots and cook, stirring, until the vegetables have softened, 6 minutes. Add the garlic, rosemary, salt, and pepper and cook for 1 minute more. Add the broth and chicken and bring to a boil over high heat.

2. Lower the heat to medium-low and simmer, partially covered, until the chicken is cooked through, about 30 minutes. Transfer the chicken to a plate and allow it to cool until it is easy to handle.

3. Add the tomatoes with their juices, butternut squash, and quinoa to the pot and bring to a boil, then simmer, partially covered, stirring occasionally, for 15 minutes. Stir in the kale and cook until the squash and kale are tender and the quinoa is cooked, 5 minutes more. Remove the chicken meat from the bone and chop it into bite-size pieces. Add the chicken to the soup to warm through, 1 to 2 minutes.

The soup will keep in an airtight container in the refrigerator for up to 4 days, or in the freezer for 3 months.

Makes 6 servings

SERVING SIZE: 2½ cups

PER SERVING: Calories 310; Total Fat 8 g (Sat Fat 1.5 g, Mono Fat 4 g, Poly Fat 1 g); Protein 29 g; Carb 28 g; Fiber 5 g; Cholesterol 70 mg; Sodium 490 mg; Total Sugar 8 g (Added Sugar 0 g)

EXCELLENT SOURCE OF: manganese, niacin, phosphorous, potassium, protein, selenium, vitamin A, vitamin B_6, vitamin C, vitamin K

GOOD SOURCE OF: copper, fiber, folate, iron, magnesium, pantothenic acid, riboflavin, thiamine

paprika chicken with vegetables and brown rice

This chicken-in-a-pot supper reminds me of the simple delights of my grandma's cooking. She was always cooking up a wholesome meal that made the house smell incredible. Her dinners invariably included lots of vegetables, and she generally favored seasonings from her Eastern European roots. This paprika-dusted chicken stewed with earthy mushrooms, root vegetables, green beans, and rice would have been right up her alley. Using bone-in chicken ensures the meat stays moist and flavorful, and quick-cooking brown rice provides whole-grain goodness in a time frame that is compatible with all the other ingredients. A tasty and plentiful gravy forms as everything cooks. Grandma would be proud.

3 pounds bone-in chicken thighs and breast, skin removed (all thighs or breast, or a mix of both)

2 teaspoons paprika

¾ teaspoon salt, divided, plus more to taste

½ teaspoon freshly ground black pepper, divided, plus more to taste

3 tablespoons olive oil, divided

1 medium-size onion, diced

1 large carrot, diced

1 large parsnip, diced

10 ounces white button mushrooms, trimmed and sliced

2 cups low-sodium chicken broth

1 cup quick-cooking "instant" brown rice (parboiled, not precooked)

8 ounces green beans, trimmed and cut into ¾ inch pieces, or frozen

1. Season the chicken on both sides with the paprika and ¼ teaspoon each of the salt and pepper. Heat 1 tablespoon of the olive oil in a wide-mouth soup pot over medium-high heat. Place half of the chicken in the pot and cook until it is browned on both sides, 1½ to 2 minutes per side, and transfer to a plate. Repeat with another tablespoon of the oil and the remaining chicken, transferring it to the plate.

2. Lower the heat to medium and add the remaining tablespoon of oil to the pot. Add the onion, carrot, parsnip, and mushrooms and the remaining ½ teaspoon of salt and ¼ teaspoon of pepper, and cook until the vegetables have softened somewhat, the water the mushrooms released has evaporated, and the mushrooms begin to brown, 8 minutes more.

3. Return the chicken to the pot, add the broth, and bring it to a boil. Lower the heat to medium-low, cover, and simmer for 10 minutes, then turn the chicken pieces over and simmer, covered, for another 5 minutes. Add the rice and green beans, stirring them in well, return to a boil, then lower the heat to medium-low and cook, covered, until the rice is tender and the chicken is cooked through, about 15 minutes more. Remove from the heat and let rest, covered, for 5 minutes before serving.

(Continued)

The dish will keep in an airtight container in the refrigerator for up to 4 days.

Makes 4 servings

SERVING SIZE: 1 chicken breast or 2 thighs and 1¼ cups rice mixture

PER SERVING: Calories 460; Total Fat 17 g (Sat Fat 3 g, Mono Fat 9 g, Poly Fat 3 g); Protein 42 g; Carb 34 g; Fiber 5 g; Cholesterol 140 mg; Sodium 610 mg; Total Sugar 6 g (Added Sugar 0 g)

EXCELLENT SOURCE OF: fiber, folate, niacin, phosphorous, potassium, protein, selenium, vitamin B_6, vitamin B_{12}, vitamin C, vitamin K, zinc

GOOD SOURCE OF: copper, iron, magnesium, manganese, molybdenum, pantothenic acid, riboflavin, thiamine, vitamin A

west african–style peanut stew with chicken

f you tend to get bored with your healthy eating routine, stick with me. There is a world of healthy flavor I can help you explore. This West African–inspired meal is case in point. It is a fragrant, satisfying combination of familiar ingredients used in an excitingly different way. The peanut butter that's stirred into the stew is what makes it so wonderfully unique, providing a creamy, toasty richness to the medley of warm, earthy spices, colorful vegetables, and chicken. It's a dish that will make you realize you have only begun to know all the healthy possibilities ahead.

1½ pounds boneless, skinless chicken breast, cut into 1-inch pieces

1 teaspoon salt, divided

¼ teaspoon freshly ground black pepper

3 tablespoons peanut oil, divided

1 large onion, diced

2 garlic cloves, minced

2 tablespoons finely minced fresh ginger

1 teaspoon ground coriander

½ teaspoon ground cumin

¼ teaspoon ground turmeric

¼ teaspoon ground cinnamon

4 cups low-sodium chicken broth

1 (14.5 ounce) can no-salt-added diced tomatoes

1 medium-size sweet potato (12 ounces), peeled, cut into 1-inch cubes

½ bunch collard greens, tough rib removed and discarded, leaves chopped (about 3 cups)

2 medium-size red bell peppers, seeded and chopped

⅓ cup natural-style peanut butter, smooth or chunky

6 tablespoons chopped peanuts

1. Season the chicken with ¼ teaspoon of the salt and the black pepper. Heat 1 tablespoon of the oil in a large pot over medium-high heat. Add half of the chicken and cook until it is browned, 2 to 3 minutes, then transfer it to a plate. Repeat with another 1 tablespoon of the oil and the remaining chicken, transferring it to the plate.

2. Add the remaining tablespoon of oil to the pot and lower the heat to medium. Add the onion and cook until it has softened, about 3 minutes. Add the garlic, ginger, coriander, cumin, turmeric, cinnamon, and remaining ¾ teaspoon of salt, and cook, stirring, for 30 seconds.

3. Stir in the broth, tomatoes with their juices, sweet potato, collard greens, and red bell peppers and bring to a boil, then lower the heat to medium-low and simmer, partially covered, until the vegetables are tender, about 20 minutes. Return the chicken with any accumulated juices to the pot. Return to a boil, then stir in the peanut butter and simmer until it is incorporated and the chicken is cooked through, 3 to 5 minutes. Serve garnished with the chopped peanuts.

The stew will keep in an airtight container in the refrigerator for up to 4 days.

Makes 6 servings

SERVING SIZE: about 2 cups

PER SERVING: Calories 450; Total Fat 22 g (Sat Fat 3.5 g, Mono Fat 10 g, Poly Fat 6 g); Protein 35 g; Carb 26 g; Fiber 6 g; Cholesterol 85 mg; Sodium 580 mg; Total Sugar 8 g (Added Sugar 0 g)

EXCELLENT SOURCE OF: fiber, manganese, niacin, pantothenic acid, phosphorous, potassium, protein, vitamin A, vitamin B$_6$, vitamin C, vitamin K

GOOD SOURCE OF: folate, iron, magnesium, riboflavin, thiamine

green posole with chicken

This gorgeous green soup is a perfect storm of contrasts. It is warm and filling, with a creamy base of pureed tomatillo, pumpkin seeds, onion, garlic, and oregano that is laden with shredded chicken and hominy, the large white corn kernels for which the traditional Mexican soup is named. But it is also light and crisp, bright with fresh lime juice and garnished with a salad's worth of shredded romaine lettuce, radishes, and cilantro leaves. It tastes complex, with layers of interesting flavors and textures, but it is simple to make. It's an exciting soup that satisfies completely, without weighing you down, and once you try it, I'll bet you crave it as often as I do.

½ cup hulled pumpkin seeds (pepitas)

1 pound boneless, skinless chicken breast, pounded to an even ½-inch thickness

1 pound tomatillos, papery skins removed and discarded, well rinsed

½ medium-size onion, peeled

3 garlic cloves, peeled

1 to 2 jalapeño peppers, stemmed, seeded, and halved

½ cup fresh cilantro leaves, plus more for garnish

1 teaspoon dried oregano

½ teaspoon salt, plus more to taste

4 cups low-sodium chicken broth

2 (15-ounce) cans hominy, drained and rinsed

2 cups shredded hearts of romaine lettuce leaves

2 medium-size radishes, sliced thinly into half-moons

4 teaspoons freshly squeezed lime juice

1. Put the pumpkin seeds into a soup pot and toast them over medium-high heat, stirring frequently, until they are fragrant and begin to pop, 2 to 3 minutes. Transfer the seeds to a blender.

2. Place the chicken, tomatillos, onion, and garlic in the same pot and add enough water to cover. Bring to a gentle boil, then lower the heat to maintain a low simmer and cook, covered, until the chicken is just cooked through and the tomatillos are tender, 10 to 12 minutes. (Check the chicken after 8 minutes and remove first, if it is done before the vegetables.) Reserve ¼ cup of the cooking liquid.

3. Transfer the chicken to a cutting board. Drain the remaining water and transfer the cooked tomatillos, onion, and garlic cloves to the blender that contains the pumpkin seeds. Then, add the jalapeño(s) (one if you want to keep it mild, two for a little more heat), cilantro, oregano, salt, and the reserved cooking water, and blend until smooth.

4. Return the puree to the soup pot (it's okay that some of the dissolved proteins from the chicken linger in the pot) and heat it over medium-high heat to bring to a boil. Lower the heat to medium-low and cook, uncovered, stirring occasionally, until the mixture is thickened and turns a deeper shade of green, 12 to 15 minutes. (The mixture splatters a bit as it cooks, so a splatter screen comes in handy here if you have one.)

(Continued)

5. Add the chicken broth and hominy and bring to a boil. Shred the chicken breast, then stir it into the pot and cook until it is warmed through, 2 minutes. Season with additional salt to taste. The soup will keep in an airtight container in the refrigerator for up to 4 days, or in the freezer for 3 months.

6. To serve, ladle into shallow bowls. Top each with ½ cup of lettuce, some radish slices, additional cilantro leaves, and a teaspoon of the lime juice.

Makes 4 servings

SERVING SIZE: about 2 cups soup and a heaping ½ cup vegetable garnishes

PER SERVING: Calories 450; Total Fat 14 g (Sat Fat 2.5 g, Mono Fat 4 g, Poly Fat 5 g); Protein 37 g; Carb 43 g; Fiber 10 g; Cholesterol 85 mg; Sodium 860 mg; Total Sugar 3 g (Added Sugar 0 g)

EXCELLENT SOURCE OF: copper, iron, magnesium, niacin, manganese, pantothenic acid, phosphorous, potassium, protein, selenium, vitamin A, vitamin B_6, vitamin C, vitamin K, zinc

GOOD SOURCE OF: folate, molybdenum, riboflavin, thiamine

chicken and dumplings

A simmer of vegetables and chicken in a thyme-infused broth with tender, fluffy dumplings cooked on top is the food equivalent of settling into a big easy chair with a book and a cup of tea—familiar, fulfilling, and nourishing. This recipe takes the nourishment aspect a step further with the addition of diced zucchini to the usual onion-carrots-celery trio, and with dumplings made with whole-grain flour and olive oil. A cup-for-cup gluten-free flour may be substituted for the whole wheat pastry flour.

2½ pounds bone-in chicken breast, skin removed

3 cups low-sodium chicken broth

1 medium-size onion, diced

3 celery stalks, diced

2 medium-size carrots, diced

2 large thyme sprigs

1 bay leaf

½ teaspoon salt, divided, plus more to taste

¼ teaspoon freshly ground black pepper

1 medium-size zucchini, diced

1 cup whole wheat pastry flour, or ½ cup each regular whole wheat flour and all-purpose flour

1 teaspoon baking powder

½ cup low-fat buttermilk, well shaken

3 tablespoons olive oil

1. Place the chicken, flesh side down, and the broth, onion, celery, carrots, thyme, bay leaf, ¼ teaspoon of the salt, and the pepper in a large pot and bring to a boil. Lower the heat to medium-low and simmer, covered, until the chicken is cooked through, about 30 minutes. Transfer the chicken to a plate and allow it to cool until it is easy to handle, about 15 minutes. Remove the pot from the heat as the chicken cools. Separate the chicken meat from the bone (discarding the bones) and chop it into bite-size pieces.

2. Return the vegetables and broth in the pot to a boil, then add the zucchini, lower the heat to medium-low, and simmer, covered, until it is firm-tender, about 8 minutes. Remove the thyme stems and bay leaf and season with additional salt to taste, if desired. Add the chopped chicken to the pot and return the broth to a boil.

3. While the zucchini cooks, whisk together the flour, baking powder, and remaining ¼ teaspoon of salt in a medium-size bowl. Whisk together the buttermilk and oil in a small measuring pitcher. Add the buttermilk mixture to the flour mixture and stir until it is just moistened. Do not overmix. Spoon the dumpling batter in eight mounds (about 3 tablespoons each) on top of the broth, then lower the heat to medium-low, cover, and simmer, without lifting the lid, until a toothpick inserted into each dumpling comes out clean, about 8 minutes. Serve the chicken and vegetable mixture on four serving plates, each topped with two dumplings. The dish will keep in an airtight container in the refrigerator for up to 4 days.

Makes 4 servings

SERVING SIZE: 1¾ cups chicken mixture and 2 dumplings

PER SERVING: Calories 450; Total Fat 16 g (Sat Fat 2.5 g, Mono Fat 9 g, Poly Fat 2 g); Protein 47 g; Carb 28 g; Fiber 5 g; Cholesterol 135 mg; Sodium 550 mg; Total Sugar 7 g (Added Sugar 0 g)

EXCELLENT SOURCE OF: calcium, magnesium, niacin, pantothenic acid, phosphorous, potassium, protein, riboflavin, selenium, vitamin A, vitamin B_6, vitamin C

GOOD SOURCE OF: fiber, folate, iron, molybdenum, thiamine, vitamin K, zinc

aromatic basmati rice and vegetable bowl with chicken

t's remarkable how central aroma is to our experience of flavor and to our food memories. You may even recall the smells of your mother's cooking more vividly than you remember its taste. This recipe fills your kitchen with a siren's call of alluring scents. They enter the pot one by one, layering upon one another and adding up to a bowl filled with fragrant flavors and exciting textures. First, the toasted almonds infuse the air with nuttiness, then the spices release their essential oils upon warming. The chicken browning in coconut oil has its own enticing call to action and then the floral basmati rice comes through. Before digging in, it is well worth taking a moment to appreciate this dish's aromatic gifts because you will be sure to remember them, and its flavors, for a time to come.

⅓ cup sliced or slivered almonds

3 cardamom pods

¾ teaspoon cumin seeds

¾ teaspoon mustard seeds

¾ teaspoon coriander seeds

1 cinnamon stick

1 pound boneless, skinless chicken breast, cut into ¾-inch pieces

1 teaspoon salt, divided

¼ teaspoon freshly ground black pepper

1½ tablespoons extra-virgin coconut oil or a neutral-flavored oil, such as canola, divided

1 medium-size onion, chopped

1 cup uncooked basmati brown rice

1¾ cups boiling water

1 cup chopped cauliflower florets (½-inch pieces)

1 large carrot, shredded (1 cup)

1 cup peas, no need to thaw if frozen

¼ cup chopped fresh cilantro leaves

1. Put the almonds into a dry 3- to 4-quart pot over medium heat and toast, stirring frequently, until fragrant and browned, 3 to 5 minutes, then transfer them to a dish. Add the cardamom, cumin, mustard, coriander, and cinnamon to the pot and toast until fragrant and the seeds begin to pop, 1 minute. Transfer the spices to a separate plate.

2. Sprinkle the chicken with ¼ teaspoon each of the salt and pepper. Heat 1 tablespoon of the oil in the same pot over medium-high heat. Add half the chicken and cook, stirring occasionally, until it is browned and cooked through, 3 to 4 minutes. Use a slotted spoon to transfer the cooked chicken to a plate. Repeat with the remaining ½ tablespoon of oil and the rest of the chicken and transfer it to the plate, then cover the plate of cooked chicken with foil.

3. Lower the heat to medium, add the onion to the pot, and cook until it is soft, stirring occasionally, 3 minutes. Stir in the rice and cook until it is coated, 30 seconds.

4. Return the spices to the pot, then add the boiling water and the remaining ¾ teaspoon of salt and return to a boil. Lower the heat to low, cover, and cook until the rice is nearly tender and almost all of the liquid is absorbed, 45 to 50 minutes.

5. Without stirring the rice, add the cauliflower to the pot directly on top of the rice, then add the carrots and peas on top of that. Cover and continue to cook over low heat until the vegetables begin to soften, 10 minutes.

6. Remove the pot from the heat, add the chicken, cover, and allow to rest until the vegetables are tender, 8 to 10 minutes more. Uncover, fluff with a fork, tossing the ingredients together, and remove the cinnamon stick and cardamom pods. Serve in bowls garnished with the cilantro and toasted almonds.

The dish will keep in an airtight container in the refrigerator for up to 4 days.

Makes 4 servings

SERVING SIZE: 1½ cups

PER SERVING: Calories 450; Total Fat 15 g (Sat Fat 6 g, Mono Fat 5 g, Poly Fat 3 g); Protein 35 g; Carb 47 g; Fiber 7 g; Cholesterol 85 mg; Sodium 680 mg; Total Sugar 6 g (Added Sugar 0 g)

EXCELLENT SOURCE OF: fiber, niacin, pantothenic acid, phosphorous, protein, selenium, vitamin A, vitamin B$_6$, vitamin C, vitamin K

GOOD SOURCE OF: folate, iron, magnesium, manganese, potassium, riboflavin, thiamine

turkey sausage and chickpea soup with butternut squash

This soup brims with so much flavor, color, and hearty texture, once you taste it, it's hard to believe how easy it is to make and with how few ingredients. As it simmers, the broth is infused with a deeply savory mix of sausage, tomatoes, onion, and garlic; it gets a hint of sweetness from tender butternut squash and carrots, an herbal note from fresh thyme, and a warming touch of cayenne pepper. (If you use spicy sausage, omit the cayenne.) It's a soup that is different enough to be an exciting departure from the usual chicken and vegetable soup, but similar enough that it keeps you well within the comfort zone.

2 tablespoons olive oil

12 ounces uncooked turkey (or chicken) sausage, casings removed, crumbled

1 large onion, diced

2 garlic cloves, chopped

2 cups seeded, peeled, and cubed butternut squash (½-inch cubes)

2 medium-size carrots, diced

½ teaspoon salt

Pinch of cayenne pepper, plus more to taste

4 cups low-sodium chicken broth

1 (14.5-ounce) can no-salt-added diced tomatoes

1 (15-ounce) can no-salt-added chickpeas, drained and rinsed

4 thyme sprigs

1. Heat the oil in a large pot over medium-high heat. Add the sausage, onion, and garlic and cook until the onion is softened and the sausage is browned and cooked through, breaking it up with a spoon, about 5 minutes.

2. Add the butternut squash, carrots, salt, and cayenne and stir to combine. Add the broth, tomatoes with their juices, chickpeas, and thyme and bring to a boil, then lower the heat to medium-low and simmer, covered, until the squash is very tender but still retains its shape, about 20 minutes. Pick out the thyme sprigs and discard before serving.

The soup will keep in an airtight container in the refrigerator for up to 4 days, or in the freezer for 3 months.

Makes 4 servings

SERVING SIZE: 2¼ cups

PER SERVING: Calories 390; Total Fat 16 g (Sat Fat 3 g, Mono Fat 8 g, Poly Fat 4 g); Protein 26 g; Carb 36 g; Fiber 8 g; Cholesterol 65 mg; Sodium 840 mg; Total Sugar 11 g (Added Sugar 0 g)

EXCELLENT SOURCE OF: fiber, iron, manganese, niacin, phosphorous, potassium, protein, vitamin A, vitamin B_6, vitamin C, zinc

GOOD SOURCE OF: calcium, copper, folate, magnesium, pantothenic acid, riboflavin, thiamine, vitamin B_{12}, vitamin K

braised chicken thighs with lemon, olives, and green beans

In this homey but elegant recipe, chicken thighs become fall-off-the-bone tender and a gloriously tasty sauce forms in the pot as the poultry simmers with browned shallots, thin slices of peel-on lemon, green beans, olives, and thyme. The peel of the lemon imbues the dish with its robust citrus flavor, softening as it cooks and becoming as delightfully mellow and tender to eat as it is beautiful on the plate. The green beans are softened into a deep green comfort food, while still retaining some firmness. It's a meal that's easy to pull together, but it has a certain French-country romance to it that makes it totally worth breaking out the nice place mats and a couple of candles for.

3 pounds bone-in chicken thighs, skin removed

½ teaspoon salt, divided

½ teaspoon freshly ground black pepper, divided

3 tablespoons olive oil, divided

5 garlic cloves, smashed and peeled

3 large shallots, peeled and cut lengthwise into 8 wedges each

1 lemon, unpeeled, sliced thinly into half-moons, seeds removed

1 pound green beans, trimmed

1 cup green olives, pitted if you prefer

2 teaspoons fresh thyme leaves, or 1 teaspoon dried

1 cup low-sodium chicken broth

¼ cup freshly squeezed lemon juice

1. Season the chicken with ¼ teaspoon each of the salt and pepper. Heat 2 tablespoons of the oil in a large, wide pot over medium-high heat. Add half of the chicken, on what would have been the skin side down, and cook until it is golden brown, about 3 minutes. Flip the chicken and cook for 2 minutes on the other side, then transfer it to a plate. Add the remaining tablespoon of oil to the pot, then repeat with the remaining chicken. Right after you flip the second batch of chicken, add the garlic to the pot (without removing the chicken) to cook for the remaining 2 minutes, until the garlic is softened slightly and lightly browned. Transfer the second batch of chicken and the garlic to the plate.

2. Add the shallots and lemon slices to the pot and cook, stirring occasionally, until they have softened and browned, 4 minutes. Add the green beans, olives, thyme, and the remaining ¼ teaspoon each of salt and pepper; and then add the chicken broth and lemon juice. Return the chicken with any accumulated juices and the garlic to the pot, nestling the chicken into the vegetable mixture, and bring to a boil. Lower the heat to medium-low, cover and simmer, stirring occasionally, until the chicken is tender and cooked through, about 30 minutes.

3. Serve the chicken with the vegetables along-side, drizzled with the pan sauce.

The dish will keep in an airtight container in the refrigerator for up to 4 days.

Makes 4 servings

SERVING SIZE: 2 pieces chicken and about 1¼ cups vegetables and sauce

PER SERVING: Calories 410; Total Fat 20 g (Sat Fat 3.5 g, Mono Fat 10 g, Poly Fat 3 g); Protein 38 g; Carb 21 g; Fiber 6 g; Cholesterol 160 mg; Sodium 780 mg; Total Sugar 9 g (Added Sugar 0 g)

EXCELLENT SOURCE OF: fiber, magnesium, manganese, niacin, pantothenic acid, phosphorous, potassium, riboflavin, selenium, vitamin B_6, vitamin C, vitamin K, zinc

GOOD SOURCE OF: copper, folate, iron, molybdenum, thiamine, vitamin A, vitamin B_{12}

quinoa bowl with turkey crumbles, toasted garlic, and spinach

This recipe brings big flavor and bold color to a basic quinoa grain bowl, turning it into a truly craveable meal. While regular quinoa works, using red quinoa makes a huge difference by adding exciting, rich color to the mix. It is cooked pilaf style—in chicken broth with toasted garlic and lemon—which infuses it with intoxicating flavor and aroma. Contrasting green leaves of fresh baby spinach are stirred right into the hot quinoa, where they wilt until they are soft but keep their fresh appeal, and then crumbles of savory, browned ground turkey are tossed in. Sprinkled with parsley and topped with buttery avocado, it's a satisfying bowl that is as alluring as it is good for you.

2 tablespoons olive oil, divided

1 pound ground turkey

¾ teaspoon salt, divided

Pinch of crushed red pepper flakes, plus more to taste

3 garlic cloves, thinly sliced

1 cup uncooked red quinoa (prerinsed)

1½ cups low-sodium chicken broth

2 tablespoons freshly squeezed lemon juice

4 cups baby spinach leaves

¼ cup chopped fresh parsley

1 medium-size avocado, pitted, peeled, and sliced

Lemon wedges, for serving

1. Heat 1 tablespoon of the oil in a 3- to 4-quart pot over medium-high heat. Add the turkey and cook, breaking it up with a spoon until it is completely browned, about 3 minutes. Season it with ¼ teaspoon of the salt and the red pepper flakes, then transfer the turkey and any accumulated juices to a dish and cover it to keep warm.

2. Lower the heat to medium-low. Add the remaining tablespoon of oil and the garlic to the pot and cook, stirring, until the garlic is golden and fragrant, 2 to 3 minutes. Add the quinoa and stir until it is coated in the oil. Add the broth, lemon juice, and the remaining ½ teaspoon of salt. Bring to a boil, then simmer, covered, over low heat until the liquid is absorbed and the quinoa is tender, 15 to 20 minutes. Fluff the quinoa with a fork.

3. Stir the spinach into the quinoa until the spinach is just wilted. Then, return the turkey and its juices to the pot, add the parsley, and stir to combine. The mixture will keep in an airtight container in the refrigerator for up to 4 days.

4. Serve in bowls topped with avocado slices and a lemon wedge.

Makes 4 servings

SERVING SIZE: about 1¼ cups

PER SERVING: Calories 480; Total Fat 24 g (Sat Fat 2 g, Mono Fat 10 g, Poly Fat 2 g); Protein 31 g; Carb 38 g; Fiber 8 g; Cholesterol 65 mg; Sodium 590 mg; Total Sugar 3 g (Added Sugar 0 g)

EXCELLENT SOURCE OF: fiber, folate, iron, manganese, protein, vitamin A, vitamin C, vitamin K

GOOD SOURCE OF: magnesium

masala chicken with cauliflower and chickpeas

This satisfying meal is a breeze to make but is layered with exciting, healthy flavors and textures thanks, in large part, to the masala spice mix taught to me by my friend Sri Rao, author of *Bollywood Kitchen*. The masala is deeply savory with a touch of heat, and boasts bona fide anti-inflammatory properties. Whole cumin seeds add contrasting texture and surprising bursts of flavor to the tender cauliflower and hearty chickpeas. Stirring some hot water onto the sheet pan after everything is plated turns the luscious browned pan juices into a drizzle of sauce, and the bright, fresh finish from a squeeze of lemon along with a sprinkle of cilantro take this dish to the next level.

1 medium-size head cauliflower (about 2 pounds) cut into 1½-inch florets

2½ tablespoons olive oil, divided

¾ teaspoon salt, divided

1 lemon

1½ teaspoons paprika

½ teaspoon ground cumin

½ teaspoon ground coriander

½ teaspoon light brown sugar

¼ teaspoon cayenne pepper

⅛ teaspoon ground turmeric

⅛ teaspoon freshly ground black pepper

4 pieces bone-in chicken breast (about 12 ounces each)

1 cup canned low-sodium chickpeas, drained and rinsed

1 teaspoon whole cumin seeds

¼ cup hot water

¼ cup coarsely chopped fresh cilantro leaves

1. Preheat the oven to 425°F. Place the cauliflower on a sheet pan, toss it with 1½ tablespoons of the oil, and sprinkle with ¼ teaspoon of the salt.

2. Zest the lemon with a fine grater into a medium-size bowl until you have about ½ teaspoon of zest. Cut the lemon into wedges and set aside. Add the paprika, cumin, coriander, brown sugar, cayenne, turmeric, black pepper, and ¼ teaspoon of the salt to the bowl and toss to combine. Drizzle 1½ teaspoons of the oil onto the chicken and rub it onto both sides, then sprinkle the chicken with the spice mixture, rubbing it all over, including under the skin.

3. Move the cauliflower to one side of the sheet pan to make room for the chicken. Place the chicken on the pan and cook until an instant-read thermometer inserted into the thickest part reads 165°F, about 30 minutes, removing the pan from the oven to stir the cauliflower after about 15 minutes. The cauliflower will develop an appealing char in places as it cooks. Meanwhile, put the chickpeas into the bowl that contained the spices. (It's fine—good even—if there is a dusting of the spice still in the bowl.) Add the remaining 1½ teaspoons of oil, the remaining ¼ teaspoon of salt, and the cumin seeds and toss to combine.

(Continued)

4. Once the chicken is done, transfer it to a plate to rest (leaving the cauliflower on the sheet pan). Add the chickpea mixture to the cauliflower, toss to combine, and return the pan to the oven and heat until the cumin seeds are toasted and the chickpeas are warmed, 5 minutes more.

5. Divide the chicken and vegetables among four serving plates. Add the hot water to the pan and scrape the pan to dissolve some of the brown bits. Drizzle the juices over each plate. Then, squeeze about ½ teaspoon of lemon juice over each, sprinkle with the cilantro, and serve garnished with remaining lemon wedges.

The chicken and vegetables will keep in an airtight container in the refrigerator for up to 4 days and may be served warm or at room temperature.

Makes 4 servings

SERVING SIZE: 1 piece chicken and 1 cup vegetables

PER SERVING: Calories 440; Total Fat 16 g (Sat Fat 3 g, Mono Fat 8 g, Poly Fat 3 g); Protein 56 g; Carb 17 g; Fiber 6 g; Cholesterol 160 mg; Sodium 590 mg; Total Sugar 5 g (Added Sugar 1 g)

EXCELLENT SOURCE OF: fiber, folate, magnesium, manganese, niacin, pantothenic acid, phosphorous, potassium, protein, riboflavin, selenium, thiamine, vitamin B_6, vitamin C, vitamin K

GOOD SOURCE OF: chloride, copper, zinc

pomegranate marinated chicken thighs with roasted carrots over romaine

This is, hands down, my favorite way to cook and eat chicken thighs—infused with savory flavor from a good, long marinating, then brushed with honey so when broiled they char and caramelize seductively outside, but stay juicy inside. In this recipe, pomegranate juice makes for a lovely sweet-tart marinade base that carries deeply earthy spices and garlic into the chicken. It is plated with roasted carrots, warm or at room temperature, on top of lemony dressed lettuce leaves, with parsley, mint, toasted pistachios, and ruby red pomegranate arils, making for a satisfying yet fresh salad imbued with exciting, Moroccan-inspired flavor and color.

⅓ cup pomegranate juice

5 tablespoons olive oil, divided

3 tablespoons honey, divided

1 tablespoon plus 2 teaspoons freshly squeezed lemon juice, divided

1 teaspoon ground cumin

1 teaspoon ground coriander

4 garlic cloves, smashed and quartered

¾ teaspoon salt, divided

¼ teaspoon crushed red pepper flakes

8 boneless, skinless chicken thighs (about 1½ pounds)

1 pound medium-size carrots, cut into 3-inch-long pieces and halved or quartered lengthwise so they are an even finger-size thickness

¼ teaspoon freshly ground black pepper, divided

¼ cup unsalted, shelled pistachios

1. Whisk together the pomegranate juice, 2 tablespoons of the oil, 2 tablespoons of the honey, 1 tablespoon of the lemon juice, the cumin, coriander, and garlic, ½ teaspoon of the salt, and the red pepper flakes in a small bowl. Place the chicken in a resealable plastic bag, pour in the marinade, close the bag and refrigerate for at least 2 hours and up to 8 hours.

2. Preheat the oven to 400°F. Toss the carrots on a sheet pan with 1 tablespoon of the olive oil, and ⅛ teaspoon each of the salt and pepper. Roast until tender and beginning to brown, 20 to 25 minutes. Push the carrots to one side of the pan and add the pistachios to the other side. Return to the oven and bake until the nuts are toasted, 2 to 3 minutes more. Transfer the carrots to a plate and coarsely chop the nuts.

3. Set an oven rack in the highest position in the oven. Preheat the broiler to HIGH. Line the sheet pan with foil and place a rack on top of the pan. Remove the chicken from the marinade and place it on the rack. (Discard the marinade.) Brush the chicken on both sides with the remaining tablespoon of honey. Broil until the chicken is cooked through and nicely charred on the outside, about 4 minutes per side. The chicken and carrots will keep in an airtight container in the refrigerator for up to 4 days and may be served warm or at room temperature.

(Continued)

4 cups lightly packed torn romaine lettuce leaves, preferably red romaine

½ cup coarsely chopped fresh parsley leaves

¼ cup pomegranate arils

1 tablespoon chopped fresh mint leaves

4. Place the lettuce in a medium-size bowl and toss with the parsley, the remaining 2 tablespoons of olive oil, the remaining 2 teaspoons of lemon juice, and the remaining ⅛ teaspoon each of salt and pepper.

5. To serve, place a bed of the dressed lettuce on each of four serving plates. Top each with two pieces of chicken, scatter carrots around the plate, then top each with 1 tablespoon of pomegranate arils, mint leaves, and chopped pistachios.

Makes 4 servings

SERVING SIZE: 1 cup greens, 2 pieces chicken, and about ½ cup carrot

PER SERVING: Calories 470; Total Fat 24 g (Sat Fat 4 g, Mono Fat 14 g, Poly Fat 6 g); Protein 37 g; Carb 27 g; Fiber 6 g; Cholesterol 160 mg; Sodium 510 mg; Total Sugar 17 g (Added Sugar 8 g)

EXCELLENT SOURCE OF: fiber, folate, manganese, niacin, pantothenic acid, phosphorous, potassium, protein, riboflavin, selenium, thiamine, vitamin A, vitamin C, vitamin K, zinc

GOOD SOURCE OF: copper, iron, magnesium, vitamin B$_{12}$

rosemary balsamic chicken with roasted grapes, zucchini, and croutons

Whenever I serve this stunning meal, I am transported to the California wine country where the food has a relaxed, rustic sensibility, often with a Tuscan accent. The rosemary-laced croutons become the bed for juicy balsamic-roasted chicken breast, tender zucchini, caramelized cloves of roasted garlic, and colorful clusters of roasted grapes. The croutons absorb the luscious pan juices, which soften them just enough so they retain some of their crunch. It all comes together for a meal that is as delicious as it is beautiful. Even eating it at home in New York City, I can imagine myself dining al fresco with a view of the West Coast hills and vineyards.

2 cups cubed crusty whole-grain bread (¾-inch cubes)

3 tablespoons plus 1 teaspoon olive oil, divided

2 teaspoons finely chopped fresh rosemary, divided

½ plus ⅛ teaspoon salt, divided

¼ plus ⅛ teaspoon freshly ground black pepper, divided

1½ tablespoons balsamic vinegar

4 pieces bone-in chicken breast (about 12 ounces each)

1 tablespoon honey

3 medium-size zucchini, quartered lengthwise, then cut into ½-inch chunks

8 medium-size garlic cloves, unpeeled

4 small clusters red grapes (15 to 20 grapes each)

1. Preheat the oven to 350°F. Place the bread on a sheet pan. Drizzle with 1 tablespoon of the oil, 1 teaspoon of the rosemary, and ⅛ teaspoon each of the salt and pepper and toss to coat evenly. Spread out the bread cubes on the pan and bake until crisped and golden brown, about 15 minutes. Transfer to a serving platter. Carefully wipe off the sheet pan with a paper towel. The croutons may be made up to 2 days ahead and stored in an airtight container.

2. Increase the oven temperature to 425°F. Whisk together 2 tablespoons of the olive oil, the balsamic vinegar, and the remaining ½ teaspoon of salt and ¼ teaspoon of pepper in a medium-size bowl. Place the chicken on one side of the sheet pan, skin side up, and brush the tops generously with the balsamic mixture, using about one third of the mixture. Then, brush the tops of the chicken with the honey.

3. Toss the zucchini and garlic cloves with the remaining balsamic mixture; place on the sheet pan with the chicken, and roast for 15 minutes. Put the grape clusters in the bowl and drizzle with the remaining teaspoon of oil, tossing gently.

4. Sprinkle the remaining teaspoon of rosemary onto the zucchini and toss. Place the clusters of grapes on the sheet pan. Continue to roast until the chicken is cooked through, with an internal temperature of 165°F, and the zucchini and garlic are tender and nicely browned, 15 to 20 minutes more.

(Continued)

5. To serve, place the chicken on the serving platter with the croutons. Spoon the zucchini on top and add the grape clusters, then drizzle the whole plate with the juices that have accumulated in the pan, adding a little hot water to the pan if more liquid is needed.

The dish will keep in an airtight container in the refrigerator for up to 4 days and may be served warm or at room temperature.

Makes 4 servings

SERVING SIZE: 1 piece chicken, ¾ cup vegetables and croutons, and 1 cluster grapes

PER SERVING: Calories 500; Total Fat 19 g (Sat Fat 3 g, Mono Fat 10 g, Poly Fat 3 g); Protein 56 g; Carb 25 g; Fiber 4 g; Cholesterol 160 mg; Sodium 590 mg; Total Sugar 11 g (Added Sugar 4 g)

EXCELLENT SOURCE OF: folate, magnesium, manganese, niacin, pantothenic acid, phosphorous, potassium, protein, riboflavin, selenium, thiamine, vitamin B$_6$, vitamin C, zinc

GOOD SOURCE OF: fiber, iron, vitamin K

sage-rubbed roasted chicken with brussels sprouts, apple, and sunflower seeds

Roasting Brussels sprouts until they are deeply browned and their outer leaves have crisped is one of the most effortless and enticing ways to cook them. This recipe builds on that trusty basic, adding easy flourish and a protein to the pan to turn it into a complete and satisfying dinner. Here, the sprouts are roasted alongside chicken breast that has been rubbed with a flavorful sage-garlic mixture. Once the chicken is cooked, it comes off the pan to rest and a sprinkle of sunflower seeds is added to the pan to toast. The seeds (you could substitute any nut or seed you like) highlight the vegetable's nutty undertone, while chunks of fresh red apple sprinkled on after plating adds contrasting sweet freshness and color. The simple vinaigrette ties the elements together and lends a bright punch of flavor to the meal.

1½ pounds medium-size Brussels sprouts, trimmed and halved lengthwise

3 tablespoons olive oil, divided

¾ teaspoon salt, divided

1 medium-size garlic clove, finely minced

1 tablespoon finely chopped fresh sage leaves

4 pieces bone-in chicken breast (about 12 ounces each)

¼ teaspoon freshly ground black pepper

2 tablespoons unsalted, hulled sunflower seeds

1½ teaspoons cider vinegar

1 teaspoon whole-grain mustard

½ teaspoon honey

½ cup diced red apple (¼-inch dice)

1. Preheat the oven to 425°F. Place the Brussels sprouts on a sheet pan; toss them with 1 tablespoon of the oil and ¼ teaspoon of the salt and spread them out evenly on the pan.

2. Place the remaining ½ teaspoon of the salt and the garlic in a small pile on a cutting board. Use the broad side and blade edge of the knife to mash the garlic and salt together to form a paste. Place the garlic in a small bowl with the sage, 1 tablespoon of the oil, and the pepper and stir to combine. Place the chicken on the sheet pan with the Brussels sprouts. Rub the sage mixture on top of and under the chicken skin.

3. Roast until the chicken is cooked through with an internal temperature of 165°F and the Brussels sprouts are deep golden brown and crisp on the outside and tender on the inside, about 30 minutes. Transfer the chicken to a plate, then add the sunflower seeds to the pan and return to the oven and toast until they are aromatic, 3 minutes.

4. Meanwhile, whisk together the remaining tablespoon of oil and the vinegar, mustard, and honey in a small bowl.

(Continued)

5. Serve the chicken alongside the Brussels sprouts. Right before serving, scatter the apple over the Brussels sprouts and then drizzle the dressing all over each plate.

The chicken and Brussels sprouts will keep in the refrigerator for up to 4 days in an airtight container.

Makes 4 servings

SERVING SIZE: 1 piece chicken and ¾ cup Brussels sprouts

PER SERVING: Calories 470; Total Fat 19 g (Sat Fat 3 g, Mono Fat 9 g, Poly Fat 6 g); Protein 56 g; Carb 21 g; Fiber 8 g; Cholesterol 160 mg; Sodium 590 mg; Total Sugar 10 g (Added Sugar 1 g)

EXCELLENT SOURCE OF: fiber, folate, magnesium, manganese, niacin, pantothenic acid, phosphorous, potassium, protein, riboflavin, selenium, thiamine, vitamin A, vitamin B$_6$, vitamin C, vitamin K

GOOD SOURCE OF: copper, iron, zinc

lemon-cumin chicken, bulgur, and vegetable packets

These fragrant and flavorful parcels of lemony, cumin-seasoned chicken with colorful vegetables and tender whole-grain bulgur are unique for a couple of reasons. First, most packet meals call for serving over a separately cooked grain, but here it's all in one with the bulgur tucked into the parcel with everything else, where it steams to perfection and absorbs the flavors from the dressing, chicken, and vegetables. A ten-minute soak in a bowl with some boiling water gives it just the head start it needs. Second, to make the packets fuss-free to close, I use a piece of foil under the parchment so you don't have to worry about fancy origami-like folding. I like to serve them right in their packets, opened on a plate.

¾ cup quick-cooking (fine) bulgur

1 cup boiling water

1 lemon

3 tablespoons olive oil

2 garlic cloves, finely minced

½ teaspoon ground cumin

½ teaspoon salt

¼ teaspoon freshly ground black pepper

¼ cup finely minced onion

1 medium-size yellow bell pepper, seeded and diced

1 cup grape tomatoes, quartered

½ medium-size zucchini, diced

4 pieces thin-cut chicken breast (½-inch thick, 4 to 5 ounces each)

4 teaspoons chopped fresh parsley

1. Preheat the oven to 400°F. Place the bulgur and boiling water in a medium-size bowl, stir, and let sit until nearly all the water is absorbed, 10 minutes. Slice the lemon in half crosswise. Juice half of the lemon and slice the other half into thin rounds. Whisk together the olive oil, lemon juice, garlic, cumin, salt, and black pepper in a small bowl.

2. Cut four pieces of aluminum foil about 18 inches long and lay them out on a work surface. Place an 18-inch-long piece of parchment on top of each piece of foil.

3. Place about ½ cup of the bulgur at the center of each piece of parchment. Top with the onion, then the pepper, tomatoes, and zucchini. Lay a piece of chicken on top of each. (If the chicken is thicker than ½ inch, pound it out with a mallet or rolling pin. If it is considerably thinner, reduce the cooking time by 5 to 10 minutes.)

4. Drizzle each with the dressing, then place a lemon slice on top. Tightly seal the packets any way you'd like; just leave some space inside to allow steam to build up. Place the packets on a sheet pan and cook until the chicken is cooked through and the vegetables are crisp-tender, 25 minutes. Serve garnished with the parsley.

Makes 4 servings

SERVING SIZE: 1 packet

PER SERVING: Calories 360; Total Fat 12 g (Sat Fat 1.5 g, Mono Fat 7 g, Poly Fat 2 g); Protein 35 g; Carb 31 g; Fiber 6 g; Cholesterol 65 mg; Sodium 380 mg; Total Sugar 2 g (Added Sugar 0 g)

EXCELLENT SOURCE OF: fiber, manganese, protein, vitamin C, vitamin K

GOOD SOURCE OF: copper, iron, magnesium, molybdenum, niacin, phosphorous, potassium, vitamin A

greek-style chicken with potatoes, peppers, olives, and feta

Since my very first swoon-worthy bite of spanakopita (spinach pie) as a child, I have had a thing for Greek food. From my perspective today it makes perfect sense—so much of the cuisine hits the bull's eye on what I call the "sweet spot" where delicious and healthy meet. This recipe brings its craveable lemon and herb–centric flavors together for a meal that is a weeknight game-changer. There is very little prep involved and everything cooks on the same sheet pan in roughly thirty minutes, so you can have an incredible meal of lemony, oregano-flecked roast chicken, sweet peppers, and potatoes garnished with a pop of feta cheese and briny olives on the table fast. That leaves you more time to savor your meal with friends or family slowly, in the true Mediterranean style.

1 lemon

2 teaspoons dried oregano, divided, plus more to taste

2 garlic cloves, finely minced

½ teaspoon salt, divided

¼ teaspoon freshly ground black pepper, divided

2 tablespoons olive oil, divided

4 pieces bone-in chicken breast (about 12 ounces each)

1 pound baby new potatoes, halved

2 large red bell peppers, seeded and cut lengthwise into 8 wedges each

⅓ cup kalamata olives

⅓ cup crumbled feta cheese

1. Preheat the oven to 425°F. Finely zest the lemon. Combine the lemon zest, 1 teaspoon of the oregano, the garlic, ¼ teaspoon of the salt, ⅛ teaspoon of the black pepper, and 1 tablespoon of the oil in a small bowl. Rub the spice mixture all over the chicken and underneath the skin.

2. Place the potatoes and peppers on a sheet pan. Drizzle with the remaining tablespoon of olive oil, squeeze about a tablespoon of lemon juice on top, sprinkle with the remaining teaspoon of oregano, ¼ teaspoon of salt, and ⅛ teaspoon of black pepper, and toss to coat. Distribute the vegetables around the pan, then nestle the chicken pieces on the pan among the vegetables.

3. Cook until the chicken is cooked through with an internal temperature of 165°F and the vegetables are tender, about 30 minutes. If the chicken is cooked before the vegetables are done, transfer it to a plate, cover with foil to keep warm, and allow the vegetables to cook a bit more.

4. Serve sprinkled with the olives, feta cheese, the remainder of the lemon juice, and more oregano to taste. The chicken and vegetables will keep in an airtight container in the refrigerator for up to 4 days.

Makes 4 servings

SERVING SIZE: 1 piece chicken and 1 cup vegetables

PER SERVING: Calories 510; Total Fat 18 g (Sat Fat 4.5 g, Mono Fat 7 g, Poly Fat 2 g); Protein 55 g; Sodium 640 mg; Total Sugar 7 g (Added Sugar 0 g)

EXCELLENT SOURCE OF: magnesium, niacin, pantothenic acid, phosphorous, potassium, protein, riboflavin, selenium, thiamine, vitamin A, vitamin B_6, vitamin C

GOOD SOURCE OF: calcium, fiber, folate, iron, vitamin B_{12}, vitamin K, zinc

asiago-crusted chicken with roasted tomatoes and garlic broccoli

This is one of those meals that inevitably has the whole family begging you to put it in regular rotation. It has the comfort-food elements everyone loves—tender, moist chicken breasts coated in crispy, cheesy breadcrumbs; garlicky broccoli florets; and juicy tomato halves topped with an herbed edition of the whole-grain panko bread crumbs. Using mustard to make the bread crumb mixture adhere adds a punch of flavor and is more healthful than the loads of mayo commonly used in crumb-coated baked chicken, and Asiago imparts bold taste and is a nice variation of more typically used Parmesan, but either cheese works well. With very little prep or cooking time involved, it is perfect for a busy weeknight.

¾ cup whole-grain panko bread crumbs

½ cup coarsely grated aged Asiago or Parmesan cheese (grated on a box grater)

½ teaspoon paprika

¼ teaspoon freshly ground black pepper

2½ tablespoons olive oil, divided

4 cups broccoli florets (12 ounces, from 1 small head broccoli)

¼ teaspoon salt, divided

⅛ teaspoon crushed red pepper flakes

1 tablespoon Dijon mustard

4 boneless, skinless chicken breasts (about 6 ounces each), pounded to ½-inch thickness

2 medium-size tomatoes, halved crosswise

1 teaspoon chopped fresh oregano, or ½ teaspoon dried

3 garlic cloves, thinly sliced

1. Preheat the oven to 425°F. Combine the panko, cheese, paprika, and black pepper in a shallow dish. Drizzle the mixture with 1 tablespoon of the olive oil and toss to combine. Transfer ¼ cup of the bread crumb mixture to a small bowl.

2. Place the broccoli on a sheet pan and drizzle it with the remaining 1½ tablespoons of oil, ⅛ teaspoon of the salt, and the red pepper flakes. Push the broccoli to one end of the sheet pan.

3. Rub the mustard onto both sides of the chicken breasts, then coat on both sides with the bread crumb mixture from the shallow dish, pressing in the mixture lightly to coat. Arrange the chicken on the sheet pan.

4. Place the tomatoes, cut side up, on the sheet pan. Stir the oregano and remaining ⅛ teaspoon of salt into the reserved bread crumbs, then distribute on top of the tomatoes.

5. Bake for 15 minutes. Then, add the garlic to the broccoli, toss, and return the pan to the oven until the chicken is cooked through and the broccoli is crisp-tender, 5 to 10 minutes more. The dish will keep in an airtight container in the refrigerator for up to 4 days.

Makes 4 servings

SERVING SIZE: 1 piece chicken, ½ cup broccoli, and ½ tomato

PER SERVING: Calories 420; Total Fat 17 g (Sat Fat 4.5 g, Mono Fat 7 g, Poly Fat 5 g); Protein 47 g; Carb 19 g; Fiber 4 g; Cholesterol 135 mg; Sodium 530 mg; Total Sugar 2 g (Added Sugar 0 g)

EXCELLENT SOURCE OF: niacin, pantothenic acid, phosphorous, protein, selenium, vitamin B_6

GOOD SOURCE OF: calcium, magnesium, potassium, riboflavin, thiamine, vitamin A, vitamin K

sheet pan thanksgiving dinner

This one-pan feast of turkey with all the fixin's puts a fabulous holiday dinner on the table without a big fuss or a sink full of dishes. It comes in handy on actual holidays when you are feeding a smaller group, or any day of the year when you want to tap into that Thanksgiving spirit. Golden turkey breast is stuffed with a gussied-up cranberry sauce—fresh cranberries, pecans, maple syrup, thyme, and orange zest. (Ask your butcher to do the work of deboning, butterflying, and pounding the poultry; then, all you need to do is slather the cranberry mixture on and roll it up. Although this recipe calls for half a turkey breast, I have found most butchers sell them only whole, so I have my butcher prep both halves and I freeze the leftover one for another day.) The stuffed breast is cooked alongside maple-seasoned sweet potatoes studded with pecans and green beans with roasted shallots. The meal even includes a "gravy" made from the deglazed pan juices. Since there is enough turkey for six but the meal itself serves four, you even wind up with some leftover turkey to enjoy the next day, in true Thanksgiving style.

½ **cup pecan halves or pieces, divided**

½ **cup fresh cranberries, halved**

3 **tablespoons pure maple syrup, divided**

1 **tablespoon fresh thyme leaves**

¼ **teaspoon finely grated orange zest**

1 **teaspoon salt, divided**

½ **boneless, skinless turkey breast (about 2½ pounds), butterflied and pounded to about ¾-inch thickness (have your butcher do this)**

½ **teaspoon freshly ground black pepper, divided**

1. Preheat the oven to 375°F. Coarsely chop ¼ cup of the pecans and combine them in a small bowl with the cranberries, 2 tablespoons of the maple syrup, the thyme and orange zest, and ¼ teaspoon of the salt.

2. Sprinkle both sides of the turkey breast with ¼ teaspoon each of the salt and pepper. Spread the cranberry mixture onto one side of the turkey, leaving a bare border of about 2 inches on all sides. Roll up and secure tightly with kitchen twine, then brush the top with 1½ teaspoons of the olive oil. Place on one side of a sheet pan and roast for 15 minutes.

3. Place the sweet potatoes on the sheet pan. Drizzle with 2 tablespoons of the olive oil, remaining tablespoon of maple syrup, and ¼ teaspoon of the salt and use tongs to toss to coat evenly. Return the pan to the oven and roast for 25 minutes.

4. Move the potatoes aside, then add the green beans and shallots to the pan. Drizzle them with the remaining tablespoon of olive oil, and ¼ teaspoon each of the salt and pepper, tossing to coat, using tongs.

5. Return the sheet pan to the oven and roast until the turkey reaches an internal temperature of 160°F, about 15 minutes. When the turkey is done, transfer it to a cutting board to rest, then sprinkle the potatoes with the remaining pecans and return the pan to the oven to allow the vegetables to cook until they are softened and lightly browned, 5 to 10 minutes more.

3½ tablespoons olive oil, divided

3 medium-size sweet potatoes (about 1½ pounds), peeled and cut into 1-inch pieces

12 ounces green beans, trimmed

3 medium-size shallots, peeled and quartered lengthwise

¼ cup boiling water

6. Transfer the vegetables to serving plates or a serving platter. Add the boiling water to the pan and stir to dissolve some of the pan juices (but avoid actively stirring any juices that may have charred). Slice the turkey into ½-inch-thick slices and serve it drizzled with the pan juices, alongside the vegetables.

Leftovers will keep in an airtight container in the refrigerator for up to 4 days.

Makes 4 servings
(with 2 servings turkey left over)

SERVING SIZE: 2 slices turkey and ¾ cup each sweet potato and green beans

PER SERVING: Calories 630; Total Fat 22 g (Sat Fat 3 g, Mono Fat 11 g, Poly Fat 3 g); Protein 51 g; Carb 58 g; Fiber 10 g; Cholesterol 110 mg; Sodium 800 mg; Total Sugar 21 g (Added Sugar 7 g)

EXCELLENT SOURCE OF: copper, fiber, magnesium, manganese, niacin, pantothenic acid, phosphorous, potassium, protein, riboflavin, selenium, thiamine, vitamin A, vitamin B_6, vitamin B_{12}, vitamin C, vitamin K, zinc

GOOD SOURCE OF: calcium, folate

chicken shawarma
with yogurt sauce

Shawarma, a cousin of the gyro, is a Middle Eastern dish of boldly seasoned meat or poultry that's stacked on a huge rotisserie and shaved into thin strips as it cooks, then usually piled into a flatbread wrap with some crisp vegetables and a creamy sauce. Here, the chicken is first marinated in a mixture of olive oil, lemon juice, and an array of aromatic spices. Just an hour will do the trick, but it's even better if you marinate it up to twelve hours. The chicken is cooked on a rack over a sheet pan and broiled until cooked though and appealingly charred. Served in warmed pita with lettuce, tomato, and cucumber with a garlic and herb yogurt sauce, it brings the essence of the crave-worthy sandwich into your kitchen—no giant vertical spit required.

CHICKEN:

3 tablespoons olive oil

2 tablespoons freshly squeezed lemon juice

2 teaspoons ground cumin

2 teaspoons paprika

¾ teaspoon salt

½ teaspoon ground allspice

½ teaspoon ground turmeric

¼ teaspoon granulated garlic

¼ teaspoon freshly ground black pepper

⅛ teaspoon ground cinnamon

1¼ pounds boneless, skinless chicken thighs

SAUCE:

¼ cup plain whole-milk Greek yogurt or labneh

1½ teaspoons freshly squeezed lemon juice

1½ teaspoons chopped fresh dill

1½ teaspoons chopped fresh parsley

1 small garlic clove, finely minced

⅛ teaspoon salt

TO ASSEMBLE:

4 whole wheat pita or lavash breads

2 cups chopped romaine lettuce

2 medium-size tomatoes, chopped

1 cup diced English cucumber

1. Marinate the chicken: Whisk the olive oil, lemon juice, cumin, paprika, salt, allspice, turmeric, garlic, pepper, and cinnamon together in a medium-size bowl. Add the chicken and toss to coat. Cover and marinate in the refrigerator for at least 1 hour and up to 12 hours.

2. Prepare the sauce: Stir together the yogurt, lemon juice, dill, parsley, garlic, and salt and 2 tablespoons of cold water in a small bowl. The sauce may be made 2 days ahead and stored in an airtight container in the refrigerator. Stir well before serving.

3. Cook the chicken: Set an oven rack in the highest position in the oven. Preheat the broiler to HIGH. Line a sheet pan with foil and place a rack on top of the pan. Remove the chicken from the marinade and place it on the rack. Broil until the chicken is cooked through and nicely charred on the outside, about 4 minutes per side. Rotate the rack at the midpoint of cooking each side to ensure even cooking.

4. Remove the sheet pan and rack from the oven, but keep the broiler on. Transfer the chicken to a cutting board and chop it. Place the bread directly on the top oven rack to warm it, 30 seconds per side.

5. Serve the chicken in the pita pockets or on the lavash, topped with lettuce, tomato, and cucumber and a drizzle of the yogurt sauce.

The chicken will keep in an airtight container in the refrigerator for up to 4 days.

Makes 4 servings

SERVING SIZE: 1 pita, ¾ cup chicken, about 1¼ cups vegetables, and 2 tablespoons sauce

PER SERVING: Calories 420; Total Fat 17 g (Sat Fat 3 g, Mono Fat 8 g, Poly Fat 3 g); Protein 37 g; Carb 32 g; Fiber 6 g; Cholesterol 135 mg; Sodium 840 mg; Total Sugar 5 g (Added Sugar 0 g)

EXCELLENT SOURCE OF: fiber, folate, niacin, phosphorous, protein, riboflavin, selenium, vitamin A, vitamin B_6, vitamin C, vitamin K

GOOD SOURCE OF: calcium, iron, magnesium, pantothenic acid, potassium, thiamine, vitamin B_{12}, zinc

chicken "antipasti" bowls with parmesan crisps

This meal in a bowl is essentially a salad, but one so satisfying and chock-full of tasty morsels, it could rightfully rid salad of its unfair rabbit-food reputation once and for all. There are juicy bites of chicken aplenty along with an array of goodies typically found piled on an antipasti platter—tomatoes, olives, roasted peppers, fresh basil—plus the irresistible, salty-savory crunch of Parmesan crisps and, yes, some romaine lettuce— all tossed in a lovely, Italian-style garlic and herb dressing. One sheet pan is all you need to cook the chicken after baking the Parmesan crisps (which are worth keeping in mind on their own as a nibble for guests). Plus, both elements can be cooked days ahead, allowing you the makings of this incredible meal at your fingertips.

⅔ cup finely grated Parmesan cheese

1 teaspoon all-purpose flour

¼ cup extra-virgin olive oil

2 tablespoons red wine vinegar

1 teaspoon dried oregano

½ teaspoon granulated garlic

½ teaspoon freshly ground black pepper, divided

¼ teaspoon salt, divided

1¼ pounds boneless, skinless chicken breast, pounded to an even ½-inch thickness

1 heart of romaine lettuce, chopped (4 cups)

1 cup grape tomatoes, halved

1 large jarred roasted red pepper, chopped (½ cup)

½ cup sliced pitted green olives

¼ cup fresh basil leaves, torn or sliced into ribbons

1. Preheat the oven to 350°F. Line a sheet pan with parchment paper.

2. Combine the cheese and flour in a small bowl. Spoon mounds of the cheese mixture (about 2 teaspoons each) onto the prepared sheet pan, leaving about 1 inch between each mound. Use your fingers to pat down the mounds slightly so each is about 2½ inches in diameter. Bake until they are golden brown, about 8 minutes. Allow to cool slightly, then slide the parchment with the Parmesan crisps to a flat surface to cool completely. The crisps may be made up to 2 days ahead and stored in an airtight container at room temperature.

3. Meanwhile, whisk together the oil, vinegar, oregano, garlic, and ¼ teaspoon of the pepper and ⅛ teaspoon of the salt in a small bowl. Transfer 2 tablespoons of this dressing to another small bowl and use that to brush onto both sides of the chicken. Then, season the chicken with the remaining ¼ teaspoon of pepper and ⅛ teaspoon of salt. Place the chicken onto the sheet pan (the same one you used for the Parmesan crisps) and bake for 8 minutes, then flip the chicken and continue to cook until it is cooked through, about 7 minutes more. Transfer the chicken to a cutting board to rest for 5 minutes, then chop it into bite-size pieces. The chicken may be served warm or chilled and may be made up to 4 days ahead and stored in an airtight container in the refrigerator.

4. To assemble, place the lettuce, tomatoes, roasted peppers, olives, and chicken in a large bowl and toss together. Add the dressing and toss to coat. Serve in bowls topped with the basil and crumbled Parmesan crisps.

Makes 4 servings

SERVING SIZE: 2 cups of the chicken and vegetables and 4 Parmesan crisps

PER SERVING: Calories 400; Total Fat 24 g (Sat Fat 5 g, Mono Fat 13 g, Poly Fat 2 g); Protein 37 g; Carb 7 g; Fiber 2 g; Cholesterol 115 mg; Sodium 830 mg; Total Sugar 3 g (Added Sugar 0 g)

EXCELLENT SOURCE OF: folate, niacin, pantothenic acid, phosphorous, potassium, protein, selenium, vitamin A, vitamin B_6, vitamin C, vitamin K

GOOD SOURCE OF: calcium, magnesium, zinc

meat

beef and zucchini noodle stir-fry

One of the stalwart restaurants in my neighborhood, Flor de Mayo, has been in business for over thirty years and I have been eating there regularly for nearly that long. They rightfully call themselves "a pioneer in Chino-Latino cuisine," serving a wonderful fusion of Chinese and Peruvian dishes. Although my family and I usually opt for the healthier choices on their menu, one of the dishes we love is Tallarin Saltado, a savory stir-fry of steak, onions, tomatoes, and spaghetti in a beefy, soy, and vinegar–spiked sauce. Craving it one evening, I decided to spin those flavors in a healthier direction—using lean sirloin and zucchini noodles—and the result is this fast and supremely scrumptious skillet dinner. I will still be a loyal Flor de Mayo customer, but I'll be sticking to my take on this particular dish, and I think you will be stuck on it, too.

1¼ pounds boneless sirloin steak, trimmed and sliced thinly against the grain

½ teaspoon salt, divided, plus more to taste

¼ teaspoon freshly ground black pepper

¼ teaspoon granulated garlic

1 teaspoon cornstarch

½ cup low-sodium beef broth

3 tablespoons canola or other neutral-tasting oil, divided

1 small red onion, sliced into ½-inch-thick wedges

2 garlic cloves, thinly sliced

1 serrano or jalapeño pepper, seeded and thinly sliced lengthwise

3 plum tomatoes, sliced into ½-inch-thick wedges

5 cups zucchini noodles (14 ounces), store-bought or spiralized from 2 medium-size zucchini

2 tablespoons reduced-sodium soy sauce

3 tablespoons red wine vinegar

½ cup fresh cilantro leaves

1 ripe avocado, pitted, peeled, and sliced

1. Toss the meat with ¼ teaspoon each of the salt, black pepper, and granulated garlic. Whisk the cornstarch into the beef broth in a small pitcher or bowl until the cornstarch is dissolved.

2. Heat 1 tablespoon of the oil in a large skillet over medium-high heat. Add half of the meat to the skillet, increase the heat to high and cook, stirring once or twice, until the meat is nicely browned, 1½ to 2 minutes. Transfer the meat to a plate. Repeat with another tablespoon of the oil and the remaining meat, transferring it to the plate.

3. Add the remaining tablespoon of oil to the skillet. Add the onion, garlic, and serrano pepper and cook over high heat for 30 seconds. Then, add the tomatoes and zucchini noodles and cook, stirring frequently, until the vegetables soften slightly but are still quite firm, 1 minute more. Add the soy sauce, vinegar, and the cornstarch mixture and cook, stirring frequently, until the broth has thickened and the zucchini noodles are firm-tender, about 2 minutes more. Return the beef with any accumulated juices to the skillet and toss to combine.

4. Serve the stir-fry topped with a heap of the cilantro leaves and sliced avocado alongside.

Makes 4 servings

SERVING SIZE: 1½ cups stir-fry mixture and ¼ avocado

PER SERVING: Calories 370; Total Fat 24 g (Sat Fat 4 g, Mono Fat 14 g, Poly Fat 4 g); Protein 29 g; Carb 13 g; Fiber 5 g; Cholesterol 75 mg; Sodium 760 mg; Total Sugar 5 g (Added Sugar 0 g)

EXCELLENT SOURCE OF: fiber, folate, niacin, phosphorous, potassium, protein, selenium, vitamin B_6, vitamin B_{12}, vitamin C, zinc

GOOD SOURCE OF: copper, iron, magnesium, manganese, molybdenum, pantothenic acid, riboflavin, thiamine, vitamin A

fennel-rubbed pork chops with apple, kale, and sweet potato

A sprinkle of coarsely crushed fennel seeds and black peppercorns give lean pork chops a compelling sausagelike flavor that marries beautifully with a sauté of onions, apples, sweet potatoes, and hearty kale. I recommend using either curly or Tuscan (lacinato) kale; its springy texture and volume work best here. Once the pork is cooked until it's juicy inside and a luscious golden brown crust forms on the outside, the deposits of flavorful fond left in the pan are absorbed by the onion. As the fond softens, it ultimately dissolves into the broth to form a light pan sauce, which is thickened with a hint of tangy mustard. All in all, it will be on the table in less than an hour—a blessing on a busy weeknight.

1 teaspoon whole fennel seeds

½ teaspoon whole black peppercorns

4 boneless loin pork chops (about 1 inch thick, about 1 pound total)

¾ teaspoon salt, divided

¼ cup olive oil, divided

2 medium-size sweet potatoes (9 to 10 ounces each), peeled and cut into ½-inch dice

½ medium-size onion, cut thinly into half-moons

1 medium-size red apple, such as Jonagold or Honeycrisp, unpeeled, sliced into ¼-inch-thick wedges

1 cup low-sodium chicken broth

1 teaspoon Dijon mustard

4 cups lightly packed, coarsely chopped kale leaves (1 small bunch)

1. Place the fennel seeds and peppercorns in a small resealable plastic bag, then use a mallet or rolling pin to hammer the mixture until it is coarsely ground. (Alternatively, you can pulse them briefly in a spice or coffee grinder.) Season the pork on both sides with fennel and pepper and sprinkle both sides with ¼ teaspoon of the salt.

2. Heat 2 tablespoons of the oil in a large, high-sided skillet over medium heat. Add the sweet potatoes to the skillet and cook, stirring occasionally, until they are fork-tender, 10 minutes. Season them with ¼ teaspoon of the salt, then transfer them to a plate.

3. Add 1 tablespoon of the oil to the skillet and heat over medium-high heat. Add the pork to the skillet, then lower the heat to medium and cook, turning once, until the meat is nicely browned on the outside and slightly blush inside, 2½ to 3 minutes per side. Transfer the pork to a plate and tent it with foil.

4. Add the remaining tablespoon of oil to the skillet, then add the onion and cook until it has softened, about 2 minutes. Add the apple slices and cook for 1 minute more. Add the broth, then stir in the mustard and return the sweet potatoes to the skillet. Increase the heat to medium-high and bring to a simmer. Cook until the apple has softened slightly and the liquid has reduced a bit, 1 to 2 minutes.

5. Add the kale and the remaining ¼ teaspoon of salt and cook, stirring occasionally, until the kale is tender but retains its shape and color, about 1 minute. Add any accumulated juices from the plate of pork to the pan. Serve the pork with the vegetable mixture alongside and drizzle with the pan sauce.

The dish will keep in an airtight container in the refrigerator for up to 4 days.

Makes 4 servings

SERVING SIZE: 1 piece pork and 1 cup vegetable mixture

PER SERVING: Calories 450; Total Fat 21 g (Sat Fat 3.5 g, Mono Fat 12 g, Poly Fat 2 g); Protein 24 g; Carb 41 g; Fiber 7 g; Cholesterol 60 mg; Sodium 640 mg; Total Sugar 13 g (Added Sugar 0 g)

EXCELLENT SOURCE OF: copper, folate, manganese, niacin, phosphorous, protein, riboflavin, selenium, thiamine, vitamin A, vitamin B₆, vitamin C, vitamin K, zinc

GOOD SOURCE OF: calcium, fiber, iron, magnesium, pantothenic acid, potassium, vitamin E

hummus with
spiced ground beef and pine nuts

This recipe is my take on one of my favorite traditional Middle Eastern preparations for hummus, where ground beef is sautéed with a medley of earthy and warm-sweet spices, then piled warm, along with toasted pine nuts, onto plates generously spread with hummus. A sprinkle of tomatoes and parsley adds a fresh burst of flavor, color, and vegetable nutrition. I usually whip up a batch of hummus using canned chickpeas, because it tastes miles better than the packaged kind and takes just minutes, but I have also used store-bought on especially hectic days. Serve this with warmed whole wheat pita or crisp romaine lettuce leaves, or both, for scooping, depending on your appetite.

¼ cup pine nuts

1 tablespoon olive oil

1 small onion, chopped

2 garlic cloves, minced

½ teaspoon ground cumin

¼ teaspoon ground coriander

¼ teaspoon ground allspice

⅛ teaspoon ground cinnamon

Pinch of crushed red pepper flakes

¼ teaspoon salt, plus more to taste

⅛ teaspoon freshly ground black pepper

12 ounces lean ground beef (90% lean or higher)

1⅓ cups hummus, freshly made (recipe follows), or store-bought

1 pint grape tomatoes, halved, or quartered if large

¼ cup fresh parsley leaves

4 teaspoons extra-virgin olive oil, for drizzling (optional)

1. Toast the pine nuts in a medium skillet over medium-high heat, stirring frequently, until they are browned and fragrant, 2 to 3 minutes. Transfer the pine nuts to a small dish. Add the oil to the skillet and heat until it is shimmering. Add the onion and cook until softened, 2 to 3 minutes, then stir in the garlic, cumin, coriander, allspice, cinnamon, red pepper flakes, salt, and black pepper. Add the meat and cook, stirring occasionally and breaking it up with a spoon, until it is browned, 4 to 5 minutes. Season with additional salt to taste. The cooked meat will keep in an airtight container in the refrigerator for up to 4 days.

2. To serve, spread ⅓ cup of the hummus on each serving plate. Mound about ½ cup of the spiced meat on top of each plate of hummus, then sprinkle with tomatoes, parsley, and pine nuts and drizzle each plate with 1 teaspoon of oil, if desired. Alternatively, pile the ingredients on a larger plate and place in the middle of the table to serve family style.

Makes 4 servings

SERVING SIZE: 1 plate

PER SERVING: Calories 430; Total Fat 27 g (Sat Fat 6 g, Mono Fat 12 g, Poly Fat 7 g); Protein 26 g; Carb 23 g; Fiber 7 g; Cholesterol 55 mg; Sodium 640 mg; Total Sugar 6 g (Added Sugar 0 g)

EXCELLENT SOURCE OF: copper, fiber, iron, magnesium, manganese, niacin, phosphorous, potassium, protein, selenium, vitamin B$_6$, vitamin B$_{12}$, vitamin C, vitamin K, zinc

GOOD SOURCE OF: folate, riboflavin, thiamine, vitamin A

(Continued)

classic hummus

1 small garlic clove, minced

½ teaspoon salt

1 (15-ounce) can low-sodium chickpeas, drained and rinsed

2 tablespoons tahini

1 tablespoon freshly squeezed lemon juice

1 tablespoon extra-virgin olive oil

Makes 4 servings

SERVING SIZE: ⅓ cup

PER SERVING: Calories 170; Total Fat 10 g (Sat Fat 1.5 g, Mono Fat 5 g, Poly Fat 3 g); Protein 7 g; Carb 16 g; Fiber 5 g; Cholesterol 0 mg; Sodium 430 mg; Total Sugar 3 g (Added Sugar 0 g)

EXCELLENT SOURCE OF: fiber, manganese, vitamin B_6

GOOD SOURCE OF: copper, phosphorous, protein, thiamine

1. Using the broad side of a knife blade, mash together the garlic and salt to form a paste. Place the garlic paste in a food processor. Add the chickpeas to the food processor along with the tahini, lemon juice, olive oil, and 3 tablespoons of water and process until smooth. The hummus will keep in an airtight container in the refrigerator for up to 4 days.

steak and mushroom "french dip" sandwiches

When you bite into this sandwich, you are immediately awash in a multilayered experience of texture and flavor. First, there's a shattering crunch from the crusty baguette. Soon, you notice the luscious way some of the bread has absorbed and yielded to the juices from its dip. Then, there is a bright snap of fresh lettuce before you get to the savory center of tender sliced beef mingling with sautéed mushrooms and caramelized onion. It's a totally satisfying, overstuffed sandwich that's good for you, too, thanks to the bounty of mushrooms, lean beef, and the whole-grain bread, which is scooped out to keep the portion smart and make space to pile on plenty of the sumptuous filling.

2 tablespoons olive oil, divided

1 medium-size onion, sliced into half-moons

8 ounces mixed mushrooms, sliced

2 garlic cloves, thinly sliced

¼ teaspoon salt, divided

½ teaspoon freshly ground black pepper, divided

12 ounces boneless sirloin or top loin steak, trimmed of all visible fat and very thinly sliced

½ cup dry sherry

1½ cups low-sodium beef broth

2 teaspoons Worcestershire sauce

1 whole wheat baguette (about 21 inches long) or 4 crusty whole-grain rolls

2 cups mixed greens or any type of lettuce

1. Heat 1 tablespoon of the oil in a large skillet over medium-high heat. Add the onion and mushrooms and cook, stirring occasionally, until the mushrooms have released their liquid and are beginning to brown, and the onion has softened, about 6 minutes. (Add a tablespoon or two of water if the pan seems to be getting too dry.) Stir in the garlic and cook until everything is deep golden brown and softened, 2 minutes more. Season with ⅛ teaspoon each of the salt and pepper, then transfer the mixture to a bowl.

2. Add the remaining tablespoon of oil to the pan and heat it over medium-high heat. Season the beef with the remaining ⅛ teaspoon of the salt and ⅛ teaspoon of the pepper, then cook it until it is nicely browned but still has a bit of pink in it, about 2 minutes. Transfer the meat to the bowl containing the mushroom mixture and cover it to keep warm.

3. Add the sherry to the skillet and cook over medium-high heat until it is reduced by half, about 2 minutes. Add the beef broth, Worcestershire, and remaining ¼ teaspoon of pepper. Return to a boil, then cook until the sauce reduces to about 1 cup, about 3 minutes more. Divide the sauce among four ramekins or small bowls for serving.

(Continued)

4. While the sauce reduces, make the sandwiches: If using a baguette, cut it crosswise into four pieces. Slice each piece of bread or roll in half lengthwise and scoop out and discard the soft insides. Fill the bottom piece of bread with the meat and mushroom mixture, top with a heap of the greens, then the top piece of bread. Serve each sandwich with a small bowl of the pan sauce alongside for dipping.

The meat mixture and the sauce will keep in the refrigerator for up to 4 days in separate airtight containers.

Makes 4 servings

SERVING SIZE: 1 sandwich and about ¼ cup pan sauce

PER SERVING: Calories 370; Total Fat 14 g (Sat Fat 3 g, Mono Fat 7 g, Poly Fat 1 g); Protein 21 g; Carb 33 g; Fiber 4 g; Cholesterol 33 mg; Sodium 710 mg; Total Sugar 5 g (Added Sugar 0 g)

EXCELLENT SOURCE OF: iron, niacin, protein, riboflavin, selenium, vitamin A, zinc

GOOD SOURCE OF: copper, pantothenic acid, phosphorous, potassium, vitamin B_6, vitamin B_{12}, vitamin C

ginger-soy marinated pork loin with bok choy

Here, lean pork loin, thinly sliced so it cooks up in minutes, is treated to a boldly tasty marinade that does double duty, both as a flavor agent for the meat and as the liquid for a lip-smacking pan sauce. After making the marinade, you simply set some aside for deglazing the pan later, then add the rest to a resealable plastic bag with the sliced pork. A thirty-minute marinade does the trick, but let it go longer, for up to eight hours, for maximum effect. Bok choy is perfect here, but broccolini or chopped green cabbage would also work well. Making use of one of my favorite healthy convenience foods—frozen brown rice—rounds out the dish and makes it a true one-pan meal.

¼ cup reduced-sodium soy sauce

⅓ cup freshly squeezed orange juice

¼ cup peanut oil or canola oil, divided

1½ tablespoons honey

2 tablespoons unseasoned rice vinegar

1 tablespoon finely grated ginger

1 tablespoon minced garlic

2 teaspoons toasted sesame oil

2 teaspoons sriracha

1¼ pounds boneless pork loin roast, trimmed and sliced thinly into ¼-inch-thick slices

1 bunch scallions

1¼ pounds baby bok choy (about 5), quartered lengthwise, or 2 medium-size, cut crosswise into 1-inch pieces

4 cups frozen, cooked brown rice (to yield 3 cups thawed)

1. Place the soy sauce, orange juice, 2 tablespoons of the oil, and the honey, rice vinegar, ginger, garlic, sesame oil, and sriracha in a small bowl and whisk until combined.

2. Remove and reserve ¼ cup of the marinade, and place the rest in a resealable plastic bag. Add the pork to the bag and marinate for at least 30 minutes and up to 8 hours in the refrigerator.

3. Trim the roots off the scallions, then cut about 3-inch lengths of the white and light green part, halving them lengthwise if they are thick. Thinly slice the dark green part crosswise until you have about ⅓ cup and reserve separately.

4. Remove the pork from the marinade and discard the marinade. Heat 1 tablespoon of the oil in a very large, high-sided, lidded skillet over medium-high heat. Place half of the pork slices in the pan, then lower the heat to medium and cook until they are browned and just cooked through, about 2 minutes per side, then transfer to a plate. Repeat with the remaining tablespoon of oil and pork, transferring it to the plate and covering with foil to keep it warm. A dark brown coating (fond) will form in the pan as you cook the meat.

5. Add the bok choy to the skillet and cook, stirring until it begins to soften slightly, and the browned bits in the pan begin to dissolve, 2 minutes. Add a tablespoon or two of water to the pan if it seems very dry.

(Continued)

6. Add the 3-inch scallion pieces and the reserved ¼ cup of the soy mixture to the pan, cover, lower the heat to medium-low, and simmer, stirring occasionally, until the bok choy is tender, about 5 minutes.

7. While the bok choy is cooking, place the rice in a microwave-safe dish with a vented cover and microwave on HIGH until it is steaming, about 6 minutes. Return any accumulated pork juices to the pan and serve the pork, bok choy, and sauce over the rice, garnished with the scallion greens.

The dish will keep in an airtight container in the refrigerator for up to 4 days.

Makes 4 servings

SERVING SIZE: 2 or 3 slices pork, about 5 wedges baby bok choy or 1¼ cups sliced bok choy, and ¾ cup rice

PER SERVING: Calories 510; Total Fat 18 g (Sat Fat 2.5 g, Mono Fat 9 g, Poly Fat 4 g); Protein 41 g; Carb 49 g; Fiber 5 g; Cholesterol 80 mg; Sodium 600 mg; Total Sugar 8 g (Added Sugar 3 g)

EXCELLENT SOURCE OF: folate, niacin, phosphorous, potassium, protein, riboflavin, selenium, thiamine, vitamin A, vitamin B$_6$, vitamin C, vitamin K

GOOD SOURCE OF: calcium, fiber, iron, magnesium, manganese, pantothenic acid, zinc

buckwheat crepes with ham, gruyère, and spinach

uckwheat—which despite its name, isn't a type of wheat at all, but a seed—powers these satisfying crepes with both intrigue and nutrition. It imparts a nutty flavor and dark color, giving the crepes a sassy Goth look, while adding a wealth of protein, fiber, minerals, and antioxidants. Buckwheat is also gluten-free, so the crepes can be, too, if you substitute a cup-for-cup gluten-free flour for the whole wheat flour. Ultimately, the tender crepes make the perfect blanket for the savory combination of smoked ham, melted Gruyère cheese, and fresh spinach that make them a meal.

I have to admit that until recently, I was pretty intimidated by making crepes, but they are really just extra-thin pancakes, so if you can make regular pancakes, you are good to go. There is a little extra batter built into this recipe for a trial run, so you can afford to mess one crepe up while getting the feel of it, and still have enough for four. They can be made up to two days ahead and require nearly zero effort to stuff and rewarm, so they are ideal to keep on hand for a quick everyday meal or a hassle-free but elegant brunch gathering.

1 cup 1% low-fat milk

3 large eggs

¼ teaspoon salt

⅔ cup buckwheat flour

⅓ cup whole wheat pastry flour or all-purpose flour

3 tablespoons olive oil, plus more for brushing pan

1 cup packed shredded Gruyère cheese

8 slices Black Forest ham (about 7 ounces)

2 cups baby spinach leaves

1. To make the crepes, place the milk, eggs, 3 tablespoons of water, and salt in a blender and blend on a low setting, such as the "mix" setting, to combine. Add the buckwheat and whole wheat pastry flours and blend until very smooth, about 15 seconds. Add the oil and blend until incorporated, 5 seconds more. Pour the batter into a bowl or pitcher, cover, and refrigerate for at least 1 hour and up to one day.

2. Heat a 12-inch nonstick skillet over medium heat. Brush it with oil. Use a ½ cup-measure to ladle the batter into the center of the pan. Tilt and rotate the pan so the batter forms a thin layer in the bottom of it. Cook until the top is no longer liquid and the bottom is nicely browned (use a large spatula and/or your fingers to check), about 1 minute. Flip the crepe, using the spatula and/or your fingers, and cook the other side lightly, 15 seconds more. Transfer to a plate.

3. Repeat with the remaining batter until you have four crepes, stacking them on the plate once each is cooked. (There is enough batter for five crepes, so you can consider the first one a trial run. You will not need to oil the pan each time, but you may want to re-oil after the second or third crepe.) The crepes may be made up to 2 days ahead and stored between layers of parchment or waxed paper in a resealable plastic bag in the refrigerator.

(Continued)

4. To assemble, lay a crepe flat on a clean work surface. Sprinkle it with the cheese, then arrange two slices of the ham and ½ cup of the spinach on the crepe. Fold the crepe in half, and then in half again to form a triangle. Repeat with the remaining crepes and filling.

5. Lightly brush the same nonstick skillet with oil and heat it over medium heat. Place the crepes in the pan and cook, turning once, until the cheese begins to melt, 1 to 2 minutes per side. Serve immediately.

Makes 4 servings

SERVING SIZE: 1 crepe

PER SERVING: Calories 350; Total Fat 21 g (Sat Fat 7 g, Mono Fat 9 g, Poly Fat 2 g); Protein 24 g; Carb 17 g; Fiber 4 g; Cholesterol 160 mg; Sodium 920 mg; Total Sugar 4 g (Added Sugar 0 g)

EXCELLENT SOURCE OF: calcium, phosphorous, protein, vitamin A, vitamin K

GOOD SOURCE OF: fiber, folate, iodine, iron, manganese, phosphorous, riboflavin, selenium, vitamin C

lamb skewers with herbed bulgur pilaf

This dish provides a full, satisfying meal with skewers of tender, spiced lamb over a warm grain pilaf with gently wilted spinach, cooked all in one skillet. Besides the one-pan convenience, cooking the meat in the skillet before the bulgur goes in means the browned juices from the meat wind up giving an extra depth of flavor to the grain. Handfuls of fresh baby spinach are added to the skillet with the cooked grain, where it softens in the accumulated heat before a fresh burst of parsley, mint, and lemon are stirred in. Served with the lamb skewers on top, it is delicious just like that, but a finishing sprinkle of briny feta makes it even better. For this dish, you will need four wooden or metal skewers that fit into your skillet.

½ teaspoon ground cumin

¼ teaspoon ground coriander

⅛ teaspoon ground cinnamon

Pinch of cayenne pepper

¾ teaspoon salt, divided

½ teaspoon freshly ground black pepper, divided

1¼ pounds boneless lamb leg, trimmed, cut into 1-inch cubes

2 tablespoons olive oil, divided

1 medium-size onion, diced

1 garlic clove, minced

1 cup quick-cooking (fine) bulgur wheat

1½ cups low-sodium chicken broth

2 cups lightly packed fresh spinach, chopped

¼ cup fresh parsley, chopped, plus more for garnish

¼ cup fresh mint, chopped, plus more for garnish

1 lemon: 1 tablespoon juice, plus wedges for garnish

¼ cup crumbled feta cheese (optional)

1. Combine the cumin, coriander, cinnamon, cayenne, and ¼ teaspoon each of the salt and pepper in a medium-size bowl. Add the lamb and toss to coat. Cut the bottom end off four wooden skewers, if necessary, so they fit into a large, lidded skillet, or use metal skewers short enough to fit into the pan. Thread the meat onto the skewers.

2. Heat 1 tablespoon of the olive oil over medium-high heat, then place the lamb skewers in the pan and cook, turning two or three times, until they are browned on all sides and cooked to your liking, about 5 minutes total for medium-rare. Transfer the skewers to a plate and cover it with foil.

3. Lower the heat to medium, add the remaining tablespoon of oil to the pan, then add the onion and cook, stirring frequently, until it has softened, about 5 minutes. Stir in the garlic and bulgur and stir until the bulgur is coated with the oil and toasted a bit, 30 seconds. Add the chicken broth, and the remaining ½ teaspoon salt and ¼ teaspoon pepper, and bring to a boil, then cover, lower the heat to low, and simmer for 10 minutes. Without stirring the bulgur, add the spinach to the pan, remove from the heat, cover, and let steam for 5 minutes. Stir with a fork to fluff, then add the parsley, mint, and lemon juice and stir to combine. Serve the skewers on top of the pilaf, garnished with additional herbs and lemon wedges, and sprinkled with feta, if desired.

The cooked skewers and the pilaf will keep in an airtight container in the refrigerator for up to 4 days.

Makes 4 servings

SERVING SIZE: 1 cup pilaf and 1 lamb skewer

PER SERVING: Calories 460; Total Fat 21 g (Sat Fat 7 g, Mono Fat 11 g, Poly Fat 2 g); Protein 37 g; Carb 32 g; Fiber 6 g; Cholesterol 110 mg; Sodium 600 mg; Total Sugar 1 g (Added Sugar 0 g)

EXCELLENT SOURCE OF: fiber, iron, magnesium, manganese, niacin, phosphorous, protein, riboflavin, vitamin A, vitamin B_6, vitamin B_{12}, vitamin C, vitamin K, zinc

GOOD SOURCE OF: copper, folate, pantothenic acid, potassium, thiamine, selenium

spring vegetable stew with lamb

This dish conjures the delight of spring on multiple levels. It features lamb—a cornerstone of many spring holiday traditions—as well as asparagus, peas, leek, and fresh herbs, vibrant green produce that also symbolizes the season of renewal. But this stew also gives you exactly the kind of satisfaction you want when the weather turns warmer but you still want something hearty that takes the edge off the lingering chill in the air. It dishes up all the low- and slow-cooked comfort that stews are known for, but in a fresher, lighter, more vegetable-forward way. Don't forget the finishing sprinkle of fresh parsley and mint—they take it to another level. To make it gluten-free, you can use half the quantity (1 tablespoon) of gluten-free cornstarch instead of the all-purpose flour.

1¼ pounds lean boneless, trimmed lamb shoulder or stew meat, cut into ½-inch pieces

1 teaspoon salt, plus more to taste, divided

½ teaspoon freshly ground black pepper, plus more to taste, divided

3 tablespoons olive oil, divided

1 large leek, white and light green parts, washed well and chopped (about 2 cups)

3 garlic cloves, minced

2 tablespoons all-purpose flour

¾ cup dry white wine, such as sauvignon blanc

2½ cups low-sodium chicken broth

12 ounces waxy white potatoes, such as fingerling or Yukon gold, unpeeled, cut into ¾-inch chunks

½ bunch asparagus, trimmed and cut on the diagonal into ¾-inch pieces

1 cup fresh or frozen peas

2 tablespoons chopped fresh parsley leaves

1 tablespoon chopped fresh mint leaves

1. Sprinkle the lamb with ¼ teaspoon each of the salt and pepper. Heat 2 tablespoons of the oil in a large, heavy pot over medium-high heat and cook the lamb, stirring once or twice, until it is well browned, about 5 minutes. Transfer the meat to a plate.

2. Lower the heat to medium, add the remaining tablespoon of oil to the pot, then add the leek and cook until softened, about 3 minutes. Add the garlic, sprinkle with the flour, and cook, stirring, for 30 seconds. Add the wine and cook, stirring, scraping up any browned bits, until thickened, about 30 seconds.

3. Add the broth and return the browned meat with any accumulated juices to the pot and bring to a simmer. Lower the heat to very low, cover, and cook for 45 minutes, stirring occasionally. Stir in the potatoes and the remaining ¾ teaspoon of salt and ¼ teaspoon of pepper and simmer, covered, until the meat and potatoes are fork-tender, about 30 minutes more. Add the asparagus and peas, return to a simmer, then cook, covered, until they are firm-tender, about 5 minutes more. Season with additional salt and pepper to taste. Serve sprinkled with the parsley and mint.

The stew will keep in an airtight container in the refrigerator for up to 4 days.

Makes 4 servings

SERVING SIZE: 1½ cups

PER SERVING: Calories 500; Total Fat 22 g (Sat Fat 6 g, Mono Fat 12 g, Poly Fat 2 g); Protein 35 g; Carb 35 g; Fiber 6 g; Cholesterol 90 mg; Sodium 820 mg; Total Sugar 5 g (Added Sugar 0 g)

EXCELLENT SOURCE OF: copper, fiber, folate, iron, manganese, niacin, phosphorous, protein, riboflavin, thiamine, vitamin A, vitamin B$_6$, vitamin B$_{12}$, vitamin C, vitamin K, zinc

GOOD SOURCE OF: magnesium, pantothenic acid, potassium, selenium

beef, barley, and many vegetable soup

On one hand there is beef barley soup, and on the other there's mushroom barley soup, but why choose between the two when you can have both in one soup? Heck, why not add a bunch of other vegetables—carrots, celery, tomatoes, and chard or spinach—to the mix for even more color, flavor, and nutrition? And how about a handful of fresh dill for an earthy herbal essence? It's that kind of thinking that led me right to this wonderful, filling, meal-in-a-bowl with tender beef in every bite balanced with a bounty of whole-grain, plant-powered goodness.

12 ounces lean beef stew meat, cut into ½-inch pieces

1 teaspoon salt, divided

½ teaspoon freshly ground pepper, divided

2 tablespoons olive oil, divided

1 large onion, diced

8 ounces cremini mushrooms, coarsely chopped

2 medium-size carrots, diced

2 celery stalks, diced

½ small bunch green Swiss chard, stems and leaves separated and chopped, or 3 cups lightly packed chopped spinach

2 garlic cloves, minced

4 cups low-sodium beef broth

1 (14-ounce) can no-salt-added diced tomatoes

½ cup pearled barley

⅓ cup coarsely chopped fresh dill

1. Season the meat with ¼ teaspoon each of the salt and pepper. Heat 1 tablespoon of the olive oil in a large soup pot over medium-high heat. Add the meat to the pot and cook, stirring occasionally, until well browned, about 5 minutes. Transfer the meat to a plate.

2. Add the remaining tablespoon of olive oil to the pot, then add the onion and mushrooms and cook until softened, about 4 minutes. Add the carrots, celery, chopped chard stems, if using (if you are using spinach, do not add it here), and garlic and cook for 2 minutes more.

3. Add the broth, 2 cups of water, the diced tomatoes with their juices, and the barley and return the meat with any accumulated juices to the pot. Bring to a boil, then lower the heat to low, cover, and simmer until the barley is cooked and the meat is tender, about 1 hour. Add the chard leaves or spinach and the dill and cook for 2 minutes more, then serve.

The soup will keep in an airtight container in the refrigerator for up to 4 days, or in the freezer for 3 months.

Makes 4 servings

SERVING SIZE: 2¼ cups

PER SERVING: Calories 340; Total Fat 13 g (Sat Fat 2.5 g, Mono Fat 7 g, Poly Fat 1 g); Protein 21 g; Carb 38 g; Fiber 16 g; Cholesterol 50 mg; Sodium 860 mg; Total Sugar 9 g (Added Sugar 0 g)

EXCELLENT SOURCE OF: copper, iron, magnesium, manganese, niacin, phosphorous, potassium, protein, selenium, thiamine, riboflavin, vitamin A, vitamin K, zinc

GOOD SOURCE OF: calcium, folate, molybdenum, pantothenic acid

beef stew with farro and mushrooms

An ancient grain—farro—gives this savory beef stew a thoroughly modern appeal. Farro, a type of whole wheat that has been enjoyed for centuries in Italy, has a wonderful toothsomeness and mildly nutty flavor—not to mention whole-grain nutrition—and it holds it shape beautifully, making it perfect for salads, soups, and stews like this one. Here, it adds a unique dimension of and taste and texture to an otherwise classic savory beef stew with a garlic, rosemary, and red wine–infused broth, cremini mushrooms, and carrots. It's full of the deep meaty flavor and homey goodness you expect from a satisfying bowl of beef stew, but with an intriguing, unexpected twist that makes it even better. (If using pearled or quick-cooking farro, skip the soaking step and add it later to the stew, so that it cooks in the time indicated on the package.)

1 pound lean boneless chuck roast, trimmed and cut into 1-inch pieces

¾ teaspoon salt, divided

½ teaspoon freshly ground black pepper, divided

3 tablespoons olive oil, divided

10 ounces cremini mushrooms, trimmed and quartered

1 medium-size onion, chopped

2 garlic cloves, minced

1 tablespoon chopped fresh rosemary, or 1 teaspoon dried

2 tablespoons tomato paste

1 cup dry red wine

2½ cups low-sodium beef broth

½ cup whole (unpearled) farro

3 medium-size carrots, cut into ½-inch-thick rounds

¼ cup fresh parsley leaves

1. Sprinkle the beef with ¼ teaspoon each of the salt and pepper. Heat 1 tablespoon of the oil in a large, heavy pot over medium-high heat and cook the beef until it is browned, about 5 minutes. Transfer the meat to a plate.

2. Add another tablespoon of oil to the pot, then add the mushrooms and cook until they release their liquid and begin to brown, 5 minutes. (Add a tablespoon or two of water to the pot if it seems too dry.) Transfer the mushrooms to another plate.

3. Lower the heat to medium, add the remaining tablespoon of oil to the pot, then add the onion and cook until it is softened, about 3 minutes. Add the garlic and rosemary and cook, stirring, for 30 seconds. Stir in the tomato paste and then the wine. Bring to a boil and allow to reduce until the liquid is reduced by about half, 2 minutes. Add the broth, return the browned meat with any accumulated juices to the pot, and bring to a boil. Lower the heat to low, cover, and simmer for 1 hour. Place the farro in a bowl and add enough warm water to cover it. Let the farro soak as the stew simmers.

4. Once the meat is tender, drain the farro and stir it into the pot, then add the carrots, the mushrooms with their accumulated liquid, and the remaining ½ teaspoon of salt and ¼ teaspoon of pepper. Return to a boil and then simmer, covered, until the farro and carrots are tender, 30 to 35 minutes more. Season with additional salt and pepper to taste. Serve garnished with the parsley.

(Continued)

The stew will keep in an airtight container in the refrigerator for up to 4 days, or in the freezer for 3 months.

Makes 4 servings

SERVING SIZE: 1½ cups

PER SERVING: Calories 470; Total Fat 22 g (Sat Fat 5 g, Mono Fat 13 g, Poly Fat 2 g); Protein 30 g; Carb 29 g; Fiber 4 g; Cholesterol 50 mg; Sodium 850 mg; Total Sugar 7 g (Added Sugar 0 g)

EXCELLENT SOURCE OF: iron, niacin, phosphorous, potassium, protein, riboflavin, selenium, vitamin A, vitamin B_6, vitamin B_{12}, vitamin C, vitamin K, zinc

GOOD SOURCE OF: copper, fiber, folate, magnesium, manganese, pantothenic acid, thiamine

smoky black bean and pork stew

My husband teases me when, during dinner, I start talking about what to have for dinner the next night. It's not that I am ignoring my own live-in-the-moment credo—it's just that some meals need to be thought of the day before, and this is one of them. This stew is simple to make, but it does require soaking the beans ahead of time. The belly-warming stew, a hearty duo of black beans and pork infused with the smoky essence of chorizo, becomes a dark canvas for contrastingly fresh, bright condiments—chopped tomatoes, cilantro, and chopped onion. It is a dish that leverages all the comforting flavor of a classic bean and pork stew but in a much healthier way, with the beans taking center stage.

12 ounces boneless pork shoulder or stew meat, trimmed of all visible fat, cut into 1-inch pieces

¾ teaspoon salt, divided

¼ teaspoon freshly ground black pepper

2 tablespoons olive oil, divided

1 large onion, diced

4 garlic cloves, minced

1½ tablespoons smoked paprika

1 bay leaf

¼ teaspoon cayenne pepper

8 ounces dried black beans, soaked for at least 8 hours, or overnight, and drained

4 cups low-sodium chicken broth

2 ounces dried chorizo sausage, finely diced (½ cup)

1 tablespoon sherry vinegar

2 medium-size tomatoes, chopped

¼ cup finely diced red onion

¼ cup chopped fresh cilantro

1. Season the pork with ¼ teaspoon each of the salt and black pepper. Heat 1 tablespoon of the oil in a large soup pot. Add the pork and cook, stirring once or twice, until it is browned, 3 minutes. Transfer the meat to a plate.

2. Lower the heat to medium and add the remaining tablespoon of oil to the pot, then add the onion and cook until it is softened, 3 minutes. Add the garlic and cook for 30 seconds more. Then, add the paprika, bay leaf, cayenne, and the remaining ½ teaspoon of salt. Return the pork to the pot and add the beans, broth, and chorizo and bring to a boil. Lower the heat to medium-low and simmer, covered, stirring occasionally, for 50 minutes, then uncover, increase the heat to medium, and continue to cook until the beans and pork are tender and the liquid is reduced to the desired thickness, 10 to 20 minutes more.

3. Remove the bay leaf and stir in the vinegar. Serve in bowls topped with the tomato, onion, and cilantro.

The stew will keep in an airtight container in the refrigerator for up to 4 days, or in the freezer for 3 months.

Makes 4 servings

SERVING SIZE: 1 cup stew plus toppings

PER SERVING: Calories 490; Total Fat 20 g (Sat Fat 6 g, Mono Fat 11 g, Poly Fat 3 g); Protein 32 g; Carb 46 g; Fiber 11 g; Cholesterol 60 mg; Sodium 720 mg; Total Sugar 5 g (Added Sugar 0 g)

EXCELLENT SOURCE OF: copper, fiber, folate, iron, magnesium, manganese, niacin, phosphorous, potassium, protein, riboflavin, selenium, thiamine, vitamin A, vitamin B$_6$, vitamin C, vitamin K, zinc

GOOD SOURCE OF: calcium, pantothenic acid, vitamin B$_{12}$

ej's beef stew

My friend EJ is a passionate food lover whose family is originally from the Philippines, and whenever we get together, I inevitably wind up craving the exciting flavors he describes. Inspired by one of those conversations, this stew is a healthy take on a typical Filipino dish called mechado, which traditionally involves adding strips of pork fat. By using chuck roast here, you wind up with perfectly flavorful, tender morsels of meat without the added lard. The meat is simmered low and slow in an umami-rich mixture of tomato sauce and soy sauce that is made tantalizingly tangy with a generous squeeze of lemon juice. With onions, garlic, carrots, and potatoes, it's the same easy method you'd use to make your usual stew, but the punchy sauce and the final addition of red bell peppers make it an extraordinary meal.

1½ **pounds lean boneless chuck roast, trimmed and cut into 1-inch pieces**

¼ **teaspoon salt, plus more to taste**

½ **teaspoon freshly ground black pepper, plus more taste**

2 **tablespoons canola oil or other neutral-tasting oil**

1 **large onion, chopped**

4 **garlic cloves, minced**

1½ **cups low-sodium beef broth**

1 **cup no-salt-added tomato sauce**

¼ **cup freshly squeezed lemon juice**

3 **tablespoons reduced-sodium soy sauce**

1 **bay leaf**

1 **pound baby potatoes, unpeeled, halved**

3 **medium-size carrots, cut into 1-inch pieces**

2 **medium-size red bell peppers, seeded and cut into 1-inch cubes**

1. Sprinkle the beef with the salt and pepper. Heat the oil in a large pot over medium-high heat. Add the beef and cook, stirring two or three times, until browned on all sides, about 5 minutes. Transfer the meat to a plate.

2. Lower the heat to medium, add the onion to the pot, and cook until it is softened, about 5 minutes, then add the garlic and cook for 1 minute more. Add the broth, tomato sauce, lemon juice, soy sauce, and bay leaf. Return the meat with any accumulated juices to the pot and bring to a boil.

3. Lower the heat to low, cover, and cook for 1½ hours, stirring occasionally. Stir in the potatoes and carrots, return to a boil, then lower the heat to low and simmer, covered, until the vegetables are nearly fork-tender, 15 minutes more. Add the bell peppers and continue to cook until they are firm-tender and the potatoes are cooked, about 10 minutes more. Remove the bay leaf. Season with additional salt to taste and serve.

The stew will keep in an airtight container in the refrigerator for up to 4 days.

Makes 4 servings

SERVING SIZE: about 2 cups

PER SERVING: Calories 400; Total Fat 17 g (Sat Fat 4 g, Mono Fat 9 g, Poly Fat 3 g); Protein 33 g; Carb 33 g; Fiber 7 g; Cholesterol 85 mg; Sodium 850 mg; Total Sugar 9 g (Added Sugar 0 g)

EXCELLENT SOURCE OF: copper, fiber, iron, manganese, niacin, phosphorous, potassium, protein, riboflavin, selenium, vitamin A, vitamin B_6, vitamin B_{12}, vitamin C, zinc

GOOD SOURCE OF: folate, magnesium, molybdenum, pantothenic acid, thiamine

lamb meatballs with lentils in an aromatic tomato sauce

Here, lamb and lentils provide a one-two protein punch that's also a knockout flavor-wise with warm spices that ring of the Middle East. Fresh spinach leaves bring ribbons of color and vegetable nutrition to the meal, and a finishing dollop of yogurt adds cool creaminess that contrasts the warm earthy flavors in the bowl.

A couple of ingredient notes: The packaged ground lamb typically found in the meat case will most likely not be lean. It will work in the recipe, although you might want to drain some of the fat out of the pot after browning the meatballs, so you wind up with about 1 tablespoon in the pot at that stage. If possible, though, ask the butcher to grind some fresh for you from lean leg and/or shoulder cuts. Also, I chose beluga lentils for this dish because I like their contrasting color and the way they hold their shape, but green or brown lentils would work in this recipe, too.

¾ teaspoon ground cumin

¾ teaspoon ground coriander

¾ teaspoon salt

½ teaspoon freshly ground black pepper

¼ teaspoon ground cinnamon

¼ teaspoon crushed red pepper flakes, plus more to taste

¼ cup dried whole wheat bread crumbs

1 large egg yolk

2 tablespoons low-fat or whole milk

4 garlic cloves, minced, divided

12 ounces lean ground lamb

2 tablespoons olive oil

1 medium-size onion, diced

½ cup dry beluga lentils (black lentils)

1 (15-ounce) can no-salt-added tomato sauce

(Continued)

1. Combine the cumin, coriander, salt, black pepper, cinnamon, and red pepper flakes in a small bowl. Transfer 1 teaspoon of the spice mixture to a medium-size bowl. Add the bread crumbs, egg yolk, milk, and half of the garlic to the spices in the larger bowl and stir to combine. Then, add the lamb and mix with your hands to combine. Form the lamb into small meatballs, about 1 inch in diameter. (You should wind up with about twenty meatballs.)

2. Heat the oil in a large, wide pot over medium-high heat. Add the meatballs to the pot and cook, turning them two or three times, until they are browned all over, about 3 minutes total. Transfer the meatballs to a plate.

3. Lower the heat to medium, add the onion to the pot, and cook, stirring, until it is softened, 4 minutes. Add the remaining garlic and cook for 30 seconds more, then stir in the reserved spice mixture and the lentils. Add the tomato sauce, diced tomatoes with their juices, and 1¼ cups of water and bring to a boil.

4. Lower the heat to medium-low and simmer, uncovered, for 15 minutes, then return the meatballs with any accumulated juices to the pot and simmer, covered, until the lentils are tender, about 20 minutes more. Stir in the honey, if using, then add the spinach and cook until it is wilted, 1 minute more. Serve topped with a dollop of yogurt.

1 (14-ounce) can
no-salt-added diced
tomatoes

1 tablespoon honey
(optional)

3 cups baby spinach,
coarsely chopped

½ cup plain whole-milk
yogurt

The dish will keep in an airtight container in the refrigerator for up to 4 days, or in the freezer for 3 months.

Makes 4 servings

SERVING SIZE: 1½ cups meatballs, lentils, and sauce

PER SERVING: Calories 400; Total Fat 14 g (Sat Fat 4 g, Mono Fat 7 g, Poly Fat 1 g); Protein 31 g; Carb 39 g; Fiber 9 g; Cholesterol 105 mg; Sodium 630 mg; Total Sugar 12 g (Added Sugar 0 g)

EXCELLENT SOURCE OF: fiber, folate, iron, manganese, niacin, protein, vitamin A, vitamin B_6, vitamin B_{12}, vitamin C, vitamin K, zinc

GOOD SOURCE OF: calcium, magnesium, phosphorous, selenium, thiamine

herbed pork tenderloin with delicata squash and brussels sprouts

When the temperatures dip and the farmers' markets are flush with a multihued, late-season bounty, this meal is the easy answer to making the most of it. At its center is lean pork tenderloin, which is rubbed with an array of fresh herbs, garlic, and mustard and cooked to juicy perfection. Flanking the pork are half-moons of orange delicata squash (an especially easy choice because its peel is so tender that there is no need to remove it)—kissed with maple syrup and roasted until tender and caramelized—and deeply browned and crisped Brussels sprouts. While it is a meal that's inspired by autumn, it's one that will certainly be a bright spot throughout the winter months, too.

1 pound medium-size Brussels sprouts, trimmed and halved

3 tablespoons olive oil, divided

¾ teaspoon salt, divided

2 garlic cloves, finely minced

1½ teaspoons chopped fresh thyme

1½ teaspoons chopped fresh rosemary

1½ teaspoons chopped fresh sage

1 teaspoon Dijon mustard

¼ teaspoon freshly ground black pepper

1 large pork tenderloin (about 1 pound)

2 delicata squash (about 1 pound each), unpeeled, halved lengthwise, seeded, then cut crosswise into ¼-inch-thick slices

1 tablespoon pure maple syrup

1. Preheat the oven to 400°F. Place the Brussels sprouts on a sheet pan and toss with 1 tablespoon of the oil and ¼ teaspoon of the salt. Roast in the oven for 15 minutes.

2. While the sprouts are roasting, stir together 1 tablespoon of the oil, the garlic, thyme, rosemary, sage, and mustard, ¼ teaspoon of the salt, and the pepper in a large bowl. Place the pork in the bowl and rub the mixture all over the pork.

3. Move the Brussels sprouts to one end of the sheet pan. Place the pork on the center of the sheet pan, then place the squash onto the other side of the pan. Drizzle the squash with the remaining tablespoon of oil and ¼ teaspoon of salt, and the maple syrup and use tongs to toss slightly. Push the pork and sprouts over so the squash can be as much in a single layer as possible. It is okay if some pieces overlap. Return the pan to the oven.

4. When the pork reaches an internal temperature of 145°F for medium doneness, 20 to 25 minutes, remove it from the pan and let it rest on a cutting board for 5 to 10 minutes. If the vegetables are tender and nicely browned, remove the pan from the oven; otherwise return them to the oven to cook some more as the pork rests. Slice the pork and serve it with the squash and Brussels sprouts alongside.

The dish will keep in an airtight container in the refrigerator for up to 4 days and may be served warm or at room temperature.

Makes 4 servings

SERVING SIZE: about 6 slices pork, ¾ cup squash, and ½ cup Brussels sprouts

PER SERVING: Calories 370; Total Fat 12 g (Sat Fat 2 g, Mono Fat 7 g, Poly Fat 2 g); Protein 31 g; Carb 14 g; Fiber 4 g; Cholesterol 65 mg; Sodium 560 mg; Total Sugar 8 g (Added Sugar: 3 g)

EXCELLENT SOURCE OF: iron, magnesium, manganese, pantothenic acid, phosphorous, potassium, protein, selenium, thiamine, vitamin B_6, vitamin C, vitamin K, zinc

GOOD SOURCE OF: calcium, copper, fiber, vitamin B_{12}

steakhouse dinner: peppercorn-crusted steak with seasoned potato wedges and roasted broccoli

regularly crave a straightforward steakhouse dinner with a top-notch cut of beef, potatoes, and a green vegetable, paired with a big glass of full-bodied red wine. But I hardly ever visit an actual steakhouse because I can make this meal just as deliciously at home, so easily, and more healthfully. This recipe is case in point, with peppercorn-crusted filet mignon (in smart 5-ounce portions), crispy, addictively seasoned potato wedges (baked, not fried), and lusciously charred roasted broccoli (who needs a heavy cream sauce?), cooked all on one sheet pan. A key to its deliciousness is the step of browning the steak under the broiler on a rack on the sheet pan before cooking the other elements, then returning the steak to the pan to warm to desired doneness toward the end of cooking. Filet mignon can be kind of pricey, so feel free to substitute a less expensive but also lean and tender steak, such as sirloin, if you prefer.

1½ teaspoons black peppercorns

4 filet mignon steaks (about 5 ounces each)

¼ teaspoon coarse salt

3 medium-size Yukon gold potatoes (about 1 pound), unpeeled, cut into 8 wedges each

3 tablespoons olive oil, divided

½ teaspoon fine salt, divided

1 teaspoon onion powder

1 teaspoon granulated garlic

1 teaspoon paprika

Pinch of cayenne pepper (optional)

1 medium-size head broccoli, cut into 1½-inch florets

1. Place the peppercorns in a resealable plastic bag and use a mallet or rolling pin to crush coarsely. Alternatively, grind coarsely in a spice grinder. Sprinkle both sides of the steaks with the pepper and the coarse salt, pressing it in slightly so it adheres.

2. Set an oven rack in the highest position in the oven. Preheat the broiler. Line a sheet pan with foil and place a rack on top of the lined pan; place the steaks on the rack on top of the pan and broil on the top oven rack (with the meat about 2 inches from the flame) until the steaks are seared on the outside, about 2 minutes per side. Turn off the broiler and preheat the oven to 400°F. Transfer the steaks to a plate and remove the rack and the foil from the sheet pan.

3. Place the potatoes on the sheet pan, use tongs to toss with 1½ tablespoons of the oil and ¼ teaspoon of salt, and distribute the potatoes in a single layer on the pan with one of the cut sides facing down. Roast in the oven until the potatoes are nicely browned on the bottom, 20 minutes.

4. Meanwhile, combine the onion powder, granulated garlic, paprika, and cayenne, if using, in a small bowl. Move the potatoes to one side of the pan and sprinkle them on both sides with the spice mixture. Place the broccoli on the other side of the sheet pan; drizzle with the remaining 1½ tablespoons of oil, sprinkle with the remaining ¼ teaspoon of salt, and use tongs to toss to coat. Return the sheet pan to the oven to roast for 15 minutes, then move the vegetables farther aside and place the steaks on the pan to cook to desired doneness, about 7 minutes for medium-rare.

5. Transfer the steaks to a clean serving plate, or individual plates, and allow to rest for 5 minutes before serving. Serve with the vegetables alongside.

Makes 4 servings

SERVING SIZE: 1 steak and about 1 cup total potatoes and broccoli

PER SERVING: Calories 430; Total Fat 21 g (Sat Fat 5 g, Mono Fat 11 g, Poly Fat 2 g); Protein 36 g; Carb 28 g; Fiber 5 g; Cholesterol 95 mg; Sodium 560 mg; Total Sugar 3 g (Added Sugar 0 g)

EXCELLENT SOURCE OF: iron, niacin, phosphorous, potassium, protein, selenium, vitamin B_6, vitamin B_{12}, vitamin C, vitamin K, zinc

GOOD SOURCE OF: calcium, copper, fiber, folate, magnesium, manganese, pantothenic acid, riboflavin, thiamine

apricot-ginger glazed pork loin and carrots over napa cabbage

Here, apricot preserves are brightened with fresh ginger, made umami-rich with soy sauce and tomato paste, and kicked up with garlic and sriracha to make a mouthwatering glaze for a juicy (but lean) pork loin roast. In the oven, the roast—which is flanked on the sheet pan by ginger-spiked carrots—caramelizes beautifully, providing flavorful pan juices that are enhanced with sweet-tangy pineapple juice. The final plate is absolutely luscious, with the thinly sliced glazed pork and intensely flavorful, roasted carrots served over a crunch of napa cabbage that has yielded slightly to a drizzle of warm, accumulated pan juices.

¼ cup apricot preserves

1 tablespoon tomato paste

2 tablespoons reduced-sodium soy sauce, divided

2½ teaspoons finely grated fresh ginger, divided

1 teaspoon unseasoned rice vinegar

1 teaspoon sriracha

1 garlic clove, minced

1½ pounds medium-size carrots, peeled

1 tablespoon canola oil or other neutral-tasting oil

¼ teaspoon salt

¼ teaspoon freshly ground black pepper

1½ pounds boneless pork loin roast

1 cup pineapple juice

3 cups low-sodium chicken broth, divided, plus more as needed

6 cups thinly sliced napa cabbage (½ medium-size head)

2 scallions, thinly sliced, green and white parts

1. Preheat the oven to 375°F. Combine the apricot preserves, tomato paste, 1 tablespoon of the soy sauce, 1½ teaspoons of the ginger, and the rice vinegar, sriracha, and garlic in a medium-size bowl.

2. Cut the carrots on the diagonal into 1½-inch-long pieces. Halve any thicker pieces lengthwise so the pieces are all about the same thickness. Place the carrots on a sheet pan and toss with the oil, remaining teaspoon of ginger, and ¼ teaspoon each of the salt and pepper. Move the carrots over to either side of the pan to make room for the pork in the middle.

3. Place the pork on the pan and spread half of the apricot glaze on top. Pour the pineapple juice onto the pan and place in the oven. Bake for 25 minutes. (Check the pan every once in a while throughout cooking and add a little extra broth if the pan is getting very dry.)

4. Remove the pan from the oven, toss the carrots, and spread the remaining glaze over the pork. Pour 1 cup of broth into the pan and return to the oven to bake for another 25 minutes. Then, remove from the oven, toss the carrots again, add another cup of broth to the pan, return to the oven, and bake until the pork reaches an internal temperature of 145°F and the carrots are tender, about 15 minutes more.

(Continued)

5. Transfer the pork to a cutting board to rest for 10 minutes and then slice thinly. Transfer the carrots to a bowl and cover to keep warm. Add the remaining cup of chicken broth and tablespoon of soy sauce to the sheet pan; return the pan to the oven to warm and reduce the liquid as the pork rests, about 8 minutes. Transfer the sauce to a small bowl or pitcher. The pork, carrots, and sauce will keep in the refrigerator for up to 4 days. Store the sauce in a separate airtight container.

6. To serve, place 1½ cups of the cabbage on each plate. Drizzle each with about 2 tablespoons of the sauce, then arrange the pork slices and carrots on top. Sprinkle with the scallions and serve.

Makes 4 servings

SERVING SIZE: 1½ cups cabbage, about 3 slices pork, and ½ cup carrots

PER SERVING: Calories 420; Total Fat 8 g (Sat Fat 2 g, Mono Fat 4 g, Poly Fat 2 g); Protein 39 g; Carb 45 g; Fiber 7 g; Cholesterol 90 mg; Sodium 850 mg; Total Sugar 28 g (Added Sugar 0 g)

EXCELLENT SOURCE OF: fiber, niacin, phosphorous, potassium, protein, riboflavin, selenium, thiamine, vitamin A, vitamin B_6, vitamin C, vitamin K, zinc

GOOD SOURCE OF: calcium, copper, folate, iron, magnesium, manganese, molybdenum, pantothenic acid, vitamin B_{12}

honey-mustard pork chops with sweet-tart warm slaw

Here, juicy pork chops are slathered with a honey-mustard mixture and cooked on a rack on top of a sheet pan full of colorful roasted slaw—red cabbage, onion, and carrots—which has been doused in a sweet-tart dressing. A finishing toss of toasted pumpkin seeds adds a delightful nutty crunch and unexpected flavor. The idea to include the pumpkin seeds came to me after a visit to Vienna, Austria, where I learned they often drizzle their vegetables with a dark, deeply flavorful toasted pumpkin seed oil. I came home with a bottle and have been enamored with the vegetable–pumpkin seed pairing ever since. I typically warm a loaf of crusty, dark rye bread in the oven, while everything is roasting, to serve with this dish.

¼ cup hulled pumpkin seeds (pepitas)

6 cups lightly packed, thinly sliced red cabbage

1 small onion, sliced thinly into half-moons

2 medium-size carrots, shredded into ribbons using a vegetable peeler

2 tablespoons olive oil

3 tablespoons plus ¼ teaspoon cider vinegar

2 tablespoons honey

½ teaspoon salt

¼ teaspoon freshly ground black pepper

1½ tablespoons grainy Dijon mustard

4 bone-in pork loin chops, 1 inch thick (about 10 ounces each)

1. Preheat the oven to 375°F. Place the pumpkin seeds on a dry sheet pan and toast in the oven until they are fragrant, about 3 minutes, then transfer them to a plate.

2. Place the cabbage, onion, and carrots on the same sheet pan, drizzle with the oil, 3 tablespoons of the vinegar, 1 tablespoon of the honey, and the salt and pepper. Use tongs to toss to coat. (Don't forget the pan may still be a bit hot.)

3. Stir together the mustard with the remaining tablespoon of the honey and ¼ teaspoon of the vinegar in a small bowl. Place a rack that fits into the sheet pan on top of the vegetables. Place the pork chops on the rack and brush the mustard mixture generously onto both sides of the pork chops.

4. Roast in the middle of the oven until the vegetables have softened and the pork reaches an internal temperature of 135°F, 20 to 25 minutes. Then, transfer the whole vegetable and pork setup to the top rack in the oven and broil on HIGH for 2 minutes, then flip the chops over and continue to broil until the chops are cooked to an internal temperature of 145°F and have a nice char on the outside, and the vegetables have softened further and begin to brown along the edges of the pan, 2 to 4 minutes more, or longer if you like the pork more well done.

(Continued)

5. Transfer the pork to serving plates. Remove the rack from the top of the sheet pan and toss the pumpkin seeds with the vegetables. Serve the warm slaw alongside the pork.

The dish will keep in an airtight container in the refrigerator for up to 4 days and may be served warm or at room temperature.

Makes 4 servings

SERVING SIZE: 1 pork chop and about ¾ cup slaw

PER SERVING: Calories 370; Total Fat 15 g (Sat Fat 3 g, Mono Fat 8 g, Poly Fat 3 g); Protein 38 g; Carb 22 g; Fiber 3 g; Cholesterol 80 mg; Sodium 590 mg; Total Sugar 14 g (Added Sugar 9 g)

EXCELLENT SOURCE OF: magnesium, manganese, niacin, phosphorous, potassium, protein, riboflavin, selenium, thiamine, vitamin B$_6$, vitamin C, vitamin K, zinc

GOOD SOURCE OF: copper, fiber, iron, pantothenic acid

sheet pan steak fajitas

ajitas lend themselves so easily to sheet pan cooking. The technique comes in especially handy when it is too chilly or rainy outside to cook on the grill. Here, one pan plays three roles—to roast, broil, and warm. The result is classic fajita flavor in a fuss-free, healthy way, with extra peppers (poblanos are ideal because they have a lot of flavor and just a hint of heat, but you could use green bell peppers instead); thinly sliced (and smartly portioned) lean meat that is tender and flavorful; and fragrant, warm, whole-grain corn tortillas (instead of white flour ones) to pile everything into. You gotta love a dinner that dishes up that much goodness with an easy cleanup to boot!

3 tablespoons freshly squeezed lime juice

¼ cup olive oil, divided

1 tablespoon dark brown sugar

1½ teaspoons chili powder

½ teaspoon ground cumin

2 garlic cloves, smashed and quartered

¾ teaspoon salt, divided

¼ teaspoon cayenne pepper

1¼ pounds flank steak

4 poblano or Anaheim peppers, cored and cut lengthwise into 1-inch-thick strips

1 large onion, cut into ¾-inch wedges

8 corn tortillas

¼ cup fresh cilantro leaves

8 lime wedges

1. Whisk together the lime juice, 3 tablespoons of the olive oil, 2 tablespoons of water, the brown sugar, chili powder, cumin, and garlic, ½ teaspoon of the salt, and the cayenne in a small bowl or pitcher. Place the steak in a resealable plastic bag; add the marinade to the bag, and marinate for at least 2 hours and up to 12 hours.

2. Preheat the oven to 425°F. Toss the poblano peppers on a sheet pan with 1½ teaspoons of the oil and ⅛ teaspoon of salt, then place in the oven and roast for 10 minutes. Move the peppers to one side of the pan, then place the onion on the other side and toss with the remaining 1½ teaspoons of oil and ⅛ teaspoon of salt. Return the pan to the oven and roast until the peppers and onion are both softened and nicely charred in spots, another 20 to 25 minutes. Transfer the vegetables to a dish and cover to keep warm.

3. Place an oven rack into the highest position in the oven. Preheat the broiler to HIGH. Line the sheet pan with foil and place a rack on top of it. Remove the steak from the marinade, discarding the marinade, and place it on top of the rack on the sheet pan. Broil until the meat is charred on the outside and medium-rare inside, 5 minutes per side. Then, transfer to a cutting board to rest for 5 minutes, before slicing thinly against the grain. While the meat rests, warm the tortillas by placing them on the same rack and sheet pan that held the meat and broiling them for 30 seconds. Remove them from the broiler and wrap them in a cloth napkin or clean kitchen towel to keep warm.

(Continued)

4. To serve, place three or four slices of meat and some of the peppers and onion onto each tortilla. Sprinkle each with cilantro and serve with lime wedges.

The steak, peppers, and onion will keep in an airtight container in the refrigerator for up to 4 days.

Makes 4 servings

SERVING SIZE: 2 fajitas

PER SERVING: Calories 430; Total Fat 18 g (Sat Fat 5 g, Mono Fat 9 g, Poly Fat 4 g); Protein 35 g; Carb 34 g; Fiber 5 g; Cholesterol 100 mg; Sodium 370 mg; Total Sugar 5 g (Added Sugar 1 g)

EXCELLENT SOURCE OF: folate, iron, niacin, phosphorous, protein, selenium, vitamin B_6, vitamin B_{12}, vitamin C, zinc

GOOD SOURCE OF: copper, fiber, iron, magnesium, manganese, pantothenic acid, potassium, riboflavin, thiamine, vitamin A

beef tenderloin with rosemary, balsamic roasted tomatoes, shallots, and polenta

When you want an impressive dinner that is on the fancy side, but still relaxed and approachable, this meal is the answer. The cut of meat—tenderloin—automatically says "this is special" and seasoning it with fresh rosemary, garlic, olive oil, salt, and pepper gives it just the flavor enhancement it deserves. The meat is browned first under the broiler, then joined on the sheet pan to roast with whole grape tomatoes, shallots, and rounds of prepared polenta—hardly any chopping or prep is required. As they roast, the tomatoes burst and brown beautifully and the shallots soften and caramelize, while the polenta becomes crisp on the outside and warm and creamy inside. A drizzle of aged balsamic vinegar finishes the vegetables with luxurious, sweet tanginess. All together on the plate they are an elegant, easy-to-love match for the rosemary-scented, ultratender beef.

1 large garlic clove, finely minced

¾ teaspoon salt, divided

3 tablespoons olive oil, divided

1 tablespoon finely chopped rosemary

¾ teaspoon freshly ground black pepper

1¼ pounds beef tenderloin roast

2 pints grape tomatoes

4 medium-size shallots, peeled and quartered lengthwise

1 (1-pound) tube prepared polenta, sliced into 8 slices about ¾-inch thick

1 teaspoon aged balsamic vinegar

2 tablespoons chopped fresh parsley

1. Preheat the broiler to HIGH. Place the garlic on a cutting board and sprinkle ½ teaspoon of the salt over it, then mash them together with the flat side of a knife blade to form a coarse paste. Place the garlic paste in a small bowl with 1 tablespoon of the olive oil, the rosemary, and ½ teaspoon of the pepper and stir to combine. Rub the mixture all over the meat.

2. Line a sheet pan with foil and place a metal rack on top of the lined pan; place the meat on the rack and broil about 2 inches from the flame until the top of the meat is browned, about 3 minutes. Turn off the broiler and preheat the oven to 425°F. Transfer the meat to a plate and remove the rack and the foil from the sheet pan.

3. Place the tomatoes and shallots on the pan. Drizzle them with 1 tablespoon of the oil and the remaining ¼ teaspoon each of salt and pepper. Toss them with tongs, then push them over to one half of the pan. Place the meat, browned side up, in the center of the pan. Brush the polenta slices with the remaining tablespoon of oil and place them on the other side of the meat on the pan.

4. Bake for 15 minutes, then stir the tomatoes and shallots and flip the polenta slices. Return the pan to the oven and continue to bake until the meat reaches an internal temperature of 130°F for medium rare, 10 to 15 minutes more. Transfer the meat to a cutting board and allow to rest for 5 to 10 minutes before

slicing against the grain into ¼-inch-thick slices. While the meat is resting, return the tomatoes and polenta to the oven to continue baking until the tomatoes have burst and the shallots are soft and both are browned in spots, 5 to 10 minutes. Drizzle the tomatoes and shallots with the balsamic vinegar. Serve the meat with the polenta, tomatoes, and shallots alongside and garnish with parsley.

The dish will keep in an airtight container in the refrigerator for up to 4 days.

Makes 4 servings

SERVING SIZE: 3 slices meat, 2 polenta rounds, and ⅔ cup tomatoes and shallots

PER SERVING: Calories 420; Total Fat 22 g (Sat Fat 6 g, Mono Fat 11 g, Poly Fat 2 g); Protein 33 g; Carb 23 g; Fiber 3 g; Cholesterol 75 mg; Sodium 610 mg; Total Sugar 7 g (Added Sugar 0 g)

EXCELLENT SOURCE OF: iron, protein, vitamin A, vitamin C, vitamin K

GOOD SOURCE OF: fiber, folate, manganese, molybdenum, potassium, vitamin B$_6$

desserts

polenta cake with red grapes

This scrumptious cake has a rustic elegance that lets you imagine yourself in a charming farmhouse in the Tuscan wine country. Yellow cornmeal (a.k.a. polenta) gives it a delightfully distinctive grainy texture; pure olive oil makes it rich and ultra-moist; and the fresh red grapes it is studded with not only look like edible gems, the fruit tastes even sweeter and plumper once baked. Without any refined sugar, white flour, or butter, it is also much better for you than a standard cake, without sacrificing a drop of flavor. Sit down and savor it with an espresso, a cup of tea, or even a glass of fruity wine.

1 cup whole wheat pastry flour

½ cup yellow cornmeal (fine to medium grind)

1½ teaspoons baking powder

¼ teaspoon salt

½ cup olive oil, plus more for brushing skillet

½ cup mild-tasting honey

2 large eggs

1 teaspoon pure vanilla extract

1 teaspoon finely grated lemon zest

1¾ cups medium-size red seedless grapes (about 10 ounces) washed and patted dry

Confectioners' sugar (optional)

1. Preheat the oven to 325°F. Brush a 10-inch cast-iron or other ovenproof skillet with olive oil. Whisk together the flour, cornmeal, baking powder, and salt in a medium-size bowl.

2. Beat the olive oil, honey, and eggs in another medium-size bowl until incorporated. Stir in the vanilla and lemon zest, then add the flour mixture in three batches, stirring to incorporate after adding each batch. Stir in half of the grapes. Transfer the batter to the skillet and bake, in the middle of the oven, for 10 minutes, then scatter the remaining grapes on top of the cake and continue to bake until it is golden and a toothpick inserted into the center comes out clean, 20 to 25 minutes more.

3. Remove from the oven and let rest in the skillet for 10 to 15 minutes before sprinkling with confectioners' sugar, if desired, and cutting into eight wedges. The cake will keep for a week in an airtight container in the refrigerator.

Makes 8 servings

SERVING SIZE: 1 wedge

PER SERVING: Calories 260; Total Fat 15 g (Sat Fat 2.5 g, Mono Fat 10 g, Poly Fat 2 g); Protein 4 g; Carb 38 g; Fiber 2 g; Cholesterol 45 mg; Sodium 90 mg; Total Sugar 24 g (Added Sugar 17 g)

GOOD SOURCE OF: calcium, vitamin K

maple pecan dessert pancake

This lovely dessert of buttery pecans cooked in a skillet with a maple-sweetened egg batter can be served warm or chilled, and has a very different personality depending on which way you go. Warm, it feels like a homey, sweet pancake; but chilled, it becomes more of an elegant, flanlike tart, thanks to its custardy batter and caramelized sugars. The pecans do double duty ground in a food processor two ways: finely, so they behave like a flour that's integrated into the pancake, and coarsely, so they provide a distinctive nutty crunch.

1 cup pecan pieces, divided

4 large eggs

⅓ cup whole milk

¼ cup pure maple syrup

¼ cup light brown sugar

¼ teaspoon ground cinnamon

Pinch of salt

1 tablespoon unsalted butter

1 teaspoon confectioners' sugar

1. Preheat the oven to 400°F. Place half of the pecans in the small bowl of a food processor and process them until they are finely ground. Transfer to a bowl. Place the remaining pecans in the processor and pulse to coarsely chop.

2. Whisk together the eggs, milk, maple syrup, brown sugar, cinnamon, and salt in a medium-size bowl. Stir in both the finely ground and coarsely chopped pecans.

3. Heat the butter in a 10-inch ovenproof skillet over medium-low heat. Add the batter to the pan. Cook (without stirring) until the edges begin to set, 5 minutes, then transfer to the oven and bake until completely set and golden brown, 10 minutes more. (The pancake will puff up in the oven and then fall into place as it cools.)

4. Allow to cool in the pan for 10 minutes and then sprinkle with confectioners' sugar and cut into eight wedges. Serve warm or chilled. The pancake will keep for up to 3 days in an airtight container in the refrigerator.

Makes 8 servings

SERVING SIZE: 1 wedge

PER SERVING: Calories 210; Total Fat 15 g (Sat Fat 3 g, Mono Fat 1 g, Poly Fat 3 g); Protein 5 g; Carb 17 g; Fiber 1 g; Cholesterol 100 mg; Sodium 70 mg; Total Sugar 14 g (Added Sugar 13 g)

GOOD SOURCE OF: iodine, manganese, riboflavin, selenium

peanut butter skillet cookie

'm one of those people who like to snack on a spoonful of peanut butter right out of the jar, so for me, the best peanut butter cookies are those that let the nutty spread do the talking. With this recipe, the peanut butter is front and center—the other ingredients just lift it into crunchy, delightfully sweet cookie form. Using a skillet saves you the step of having to roll each cookie into little balls and smoosh them down like you typically would. And these are better for you than the usual peanut butter cookie, too, with considerably less sugar and butter than many recipes, plus whole-grain flour instead of refined. This cookie is simple and classic as is, but if you want to add some wow factor, drizzle the top with melted chocolate. You can't go wrong with that combination. (Use a cup-for-cup gluten-free flour to make this gluten-free.)

½ cup whole wheat pastry flour

½ teaspoon baking soda

¼ teaspoon salt

⅓ cup packed light brown sugar

⅓ cup granulated sugar

¼ cup unsalted butter, softened, plus more for coating skillet

¾ cup smooth peanut butter

1 large egg

½ teaspoon pure vanilla extract

1. Preheat the oven to 350°F. Coat a 10-inch ovenproof skillet with butter.

2. Whisk together the flour, baking soda, and salt in a large bowl. Place the brown sugar, granulated sugar, and the butter in another large bowl and beat until well combined and fluffy. Then, beat in the peanut butter. Add the egg and the vanilla and beat until well combined. Gradually stir in the flour mixture.

3. Transfer the dough to the prepared skillet, spreading it to the edges and smoothing the top. Make a crosshatch pattern on the surface of the dough with the tip of a butter knife.

4. Bake in the middle of the oven until the edges are brown and crisp and the center is still soft, 25 to 30 minutes.

5. Remove from the oven and let cool in the skillet on a wire rack for 30 minutes (the cookie will firm as it cools), then cut into twelve wedges. The cookie wedges will keep for a week in an airtight container at room temperature, or may be frozen for up to three months.

Makes 12 servings

SERVING SIZE: 1 wedge

PER SERVING: Calories 190; Total Fat 12 g (Sat Fat 4 g, Mono Fat 5 g, Poly Fat 2 g); Protein 4 g; Carb 18 g; Fiber 1 g; Cholesterol 25 mg; Sodium 190 mg; Total Sugar 13 g (Added Sugar 12 g)

GOOD SOURCE OF: manganese, niacin, selenium

mixed berry coconut crisp

In this skillet-cooked fruit crisp, a medley of fresh berries—any combination you choose—is cooked until bursting and bubbling under a sumptuous, crispy, coconutty topping. A little coconut oil goes a long way to provide richness and aromatic flavor to the crust, and just enough sugar is used to highlight the fruit's natural sweetness, while keeping the whole crisp in the healthy zone. It's just the thing to make after a berry-picking excursion, or when the fruit is bountiful at the market. (Substitute gluten-free oat flour for the wheat flour, and be sure to get gluten-free oats, to make this a gluten-free dessert.)

6 cups mixed fresh berries, larger berries cut to match the size of the smaller berries

½ cup dark brown sugar or coconut sugar, divided

1½ tablespoons cornstarch

1 teaspoon ground cinnamon, divided

½ cup rolled oats

¼ cup unsweetened shredded coconut

¼ cup whole wheat pastry flour

¼ teaspoon salt

3 tablespoons virgin coconut oil, melted

1. Line the middle rack of the oven with a sheet of foil (to prevent any juices from dripping), then preheat the oven to 350°F.

2. Place the berries in a 10-inch ovenproof skillet. Sprinkle them with ¼ cup of the brown sugar, the cornstarch, and ½ teaspoon of the cinnamon, then toss gently to combine.

3. Put the oats, shredded coconut, flour, salt, and the remaining ¼ cup of brown sugar and ½ teaspoon of cinnamon into a medium-size bowl and mix to combine. Add the coconut oil and use your fingers to work the mixture together so it is evenly coated.

4. Sprinkle the topping over the berries and bake until the berries are bubbling and the topping is crisp and nicely browned, 30 to 35 minutes.

5. Remove from the oven and allow to rest for 15 to 20 minutes before serving in small bowls. The crisp will keep for 4 days in an airtight container in the refrigerator.

Makes 8 servings

SERVING SIZE: ½ cup

PER SERVING: Calories 190; Total Fat 8 g (Sat Fat 6 g, Mono Fat 1 g, Poly Fat 1 g); Protein 2 g; Carb 32 g; Fiber 5 g; Cholesterol 0 mg; Sodium 75 mg; Total Sugar 20 g (Added Sugar 12 g)

EXCELLENT SOURCE OF: manganese, vitamin C

GOOD SOURCE OF: fiber, vitamin K

caramelized bananas à la mode

Why settle for a plain dish of ice cream for dessert, when you can easily have something that's infinitely more craveable and also better for you? Here, a petite scoop of vanilla ice cream or coconut sorbet is served so it melts just enough atop a heap of warm caramelized bananas that are wafting with cinnamon and allspice. Topped with a crunch of toasted walnuts, it is a totally swoon-worthy and smart way to treat yourself.

⅓ cup walnut pieces

1½ tablespoons dark brown sugar

⅛ teaspoon ground cinnamon

Pinch of ground allspice

4 small or 2 large firm-ripe bananas

1 tablespoon unsalted butter

1 cup vanilla ice cream or coconut sorbet

1. Toast the nuts in a large, dry nonstick skillet over medium-high heat, stirring frequently, until they are fragrant, about 3 minutes. Set them aside to cool, then coarsely chop. Combine the brown sugar, cinnamon, and allspice in a small bowl.

2. Peel the bananas, then slice them on the bias into ¾-inch-thick slices. Wipe out the skillet, then heat the butter in the skillet over medium-high heat. Add the bananas and cook, turning once, until browned, about 1 minute per side. Sprinkle with the sugar mixture and cook, tossing gently once or twice with a spatula until the sugar melts, about 30 seconds. Add a tablespoon or two of water if the pan seems dry.

3. Divide the bananas among four serving bowls. Top each with a ¼-cup scoop of ice cream or sorbet and a sprinkling of walnuts.

Makes 4 servings

SERVING SIZE: heaping ½ cup bananas, ¼ cup vanilla ice cream, and 1 tablespoon walnuts

PER SERVING: Calories 260; Total Fat 13 g (Sat Fat 4.5 g, Mono Fat 3 g, Poly Fat 5 g); Protein 4 g; Carb 34 g; Fiber 3 g; Cholesterol 20 mg; Sodium 30 mg; Total Sugar 23 g (Added Sugar 10 g)

EXCELLENT SOURCE OF: manganese

GOOD SOURCE OF: copper, fiber, iodine, magnesium, potassium, vitamin B_6, vitamin C

strawberry shortcake skillet cobbler

This dessert is a lot like skipping down the street—you can't help but feel lighthearted and gleeful when you go for it. It is a mash-up of a strawberry shortcake and a cobbler that manages to bring the best of both to the table in a single skillet. The berries are tossed with lemon zest, cornstarch, and honey—just enough of each to enhance the berries' fresh flavor and thicken their juices, while avoiding the trap of turning them into a gummy, sweet pie filling. They are topped with an easy, whole wheat drop biscuit batter that is made mostly with olive oil but also a touch of butter for that essential biscuit flakiness. With or without whipped cream, this dessert is sure to put a smile on your face. (A cup-for-cup gluten-free flour may be substituted for the wheat flour to make this cobbler gluten-free.)

5 cups sliced, hulled strawberries

3 tablespoons honey

1½ tablespoons cornstarch

1 teaspoon finely grated lemon zest

½ cup low-fat buttermilk, well shaken

3 tablespoons olive oil

1 cup whole wheat pastry flour

2 tablespoons sugar

1 teaspoon baking powder

¼ teaspoon baking soda

¼ teaspoon salt

2 tablespoons cold, unsalted butter, cut into small pieces, plus more for coating pan

Whipped cream, for serving (optional)

1. Line the middle rack of the oven with a sheet of foil (to prevent any juices from dripping), then preheat the oven to 350°F. Coat a 10-inch ovenproof skillet with butter. Place the strawberries, honey, cornstarch, and lemon zest in the skillet and toss to combine.

2. Whisk together the buttermilk and oil in a medium-size bowl or small pitcher. Place the flour, sugar, baking powder, baking soda, and salt in the small bowl of a food processor and pulse together. Add the butter and pulse until the butter is the size of pebbles. Add the buttermilk mixture to the flour mixture and pulse until it is just moistened. Do not overmix. (Alternatively, you can whisk the dry ingredients together in a medium-size bowl, cut in the butter with a pastry cutter or two knives, and then stir in the buttermilk mixture.)

3. Drop the batter on top of the strawberry mixture in six mounds, then bake on the foil-lined rack until the fruit is bubbling and the biscuits are golden, 40 to 45 minutes. Carefully remove from the oven (the fruit will be liquidy at this stage, but will thicken as it cools).

4. Allow to cool for 15 to 20 minutes before serving, topped with whipped cream, if desired. The cobbler will keep for 4 days in an airtight container in the refrigerator.

Makes 6 servings

SERVING SIZE: ¾ cup strawberries and 1 biscuit

PER SERVING: Calories 220; Total Fat 11 g (Sat Fat 3.5 g, Mono Fat 6 g, Poly Fat 1 g); Protein 3 g; Carb 31 g; Fiber 3 g; Cholesterol 10 mg; Sodium 190 mg; Total Sugar 17 g (Added Sugar 13 g)

EXCELLENT SOURCE OF: vitamin C

GOOD SOURCE OF: calcium, fiber

oatmeal walnut skillet cookie

This recipe gives you all you yearn for in an oatmeal cookie, but in a much easier and healthier way. It's tender and chewy, scented with vanilla and cinnamon and textured with hearty rolled oats. But making it is completely fuss-free because all the ingredients are mixed in one bowl, then patted into one ovenproof skillet and baked into a giant cookie that is cut into wedges. It's better for you than the average cookie, too, made entirely with whole grains (whole wheat pastry flour and oats), and with healthy olive oil to replace some of the butter typically used. (Substitute a cup-for-cup, all-purpose, gluten-free flour for the wheat flour and make sure you buy gluten-free oats to make this cookie gluten-free.)

3 tablespoons unsalted butter, softened, plus more for skillet

2 tablespoons olive oil

½ cup packed dark brown sugar

1 large egg

½ teaspoon pure vanilla extract

⅔ cup whole wheat pastry flour

½ teaspoon baking soda

½ teaspoon ground cinnamon

¼ teaspoon salt

1 cup rolled oats

⅓ cup raisins or chocolate chips

⅓ cup chopped walnuts

1. Preheat the oven to 350°F. Lightly butter the bottom of a 10-inch cast-iron or other ovenproof skillet.

2. Place the butter, oil, brown sugar, egg, and vanilla in a large bowl and beat with a wooden spoon until creamy and well mixed. Add the flour, baking soda, cinnamon, and salt and mix well to combine. Stir in the oats, raisins, and walnuts. Transfer the batter to the prepared skillet and distribute it evenly on the bottom of the skillet.

3. Bake until browned lightly around the edges and set in the center, about 18 minutes. Remove from the oven and allow to cool in the skillet for 5 minutes before slicing into ten wedges and serving. The cookie wedges will keep for a week in an airtight container at room temperature.

Makes 10 servings

SERVING SIZE: 1 wedge

PER SERVING (MADE WITH RAISINS): Calories 200; Total Fat 10.5 g (Sat Fat 3.5 g, Mono Fat 4 g, Poly Fat 3 g); Protein 3 g; Carb 26 g; Fiber 2 g; Cholesterol 30 mg; Sodium 135 mg; Total Sugar 14 g (Added Sugar 11 g)

black rice coconut pudding

This dark and delicious dessert is like the more fashionable, hipster alter-ego of the good, but predictable, white rice pudding you grew up with. Both are made in a similar way, by simmering rice with sweetened milk. But here, the rice is whole-grain black rice, also called forbidden rice, which is more toothsome, imparts a beautiful purple hue to the milk, and adds a bounty of nutrition. Coconut milk adds a fun flavor change-up that pairs perfectly with the fragrant, fruity cardamom and warm cinnamon spices. (Be sure to use the coconut milk found in the refrigerator section of the store, which has a consistency similar to that of dairy milk. The canned version will be overly thick here.) Chia seeds act as a thickener and add another textural element. For maximum coconut flavor, the pudding is topped off with shredded coconut flakes.

¾ cup black "forbidden" rice

3⅓ cups unsweetened coconut milk (from the refrigerator case), divided

⅓ cup honey

¼ teaspoon ground cardamom

¼ teaspoon ground cinnamon

⅛ teaspoon salt

1 tablespoon chia seeds

¼ cup unsweetened shredded coconut, divided

1. Combine the rice and 1½ cups of water in a 3- to 4-quart pot, cover, and bring to a boil. Lower the heat to low and simmer, covered, until the water has been absorbed, 25 to 30 minutes.

2. Stir in 3 cups of the coconut milk and the honey, cardamom, cinnamon, and salt and bring to a simmer over medium heat. Lower the heat to low and simmer, uncovered, stirring frequently, until the mixture has thickened to the texture of oatmeal, 30 to 35 minutes.

3. Remove from the heat and stir in the chia seeds. Allow to sit at room temperature for 5 minutes, then stir in half of the shredded coconut. Transfer to a bowl, cover, and refrigerate for at least 4 hours and up to 4 days. Stir in the remaining ⅓ cup of coconut milk before serving, to loosen. Serve sprinkled with the remaining shredded coconut.

Makes 6 servings

SERVING SIZE: about ½ cup

PER SERVING: Calories 210; Total Fat 6 g (Sat Fat 4.5 g, Mono Fat 0 g, Poly Fat 0 g); Protein 3 g; Carb 38 g; Fiber 3 g ; Cholesterol 0 mg; Sodium 60 mg; Total Sugar 16 g (Added Sugar 15 g)

EXCELLENT SOURCE OF: vitamin B$_{12}$

GOOD SOURCE OF: fiber, vitamin D

jasmine tea and honey poached apricots

You know summer is officially in full swing when apricots appear at your local market. I always snap up plenty to get my fill while the getting's good. Besides eating them fresh out of hand, I find them to be ideal for poaching, since they are the perfect size for a dessert plate and they hold their shape beautifully when simmered. The quick, stovetop method is perfect for the season, too, when the last thing I want to do is turn on the oven. Here, the fruit is simmered in honey-sweetened jasmine tea with a few cardamom pods, which together give the dish a delicate, floral fruitiness that echoes the apricots' essence. Served over creamy, thick yogurt, it is an elegant way to cap off a summer meal. It can be served warm or at room temperature right after it is made, but it becomes more decadent once chilled for a few hours, as the fruit absorbs the sweet syrup and the liquid thickens further. Edible flowers are a wonderful additional garnish.

2 tea bags jasmine white or jasmine green tea

6 cardamom pods

⅓ cup honey

6 medium-size firm-ripe apricots (about 12 ounces)

1½ cups plain whole-milk or low-fat Greek yogurt, for serving

Fresh mint leaves, for garnish

1. Bring 2 cups of water to a simmer in a 3- to 4-quart pot. Remove from the heat, add the tea bags, and steep for 1 minute to create a light tea. (Do not steep the tea longer, to avoid developing bitter flavors.) Remove and discard the tea bags, add the cardamom pods and honey to the tea, and bring to a gentle boil, stirring a little to help dissolve the honey. Place the apricot halves in the pot, cut side down, in a single layer. Return the liquid to a boil, then lower the heat to medium-low and simmer, covered, until the fruit has softened but still retains its shape, 3 to 6 minutes depending on the ripeness of the fruit.

2. Use a slotted spoon to transfer the apricots from the liquid to a bowl. Increase the heat to high and boil the liquid until it is reduced to about ⅓ cup and has the texture of a thin syrup, 10 to 12 minutes. Remove the cardamom pods and pour the syrup over the apricots.

3. The apricots may be eaten warm, or, for sweeter fruit, may be chilled in the syrup for 2 hours or up to 4 days. The fruit will sweeten further the longer it sits in the syrup. Serve the apricots over the yogurt, drizzled with the syrup and garnished with mint.

Makes 6 servings

SERVING SIZE: 2 apricot halves, ¼ cup yogurt, and about 1 tablespoon syrup

PER SERVING: Calories 140; Total Fat 2.5 g (Sat Fat 1.5 g, Mono Fat 0 g, Poly Fat 0 g); Protein 6 g; Carb 24 g; Fiber 1 g; Cholesterol 10 mg; Sodium 25 mg; Total Sugar 22 g (Added Sugar 15 g)

EXCELLENT SOURCE OF: vitamin A

maple bourbon dark chocolate fondue

What's better than a pot full of dark chocolate fondue? That's easy—one that is flavored with real maple syrup and spiked with bourbon. It doesn't take much of each to give the dippable chocolate that extra something—a warm depth of flavor to make it truly unforgettable. It is the perfect dessert to cozy up to when there is a chill in the air, and it pairs well with the fruits of that season. It's also crazy-good with crunchy, salted pretzels.

FONDUE:

2 tablespoons unsweetened natural cocoa powder

½ cup evaporated milk

¼ cup pure maple syrup

3 ounces dark chocolate (50%–60% cacao solids), chopped, or high-quality semisweet chocolate chips

2 teaspoons bourbon

1 teaspoon pure vanilla extract

TO SERVE:

An assortment of sliced apples, pears, bananas, dried figs, and pretzels

1. Whisk together the cocoa powder and half of the milk in a 3- to 4-quart pot to form a paste. Then, whisk in the remaining milk and the maple syrup. Place the pot over low heat and cook, whisking frequently, until simmering.

2. Stir in the chocolate and cook until it is just melted. Then, remove it from the heat, add the bourbon and the vanilla, and stir until smooth. Transfer the fondue to a serving bowl and serve with the accompaniments for dipping.

Makes 4 servings

SERVING SIZE: 3 tablespoons fondue

PER SERVING (FONDUE ONLY): Calories 230; Total Fat 9 g (Sat Fat 6 g, Mono Fat 3 g, Poly Fat 0 g); Protein 4 g; Carb 31 g; Fiber 1 g; Cholesterol 10 mg; Sodium 40 mg; Total Sugar 26 g (Added Sugar 17 g)

EXCELLENT SOURCE OF: manganese, riboflavin

GOOD SOURCE OF: calcium, copper, iron, magnesium, phosphorous

sweet corn dessert pudding

I f rice can be made into a delicious dessert pudding, why not kernels of corn? When you think about it, fresh corn is perfect for dessert, since its baseline is already delightfully sweet. Here, the very essence of it—both the tender kernels and milky juices from the cob—is simmered with thickened whole milk spiked with maple syrup and a light touch of vanilla until the mixture is rich and creamy. It's then chilled to form a luxurious yet healthy pudding that is a true celebration of the summer harvest. Be sure to use the freshest, most tender sweet corn possible for this recipe.

3 large or 4 medium-size ears fresh sweet corn

1½ cups cold whole milk, plus more as needed

2 tablespoons cornstarch

¼ cup pure maple syrup, plus more for drizzling (optional)

½ teaspoon pure vanilla extract

Pinch of salt

Whipped cream, for garnish (optional)

1. Cut the kernels from the cobs over a large bowl, using a paring knife. Then, using the back of the blade, scrape against the cob to press out the milky liquid. You should wind up with about 2 cups of corn.

2. Whisk the milk and cornstarch together in a 3- to 4-quart pot until the cornstarch is dissolved. Then, place the pot over medium heat and cook, whisking constantly, until the mixture comes to a gentle boil. Stir in the corn with its juices and the maple syrup, vanilla, and salt. Return the liquid to a boil, then continue to simmer, stirring frequently, until the mixture thickens to the texture of a pudding and the corn is tender, 15 to 20 minutes. (It will thicken further as it cools.)

3. Transfer the mixture to a bowl, cover, and chill in the refrigerator for at least 4 hours and up to 4 days. Stir well before serving and add a tablespoon or two of milk to loosen, if needed. Spoon into small serving dishes and serve, topped with a dollop of whipped cream and a drizzle of maple syrup, if desired.

Makes 4 servings

SERVING SIZE: about ½ cup

PER SERVING: Calories 220; Total Fat 4.5 g (Sat Fat 2 g, Mono Fat 1 g, Poly Fat 1 g); Protein 6 g; Carb 42 g; Fiber 2 g; Cholesterol 10 mg; Sodium 115 mg; Total Sugar 23 g (Added Sugar 12 g)

EXCELLENT SOURCE OF: manganese, riboflavin

GOOD SOURCE OF: calcium, folate, iodine, magnesium, pantothenic acid, phosphorous, potassium, protein, thiamine, vitamin C, vitamin D

chai infused applesauce

nstead of the water used in most applesauce recipes, here the liquid is a cup of just-brewed chai tea that imparts a subtle layer of flavor, not making the applesauce taste like chai per se, but making it more profoundly apple-y, its warm, sweet spices and tannins highlighting those notes inherent in the fruit. Because different varieties of apples have different taste profiles, its best to use a mix for optimal complexity, but be sure to include some sweeter varieties to minimize the need for added sweetener. I find there is no better way to make use of all the bounty when I have gotten carried away, as I always seem to do, from a day spent apple-picking.

3 tea bags chai tea

1 cup boiling water

4 pounds apples (a mix of different varieties), peeled, cored, and cut into eighths

1 small cinnamon stick

Honey (optional)

1. Place the tea bags in a mug and pour the boiling water over them. Steep for 4 minutes, then remove and discard the tea bags. (Do not steep for too long, as it may become bitter.) Place the tea in a 6-quart pot with the apples and the cinnamon stick and bring to a boil. Lower the heat to medium-low, cover, and cook until the apples have softened, 20 to 25 minutes.

2. Remove the cinnamon stick and mash the apples with a potato masher to your desired consistency. Stir in a tablespoon or two of honey to taste, if desired. Serve warm or chilled. The applesauce will keep in a tightly covered container in the refrigerator for up to 4 days.

Makes 8 servings

SERVING SIZE: about ½ cup

PER SERVING: Calories 120; Total Fat 0 g (Sat Fat 0 g, Mono Fat 0 g, Poly Fat 0 g); Protein 1 g; Carb 31 g; Fiber 5 g; Cholesterol 0 mg; Sodium 0 mg; Total Sugar 24 g (Added Sugar 0 g)

EXCELLENT SOURCE OF: fiber

GOOD SOURCE OF: vitamin C

roasted pears with ginger cookie crumble and mascarpone

Roasted pears are a simple pleasure on their own. A little lemon, honey, and cinnamon and a half hour in the oven concentrates their flavors and turns them sensually soft and golden brown. But serve them on top of a pile of crunchy crumbled gingersnaps and dollop them with a richly creamy, earthy, honey-sweetened mascarpone and you have a practically effortless company-worthy dessert. The pears can be served right out of the oven, or made ahead and served at room temperature. If you can't find mascarpone—an Italian cream cheese typically used for tiramisu—you can substitute crème fraîche or Greek yogurt for a lighter take.

2 large firm ripe pears

1 tablespoon freshly squeezed lemon juice

2 tablespoons honey, divided

⅛ teaspoon ground cinnamon, plus more for garnish

¼ cup mascarpone cheese

1 to 3 teaspoons milk, as needed (optional)

1¼ ounces gingersnap cookies (about 5)

1. Preheat the oven to 375°F. Line a sheet pan with parchment paper.

2. Peel the pears, then quarter them and use a small spoon or melon baller to scoop out their core. Place the pears in a medium-size bowl and toss with the lemon juice. Then, drizzle them with 1 tablespoon of the honey and ⅛ teaspoon of the cinnamon and toss to coat. Place the pears on the prepared sheet pan, drizzle with the juice in the bowl, and roast in the oven, turning them once or twice until they are tender and browned but still retain their shape, 25 to 30 minutes.

3. Meanwhile, combine the mascarpone with the remaining tablespoon of honey in a small bowl, mixing well with a spoon. If the mascarpone is very thick, add some milk, a teaspoon at a time, to loosen so the cream is easily dolloped. Place the gingersnap cookies in a resealable plastic bag and use a mallet or rolling pin to crush them into coarse crumbs. (You should wind up with about ⅓ cup of crumbs.)

4. To serve, place about 1½ tablespoons of crushed cookies in a mound on each plate. Arrange two pear wedges on top of each, then dollop each with a tablespoon of the mascarpone and sprinkle with cinnamon. The pears will keep in an airtight container in the refrigerator for up to 4 days.

Makes 4 servings

SERVING SIZE: 1½ tablespoons cookie crumbs, 2 pear wedges, and 1 tablespoon mascarpone

PER SERVING: Calories 210; Total Fat 7 g (Sat Fat 4 g, Mono Fat 2 g, Poly Fat 1 g); Protein 2 g; Carb 35 g; Fiber 4 g; Cholesterol 15 mg; Sodium 30 mg; Total Sugar 23 g (Added Sugar 9 g)

GOOD SOURCE OF: fiber, vitamin C

cinnamon apple chips

This recipe turns two simple ingredients into a fun treat with surprisingly complex layers of taste. Each crunch reveals a concentrated apple flavor with a light caramelized sweetness that is balanced by a gentle hint of tartness. Different varieties of the fruit will give you subtly different flavors, all of which are enhanced by the fragrant sprinkle of cinnamon, and, if you want them on the slightly sweeter side, a sprinkle of brown sugar.

They are a wonderfully light sweet-tooth satisfier when you're hankering for a little something after dinner, and they make an ideal snack to tuck into a lunch box.

2 medium-size sweet apples, such as Golden Delicious, Gala, or Honeycrisp, unpeeled

¼ teaspoon ground cinnamon

1 tablespoon brown sugar (optional)

1. Preheat the oven to 225°F. Line a sheet pan with parchment paper.

2. Slice the apples into ⅛-inch-thick rounds crosswise through the core, using a chef's knife or a mandoline. Remove the seeds. (Stop cutting before you get too close to the end when it gets difficult to cut safely. Save the remaining apple for another use.)

3. Place the apple slices in a single layer on the prepared sheet pan, sprinkle both sides with the cinnamon, and the tops with the brown sugar, if using, and bake for 1½ hours. Flip and bake until the apples are dried, slightly darkened, and the edges have curled, 1 to 1½ hours more. They will still be pliable when they are done, but will crisp further as they cool.

4. Remove from the oven and allow to cool completely on the sheet pan. The chips will keep in a paper bag for up to a week.

Makes 4 servings

SERVING SIZE: about 5 chips

PER SERVING: Calories 35; Total Fat 0 g (Sat Fat 0 g, Mono Fat 0 g, Poly Fat 0 g); Protein 0 g; Carb 8 g; Fiber 1 g; Cholesterol 0 mg; Sodium 0 mg; Total Sugar 6 g (Added Sugar 0 g)

dark chocolate salted almond bark

Some might say chocolate is my weakness, but I consider it a strength! Having a treat like this around—which I try to make a point of at all times—means I can satisfy my sweet tooth more healthfully, preventing me from going overboard on lesser-quality treats. It especially comes in handy when I am on the road. Even half of a piece lifts me out of an afternoon slump or provides just the right sweet finish after dinner. It also serves as a crowd-pleasing make-ahead party treat, and makes a lovely hostess or holiday gift when wrapped up in a pretty box or jar. You can substitute any nut you like, or make it nut-free by using pumpkin or sunflower seeds. Just don't skip the salt—it takes it over the line from very good to wow!

1½ cups whole, skin-on almonds

18 ounces dark chocolate (60%–70% percent cacao solids, or bittersweet), finely chopped

½ teaspoon coarse sea salt

1. Preheat the oven to 375°F. Place the almonds on a dry sheet pan and toast in the oven until fragrant, 7 to 8 minutes. Transfer the almonds to a dish and allow to cool. Line the sheet pan with parchment.

2. Place the chocolate in a large microwave-safe bowl and microwave on HIGH for 1 minute. Stir well, then microwave for another 20 seconds and stir well again. Microwave for another 20-second interval, or two if needed, stirring well in between, until all the chocolate is melted.

3. Pour the melted chocolate onto the prepared sheet pan, spreading it out with a spatula so it is evenly distributed into a rectangle that measures about 10 by 14 inches. Scatter the almonds over the top.

4. Chill in the refrigerator for 5 minutes, then sprinkle with the sea salt and refrigerate for 1 hour to set. Once set, remove from the parchment and break up into two dozen pieces. The bark will keep in an airtight container in the refrigerator for up to 2 weeks.

Makes 24 servings

SERVING SIZE: 1 piece

PER SERVING: Calories 170; Total Fat 13 g (Sat Fat 5 g, Mono Fat 5 g, Poly Fat 3 g); Protein 3 g; Carb 13 g; Fiber 1 g; Cholesterol 0 mg; Sodium 40 mg; Total Sugar 8 g (Added Sugar 8 g)

EXCELLENT SOURCE OF: manganese

GOOD SOURCE OF: copper, magnesium

peach blueberry galette

A galette, which is essentially an open-faced, seasonal fruit pie, is the ultimate showcase of how good a "rustic" dessert can be. Not only is a galette formed and baked right on a parchment-lined sheet pan, it is also inherently better for you than a typical double-crusted fruit pie because it uses just one pastry crust. This recipe takes the health of the crust further—without giving up any tender, flaky texture—by using whole-grain pastry flour instead of all-purpose, and olive oil to replace some of the usual butter. The peach and blueberry filling is sweetened just enough with honey to punctuate the inherent sweetness of the fruit, for a splendid way to cap off a summer meal.

If using fresh peaches, score the skin of each peach from top to bottom with a paring knife. Place the peach in boiling water for 30 seconds, then transfer to an ice bath. Remove from the ice bath and use your hands and/or a paring knife to remove the peel, which should slip off easily.

1 cup whole wheat pastry flour, plus more for dusting

⅛ teaspoon salt, plus a pinch, divided

1 tablespoon olive oil

¼ cup honey, plus more to taste

¼ cup cold, unsalted butter, cut into small pieces

3 tablespoons ice water

2 cups peeled sliced peaches, fresh or frozen, thawed

1 cup blueberries

½ teaspoon pure vanilla extract

¼ teaspoon ground cinnamon

1½ tablespoons cornstarch

Makes 6 servings

SERVING SIZE: 1 wedge

PER SERVING: Calories 270; Total Fat 10 g (Sat Fat 5 g, Mono Fat 4 g, Poly Fat 1 g); Protein 3 g; Carb 42 g; Fiber 2 g; Cholesterol 20 mg; Sodium 50 mg; Total Sugar 18 g (Added Sugar 12 g)

GOOD SOURCE OF: vitamin K

1. To make the crust, put the flour and ⅛ teaspoon of salt in the small bowl of a food processor and pulse to combine. Drizzle the olive oil and 1 tablespoon of the honey on top, then add the butter and pulse about twelve times, or until the butter is the size of small pebbles. Add the ice water to the food processor and pulse three to five times, just until incorporated. Shape the dough into a flat disk, wrap it in waxed paper, and chill for at least 1 hour and up to 2 days in advance of baking.

2. Preheat the oven to 400°F. Place the peaches and berries in a large bowl and toss with the remaining 3 tablespoons of honey, and the vanilla, cinnamon, and pinch of salt. Sprinkle with the cornstarch and toss until evenly coated.

3. On a floured surface, roll the chilled dough into a circle about 10 inches in diameter. Line a sheet pan with parchment paper, and draping the dough over the rolling pin, transfer it to the prepared pan. If the dough breaks at all, patch it up with your fingers.

4. Arrange the fruit mixture in a mound in the center on the dough, leaving a 2-inch fruit-free border. Fold the border over the filling. It will cover the berries only partially and does not need to be even.

5. Bake the tart for 10 minutes, and then lower the oven temperature to 325°F, keeping the tart in the oven all the while, and bake for another 30 minutes, until the filling is bubbling and the crust is golden brown. Remove from the oven and allow to cool completely on the sheet pan before cutting into wedges. The galette will keep in an airtight container in the refrigerator for up to 4 days.

chocolate-dipped orange crisps with pistachio

Chocolate and orange is such a power couple I think it deserves a celebrity nickname—maybe "chorange"? Okay, that's pushing it. But seriously, they are good together and this recipe marries them in the most wonderful way. It harkens to the chocolate-dipped orange peel popular around holiday time, but here, rather than boil orange peel in a thick sugar syrup, you slice a whole orange into very thin rounds and bake the slices at a low temperature—dehydrate them, really. The resulting crispy, stained glass–like circles of concentrated orange flavor are then dipped in melted chocolate and showered with chopped pistachios for a treat that is as gloriously beautiful as it is scrumptious. (If your mandoline does not come with a hand guard, I suggest using two oranges to safely get the two dozen slices needed for this recipe.)

¼ cup unsalted shelled pistachios

1 small navel orange, well scrubbed (see note)

2 tablespoons confectioners' sugar

4 ounces dark chocolate (50–60% cocoa solids) or high-quality semisweet chocolate, chopped

Makes 6 servings

SERVING SIZE: 4 pieces

PER SERVING: Calories 110; Total Fat 6 g (Sat Fat 2.5 g, Mono Fat 0 g, Poly Fat 0 g); Protein 2 g; Carb 15 g; Fiber 1 g; Cholesterol 0 mg; Sodium 0 mg; Total Sugar 12 g (Added Sugar 5 g)

EXCELLENT SOURCE OF: vitamin C

1. Preheat the oven to 350°F. Place the pistachios on a dry sheet pan and toast until they are fragrant, about 4 minutes. Transfer them to a cutting board. Once they are cool enough to handle, chop them very finely.

2. Lower the oven temperature to 200°F. Line the same sheet pan with parchment paper.

3. Use a mandoline to cut the orange into very thin (⅛-inch-thick) slices. Remove and discard any pits and the outermost slices, which are mostly peel, then place the orange slices onto the sheet pan in a single layer. Dust them generously with the confectioners' sugar, then bake until the oranges are dry and crisp, about 2 hours. Allow to cool completely. (The orange slices may be baked several days ahead and stored in the refrigerator.)

4. Place the chocolate in a small microwave-safe bowl and microwave in 30-second bursts, stirring well after each burst until the chocolate is just melted.

5. Dip the orange slices in the chocolate to cover them halfway, creating a chocolate half-moon, then sprinkle the chopped nuts on both sides of the chocolate-dipped half and return the dipped oranges to the parchment-lined sheet pan. (Tip the bowl as needed to get coverage once the chocolate level gets low. You will wind up with leftover chocolate, which you can save in the refrigerator for another use.) Place the sheet pan with the dipped oranges in the refrigerator for 30 minutes to set. The dipped oranges will keep in an airtight container in the refrigerator for up to 2 weeks.

chocolate–chocolate chip sheet cake

This moist, double-chocolate cake takes one-pan cooking to the extreme since it doesn't even require a mixing bowl to make it. It's a sheet pan–size, better-for-you take on a unique cake recipe—called a war cake or Depression cake—that was developed during times of egg, milk, and butter shortages. (Because it has none of those ingredients, it happens to be vegan—if you use vegan chocolate chips.) The result is so craveably delicious and the steps for making it so easy and different that I get practically giddy thinking about it. It bakes up into a big, homey chocolate sheet cake, riddled with melty chocolate chips, that is perfect to please a crowd. It's beautiful simply sprinkled with confectioners' sugar, but it also provides a nice big canvas for more fanciful decorations.

2 cups whole wheat pastry flour

1 cup all-purpose flour

1 cup granulated sugar

½ cup light brown sugar

⅔ cup unsweetened natural cocoa powder

2 teaspoons baking soda

1 teaspoon salt

2 cups cold water

2 tablespoons cider vinegar

⅔ cup canola or other neutral-tasting oil

2 teaspoons pure vanilla extract

1 cup chocolate chips

1 tablespoon confectioners' sugar

1. Preheat the oven to 350°F. Directly on a sheet pan, whisk together the pastry flour, all-purpose flour, granulated sugar, brown sugar, cocoa powder, baking soda, and salt.

2. Combine the cold water and vinegar in a small bowl or pitcher.

3. Make a well in the middle of the flour mixture and pour the oil and vanilla into the well. Sprinkle the vinegar mixture over the top of the flour mixture and then stir well to blend all the ingredients. Stir in the chocolate chips, distributing them evenly around the pan. Wipe the rim of the pan, then place in the oven.

4. Bake until set and a toothpick inserted into the center comes out clean, about 20 minutes. Remove from the oven and place the cake on a wire rack to cool in the pan. Once cool, sprinkle with confectioners' sugar and cut into squares. The cake will keep in an airtight container in the refrigerator for up to a week.

Makes 24 servings

SERVING SIZE: one 2½-inch square

PER SERVING: Calories 230; Total Fat 10 g (Sat Fat 2.5 g, Mono Fat 4 g, Poly Fat 3 g); Protein 3 g; Carb 32 g; Fiber 1 g; Cholesterol 0 mg; Sodium 200 mg; Total Sugar 17 g (Added Sugar 15 g)

Recipe List

Plant Protein, Eggs, & Dairy

Seafood

Poultry

Desserts

Index